Hypertension in Practice

Hypertension
in Practice
Second Edition

D Gareth Beevers MD FRCP
Professor in Medicine
University of Birmingham
Honorary Consultant Physician
City Hospital Dudley Road
Birmingham

Graham A MacGregor FRCP
Professor of Cardiovascular Medicine
University of London
Honorary Consultant Physician
Blood Pressure Unit
St George's Hospital
London

MARTIN DUNITZ

© D Gareth Beevers and Graham A MacGregor 1987, 1995

First published in the United Kingdom in 1987 by

Martin Dunitz Ltd
The Livery House
7–9 Pratt Street
London NW1 0AE

First edition 1987
First edition revised, paperback 1988
Second edition 1995

A CIP catalogue record for this book is available from the British Library

ISBN 1–85317–073–9

Composition by Scribe Design, Gillingham, Kent
Printed and bound in Spain

Contents

Contents

Preface

PREFACE

This second edition of *Hypertension in Practice* has been completely updated although the basic format of 17 chapters remains the same. It is a tremendous tribute to hypertension research worldwide that so much new information has become available since the first edition in 1987 (e.g. greater diagnostic ability). Every chapter had to be rethought and updated in order to provide our readers with our considered overview of the new ideas on aetiology and the results of the latest clinical trials. We have retained our original intention to provide a clinically relevant textbook aimed at practising clinicians and nurses. We have tried to avoid the tendency seen in so many massive volumes to go into excessive detail on the latest research into esoteric and highly theoretical aspects of the pathophysiology of hypertension. We do, however, feel that clinicians should be aware of what is going on in the field of basic scientific research and the direction of current though so we have briefly covered these topics.

Perhaps, from a clinical point of view, the most important new information concerned the immense benefit of treating older patients with hypertension and recent meta-analysis that demonstrates antihypertensive drug therapy is definitely effective in the prevention, not only of strokes, but deaths from all causes as well as coronary heart disease. We now have proof that our treatments are effective and the next challenge is to ensure that we deliver this validated care on a large scale to the millions of hypertensive patients worldwide. On a longer term scale, we need to concentrate more on the prevention of hypertension in the first place, and there are some encouraging new studies in this area.

We are gratified, and perhaps a little surprised, by the enthusiastic reception for our first edition. We hope that this new edition will occupy the same niche and provide a useful guide for clinicians in all countries as they struggle to bring down blood pressure and therefore, prevent heart attacks and strokes.

D Gareth Beevers
Graham A MacGregor

1

Section One

1

THE IMPORTANCE OF HYPERTENSION

BACKGROUND

Hypertension is the commonest chronic medical condition in the developed world. Depending on the criteria for the diagnosis, hypertension can be said to be present in 20–30% of the adult population. Furthermore, it is now rapidly becoming a major problem in developing countries as well. It should not be regarded so much as a disease (although some patients may be clinically unwell) but more as one of three treatable or reversible risk factors for premature death due to arterial disease. In this chapter, the structural lesions in the blood vessels that are either a cause of, or are caused by, hypertension are described. Also detailed is the effect of these lesions on the heart and brain in what may be termed 'end-organ damage'.

In general, the amount of end-organ damage is directly proportional to the height of the blood pressure and this gradient of risk extends down into the range of blood pressure that is conventionally described as normal. Thus, an individual with a diastolic blood pressure of 80 mmHg is demonstrably more at risk in terms of cardiovascular disease than a similar individual with a diastolic blood pressure of 70 mmHg, although neither of these individuals would be considered to be hypertensive. However, one individual has a measurably higher blood pressure than the other and this difference in pressure is explicable on the basis of a higher peripheral resistance.

THE BLOOD VESSELS IN HYPERTENSION

Peripheral resistance

The elevation of blood pressure in hypertension is directly related to the degree of peripheral arteriolar narrowing (peripheral resistance). In essential hypertension, the cardiac output is normal in all patients until end-organ cardiac damage causes a fall in output. This peripheral arteriolar narrowing is due to two closely interlocking factors.

1. Arteriolar smooth muscle constriction
2. Growth (proliferation) of arteriolar cells.

The factors causing this vasoconstriction and vascular growth are described in more detail in Chapter 4. The other lesions of small and large blood vessels are described in more detail here (Fig. 1.1).

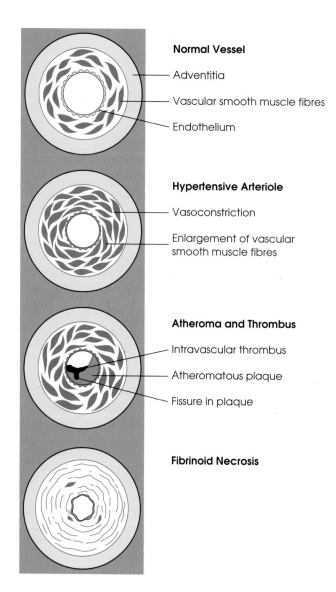

Figure 1.1
The vascular lesions of hypertension.

Normal Vessel

— Adventitia

— Vascular smooth muscle fibres

— Endothelium

Hypertensive Arteriole

— Vasoconstriction

— Enlargement of vascular smooth muscle fibres

Atheroma and Thrombus

— Intravascular thrombus

— Atheromatous plaque

— Fissure in plaque

Fibrinoid Necrosis

Arteriolar fibroid necrosis

Arteriolar fibroid necrosis is the hallmark of the accelerated or malignant phase of hypertension. Microvascular necroses are found in the arterioles of brain, heart, kidneys, retina and many other sites but not in skeletal muscle or skin.

Arteriolar thickening

As described earlier, arteriolar thickening is the basic lesion of hypertension leading to the increased peripheral resistance. There is realignment smooth muscle cells, which are also larger than normal, and in vivo they are relatively constricted. As the external diameter of these arterioles is normal, the internal (luminal) diameter is reduced.

Atheroma

Hypertensive patients are particularly prone to developing atheroma in larger vessels due to lipid-rich deposits in the arterial wall. Cigarette smoking and hyperlipidaemia also increase this rate of deposition. When blood pressure is high, atheroma is particularly prominent in regions of haemodynamic turbulence. Also, high blood pressure facilitates fissuring of the atheromatous plaque which leads to further atheroma related to platelet adhesion and cholesterol incorporation. Atheroma causes patchy or confluent narrowing of cerebral and coronary arteries as well as of the aorta and leg arteries. In renal arteries, this can cause atheromatous renal artery stenosis. Hypertensives with very low plasma cholesterol levels are very much less prone to develop atheroma although they do develop the haemorrhagic complications of raised blood pressure.

Intravascular thrombosis

There is a tendency for intravascular thrombosis to develop in atheromatous vessels, particularly in the cerebral and coronary arteries. This may lead to complete occlusion of the vessel with infarction of the tissues supplied by that vessel. There is evidence that people with raised blood pressure have a greater tendency to intravascular thrombosis partly because of increased platelet activation and also raised plasma fibrinogen levels.

Aneurysm

Large vessel saccular or fusiform aneurysms are commoner in hypertensives, who also have the increased chance of developing aortic dissection.

Charcot–Bouchard aneurysms

Microvascular aneurysms of the intracerebral arteries, Charcot–Bouchard aneurysms are almost specific to hypertension. When they rupture, they cause intracerebral haemorrhage.

Berry aneurysms

Aneurysms of the circle of Willis are common in severe hypertension, particularly if this is due to autosomal dominant polycystic kidney disease.

Arterial fibroplasia

Renal artery narrowing in younger hypertensive patients may be due to fibrous dysplasia with intimal, medial, fibromuscular and periarterial involvement. The arteries assume an irregular 'string of beads' appearance. In children, these may also be seen in the mesenteric and other abdominal arteries. When the renal arteries are affected, this is a cause rather than the consequence of the hypertension; the aetiology is unknown.

VASCULAR END-ORGAN DAMAGE

The heart

Left ventricular hypertrophy

Clinical, radiological, ECG or echocardiographic evidence of left ventricular hypertrophy (LVH) is closely correlated to the height

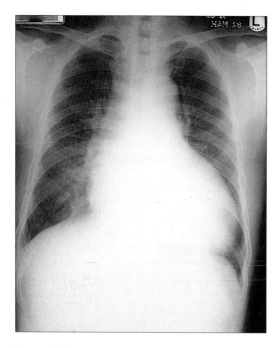

Figure 1.2
Chest X–ray showing cardiomegaly owing to severe hypertension.

of the blood pressure (Fig. 1.2). About 50% of patients with moderate hypertension (diastolic pressures of 110–120 mmHg) have the ECG criteria for definite LVH. There is some evidence that LVH is not solely due to the degree of elevation of blood pressure but may be related to circulating growth factors and a direct effect of those hormones which also elevate the blood pressure. When LVH is present, the prognosis is bad. A hypertensive patient with LVH has four times the chance of developing a heart attack compared with a patient with a similar level of blood pressure but no hypertrophy. Such patients also have their risk of stroke increased 12-fold and a three-fold higher risk

of intermittent claudication. For this reason, a routine ECG in a new hypertensive patient is a very powerful predictor of outcome. Whilst the ECG features of LVH are reasonably specific, they are not very sensitive. Thus, hypertrophy may be present even if the ECG is normal. Echocardiography is a more sensitive method of detecting LVH but this test is not generally available in routine general practice.

Hypertensive patients with large left ventricles are more prone to cardiac arrhythmias, particularly if they have hypokalaemia related to diuretic therapy.

Myocardial infarction

Coronary heart disease is twice as common in hypertensive patients than in the remainder of the population. The risk of heart attack is directly related to the height of the blood pressure. About 1% of hypertensive patients suffer a myocardial infarction each year whereas the figure is only about half of this number for people with diastolic blood pressures below 90 mmHg. A patient with myocardial infarction who has had previous hypertension has a worse prognosis than a similar patient with no such history (Fig. 1.3). Hypertensive patients who also smoke cigarettes have an even worse prognosis, particularly from sudden death, their risk being about half as much again. Similarly the risk is increased if there are also raised plasma total cholesterol levels with or without low HDL cholesterol levels (see Chapter 2).

Angina pectoris

Angina is about twice as common in hypertensives as in normotensives. This may partly be due to atheroma of coronary arteries causing ischaemia but may also be

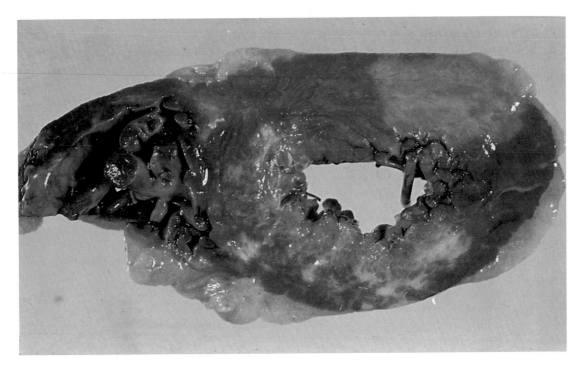

Figure 1.3
Hypertrophied left ventricle with pale wedge–shaped myocardial infarction.

compounded by the relatively larger left ventricular mass with no corresponding increase in the blood supply. Lowering the blood pressure may relieve angina even if beta-adrenoceptor blockers are not used. Exercise tests according to the Bruce protocol and 24-hour ECGs demonstrate an increased frequency of symptomless ECG changes of ischaemia in hypertensive patients.

Heart failure

Heart failure is four times commoner in hypertensive women and seven times commoner in hypertensive men in comparison with age- and sex-matched normotensive people and the risk rises with advancing age. Left ventricular failure may occur in a hypertensive patient following a myocardial infarction but it may also develop in severe hypertensives who have gross LVH. This form of heart failure should, therefore, be preventable if blood pressures are well controlled (Fig. 1.4).

The diagnosis of hypertensive heart failure is less common nowadays and this may represent a real fall in incidence owing to more effective control of blood pressure. Alternatively, the reduction may be due to previous underdiagnosis of painless myocardial infarction in hypertensive patients. Now, with more sophisticated myocardial enzyme

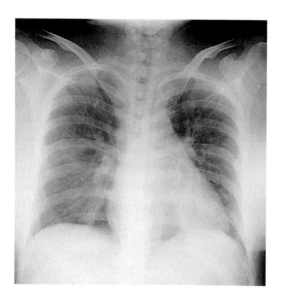

Figure 1.4
Chest X–ray showing cardiomegaly with pulmonary oedema and marked upper lobe diversion.

measurements, myocardial infarctions are more easily diagnosed in patients presenting with acute left ventricular failure. In elderly hypertensive patients, heart failure is particularly common and the major predisposing factor after coronary heart disease is longstanding hypertension.

Cardiomyopathy

Some hypertensive patients with big, poorly contracting hearts with all four chambers dilated, often with atrial fibrillation, may be heavy alcohol consumers. High alcohol intake can cause a congestive cardiomyopathy as well as hypertension. There is no convincing evidence of the existence of a syndrome of 'hypertensive cardiomyopathy'.

The brain

Subarachnoid haemorrhage

About 50% of patients with subarachnoid haemorrhage have pre-existing hypertension and about 30% do not have berry aneurysms of the circle of Willis. Cigarette smoking is also closely associated with subarachnoid haemorrhage. When a vessel ruptures, the patient develops acute meningeal irritation with severe headache and usually rapid loss of consciousness. About half of all patients die after their first haemorrhage but this figure may be reduced by surgical clipping of aneurysm and with the treatment of hypertension. There is some evidence that the calcium channel blocker, nimodipine, reduces the risk of a second subarachnoid haemorrhage and similarly some evidence of benefit from beta-adrenergic blockade. However, rapid reductions of blood pressure may be hazardous to those areas of the brain close to the ruptured blood vessel. Intracerebral arteries may exhibit intense spasm leading to a reduction in cerebral blood flow. Over-rapid reduction of blood pressure could make this situation worse.

Cerebral infarcts

In hypertensive patients, the most common cerebral lesion is a cerebral infarction (Fig. 1.5). This is related to cerebral thrombosis associated with atheroma of the intracranial vessels. The overall risk of development of stroke in a hypertensive man is about 25% of the risk of developing a myocardial infarction. The incidence is about 2% per year with patients with diastolic blood pressures about 110 mmHg. In mild hypertension, where diastolic pressures are

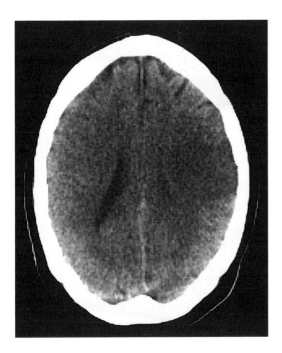

Figure 1.5
CT scan showing large cerebral infarct in the right cerebral cortex.

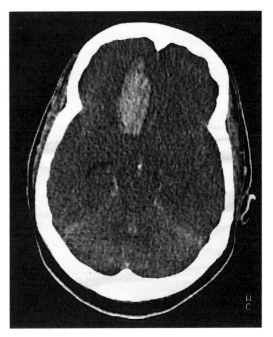

Figure 1.6
CT scan showing left anterior cerebral haemorrhage.

around 100 mmHg, the incidence is 0.5%. Of patients under the age of 70 years admitted to hospital with stroke, about half have pre-existing hypertension. There is recent evidence to suggest that high alcohol intake may be an important precipitating factor in premature stroke. This may be due to an acute rise in blood pressure following heavy drinking or possibly to alcohol-induced cerebral vasoconstriction. There is now compelling evidence that cigarette smoking is a major risk factor for cerebral infarction; serum cholesterol levels are also a risk factor for strokes as is the presence of concomitant diabetes mellitus.

Cerebral haemorrhage

The more frequent use of CT scanning in patients who have sustained a stroke has demonstrated that cerebral haemorrhage is not, in fact, the commonest cerebral complication of hypertension (Fig. 1.6 and 1.7). Previously, if a hypertensive patient developed a stroke, it was assumed that this was due to a cerebral haemorrhage. Cerebral haemorrhages occur as a result of high blood pressure in the intracerebral microaneurysms of Charcot and Bouchard. Again, cigarette smoking is an important added risk factor.

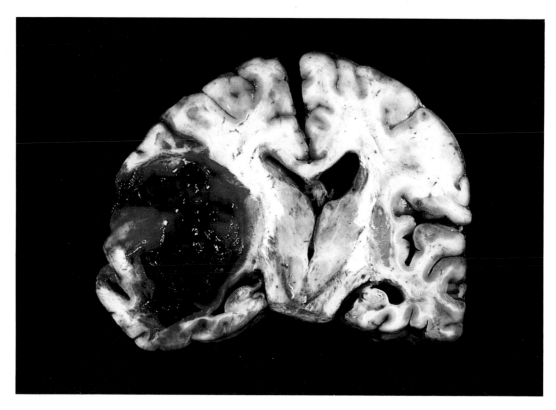

Figure 1.7
Brain showing intracerebral haemorrhage.

Cerebral embolus

Embolization can occur from a left ventricular thrombus in patients following a myocardial infarction or from a left atrial thrombus in patients who have atrial fibrillation with or without mitral stenosis. Another source of embolus is from atheromatous carotid artery stenosis. The clinical presentation is either of a transient cerebral ischaemic attack (TIA) or of a completed stroke. Both are commoner in patients with high blood pressure.

Cerebral blood flow

In normal circumstances, the blood flow to the brain is remarkably constant despite marked fluctuations in blood pressure. This state of cerebral autoregulation does, however, break down when blood pressure is either very high or very low. Autoregulation also breaks down following a stroke. When blood pressure is reduced rapidly by more than about 35%, cerebral blood flow falls and cerebral ischaemia may develop. When blood pressures are very high (for example, diastolic blood pressure 140 mmHg or more), cerebral blood flow rises and cerebral oedema may develop and lead to the clinical state of hypertensive encephalopathy. In hypertensive patients, the state of cerebral autoregulation is reset at a slightly higher level and blood flow remains constant as long as pressures are not lowered too rapidly.

Encephalopathy

The syndrome of hypertensive encephalopathy is very rare but it may be seen in association with the malignant or accelerated phase of hypertension. However, if a hypertensive patient develops a sudden onset of focal neurological deficit, then this is much more likely to be due to a stroke and, under these circumstances, rapid reduction of blood pressure is dangerous. Very rarely, focal neurological signs may develop in a very severe hypertensive patient where there is no cerebral infarct or haemorrhage. The syndrome of encephalopathy is almost impossible to diagnose without performing a CT scan to exclude a structural cerebral lesion. Encephalopathy may be considered as a diagnosis if there are fluctuating neurological signs with restlessness, confusion and sometimes generalized convulsions. Here, rapid reduction of blood pressure is necessary as cerebral blood flow is raised although blood pressures again should not be reduced too rapidly.

Lacunae

There is now increasing evidence from CT scanning that many hypertensive patients with no focal neurological signs do have small intracerebral neurological lesions (Fig. 1.8). Clinically these patients may have

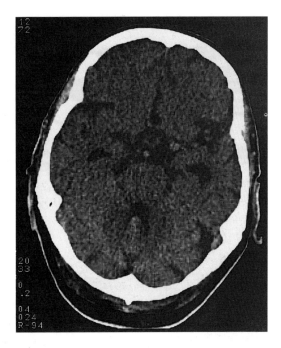

Figure 1.8
CT scan showing multiple cerebral infarcts and dilated sylvian fissures.

memory impairment with reduction of cognitive skills. More extreme cases are encountered when hypertension is associated with general deterioration of cerebral function, dementia, hyperreflexia and a steadily downward clinical progress. This is sometimes referred to as 'Binswanger's disease'.

The peripheral vessels

Aneurysm

Atheromatous plaques develop in the aorta and the common iliac vessels and these may

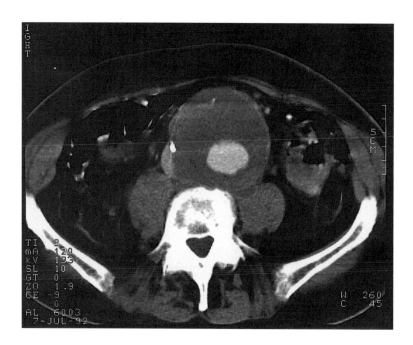

Figure 1.9
CT scan showing large abdominal aortic aneurysm.

progress to aortic aneurysm or aortic dissection (Fig. 1.9). Death from rupture of an aortic aneurysm is three times commoner in hypertensive patients than in normotensives.

Intermittent claudication

Intermittent claudication is twice as frequent in hypertensive patients as in people with normal blood pressure. The other cardiovascular risk factors, cigarette smoking and hyperlipidaemia, are often present. It should be remembered that beta-adrenoceptor blockers, used to control blood pressure, may induce or aggravate claudication in patients with pre-existing peripheral vascular disease (Fig. 1.10). Many patients with peripheral vascular disease may also have previously undiagnosed atheromatous renal artery stenosis which may be contributing to

the hypertension and to the deterioration of renal function. Atheromatous renal artery stenosis is also seen in normotensive patients with peripheral vascular disease.

The kidney

Hypertensive nephrosclerosis

Mild symptomless haematuria and proteinuria are common in hypertension even when this is not associated with the malignant/accelerated phase or with evidence of an underlying intrinsic disease. When proteinuria is present by dipstick testing, the mortality rate from vascular complications for hypertension is approximately doubled. Similarly, in hypertensive patients with a serum urea level of 10 mmol/l, the mortality is twice that of patients

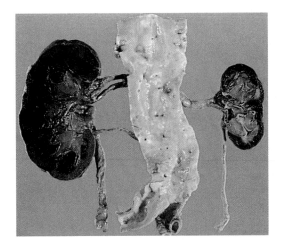

Figure 1.10
Aortic atheroma and left renal artery stenosis.
(Reproduced with permission from Swales JD,
Sever PS, Peart S. *Clinical Atlas of Hypertension*
(Gower Medical Publishing, 1991); Fig. 5.10).

with no renal impairment. Uncontrolled severe hypertension causes progressive renal damage and irreversible renal failure may develop. The overall risk of developing chronic renal failure in hypertensive patients is about five times higher than in normotensive patients with renal damage. There remains, however, some debate as to whether non-malignant essential mild hypertension can cause kidney failure. Whilst there is no doubt whatsoever that mild hypertension does cause heart attacks and strokes, there does not appear to be an increased risk of developing chronic renal failure. If a mildly hypertensive patient has proteinuria or evidence of renal impairment, then often some underlying renal disease is present which may have initiated a raised blood pressure and a vicious cycle may follow where hypertension causes further renal damage.

Hypertension is present in 70% of patients undergoing chronic renal dialysis. Furthermore hypertension complicates up to 70% of cases with intrinsic renal disease including glomerulonephritis.

Renal artery stenosis

Atheromatous renal artery narrowing or occlusion may occur as a consequence of high blood pressure in older patients, particularly if they are smokers. Sometimes, however, it is worth diagnosing and treating as surgical repair of the renal artery or angioplasty may reduce the blood pressure or make it easier to control with drugs and may also lead to some preservation of renal function.

In younger patients, renal artery stenosis may be due to fibrodysplasia of the renal arteries and again surgery or angioplasty may lead to normalization of the blood pressure.

Atheromatous or fibrodysplastic renal artery stenosis goes undiagnosed unless angiography or isotope renography is undertaken. Older hypertensive patients who smoke cigarettes and have evidence of arterial disease elsewhere (claudication, femoral or carotid bruits) may have renal artery stenosis and this may influence the choice of antihypertensive drugs.

MALIGNANT HYPERTENSION

Malignant and accelerated hypertension are now considered to be the same condition as their aetiology, prognosis and treatment are the same. Malignant hypertension is a multisystem disorder, characterized by arteriolar fibrinoid necrosis. Deaths are usually due to progressive renal failure, heart failure or stroke. If left untreated, most cases are dead fibrinoid necrosis. Deaths are usually due to progressive renal failure, heart failure or stroke. If left untreated, most cases are dead within two years. While in the malignant phase underlying renal or adrenal causes of hypertension are frequent, still about 65% of cases have essential rather than secondary hypertension. Malignant hypertension is the only form of hypertension which is directly associated with cigarette smoking. In all other vascular diseases, cigarette smoking has an independent effect on mortality, but is not related itself to blood pressure.

The ophthalmological features of malignant hypertension are retinal flame-shaped haemorrhages, cotton wool spots and hard exudates, particularly forming a macular star, and there may or may not be papilloedema. Patients who have all retinal features except papilloedema were once labelled as accelerated hypertensives but this distinction is now obsolete.

As part of this multisystem disorder, microangiopathic haemolytic anaemia may be seen whereas this is not seen in non-malignant hypertension unless there is severe renal failure. About half of patients with malignant hypertension do not have cardiomegaly even on echocardiography and this implies that not all cases are due to longstanding hypertension but may instead have a relatively acute onset. The incidence of malignant phase hypertension appears to be declining, possibly as a result of the more efficient detection and management of hypertension in its earlier stages. A large proportion of patients present with visual symptoms, which results in their first presenting to an ophthalmologist.

MULTIPLE RISK FACTORS

As stated earlier, hypertension must be seen as one of three cardiovascular risk factors and in clinical practice all these factors need attention. Chapter 2 enlarges upon the concept of multiple risk and discusses recent advances in our understanding of the epidemiology of hypertension.

FURTHER READING

Bamford J, Sandercock P, Dennis M, Burn J, Warlow C. Classification of natural history of clinically identifiable subtypes of cerebral infarction. *Lancet* 1991; **337**:1521–6.

Davies MJ, Woolf N, Rowles PM, Pepper J. Morphology of the endothelium over atherosclerotic plaques in human coronary arteries. *Br Heart J* 1988; **60**:459–64.

Folkow B, Grimsby G, Thulesius OE. Adaptive structural changes of the vascular walls in hypertension and their relation to the control of the peripheral resistance. *Acta Physiol Scand* 1958; **44**:252–72.

Lip GYH, Gammage MD, Beevers DG. Hypertension in the heart. *Br Med Bull* 1994; **50**:299–321.

Pulsinelli W. Pathophysiology of acute ischaemic stroke. *Lancet* 1992; **339**:533–6.

Raine AEG. Hypertension and the kidney. *Br Med Bull* 1994; **50**:322–41.

2 HYPERTENSION AND CARDIOVASCULAR RISK

BACKGROUND

In terms of life expectancy, mortality and morbidity, the height of the blood pressure must be seen in the context of the other important reversible cardiovascular risk factors such as raised plasma lipid levels and cigarette smoking. In this chapter, the multiple risk factor approach to hypertension is enlarged upon. Also discussed is the magnitude of this risk to the individual and to populations. The chapter opens with a series of definitions of hypertension which, though arbitrary, are relevant to clinical medicine and to epidemiology.

THE DEFINITION OF HYPERTENSION

In the last 30 years, the importance of hypertension as a cause of heart attacks and strokes has become increasingly recognized, largely because of the advent of acceptable antihypertensive drugs. However, the prevailing confusion as to the criteria for diagnosing hypertension may be attributed to the fact that there is still no universally recognized definition of the condition. Attempts to provide a universal definition have so far been unsuccessful. Given below is a pragmatic view relevant to clinical practice although the epidemiological view also requires detailed consideration.

The pragmatic definition of hypertension

The late Professor Geoffrey Rose has suggested that the best clinical definition can be taken as 'that level of blood pressure above which investigation and treatment do more good than harm'. In following this pragmatic approach the clinician should be fully up to date with the published clinical trials on the usefulness of the treatment of hypertension in a field where new information is constantly being made available. This definition may further change as more trials are completed. Over the last 10 years the pragmatic definition of hypertension, particularly in the elderly, has changed substantially as a result of a series of randomized controlled trials.

The pragmatic definition of hypertension is a diastolic blood pressure, in patients below the age of 80 years, measured at the fifth phase (disappearance of diastolic sounds), which after four clinical examinations exceeds 95 mmHg. In very elderly patients, there is less clarity as to the level where treatment is worthwhile but hypertension might then be defined as a diastolic blood pressure measured under the same conditions which is persistently greater than 100 to 110 mmHg. Patients whose blood pressures are at or above these levels need elementary investigation and follow-up and, in severer cases, require more detailed tests to identify underlying causes. At lower blood pressure levels, drug therapy has not ben shown to be useful. In some cases it might even be harmful in terms of the anxiety or distress caused to the patients and the side effects of antihypertensive drugs, with only minimal benefits in terms of coronary or stroke prevention. The WHO criteria (Table 2.1) have the disadvantage that they do not take into account the individua's age, or the number of times the pressure is increased.

Systolic hypertension

The foregoing definition takes no account of the height of the systolic blood pressure. Recent impressive evidence shows that elevated systolic blood pressures are worth treating even when the diastolic blood pressures are unequivocally normal. Epidemiologists have long considered that the concentration on the part of clinicians on the diastolic blood pressure alone is not logical. Population surveys and large studies of hypertensive patients have shown that the height of systolic blood pressure is usually a better predictor of death than the height of the diastolic blood pressure. For example,

Table 2.1

Definitions of hypertension (WHO criteria)

Normal	Systolic BP less than 140 mmHg and diastolic BP less than 90 mmHg
Borderline	Systolic BP 140–159 mmHg and/or diastolic BP 90–94 mmHg
Hypertension	Systolic BP 160 mmHg or more and/or diastolic BP 95 mmHg or more
Mild Hypertension	Systolic BP 160–179 mmHg and/or diastolic BP 95–104 mmHg
Isolated Systolic Hypertension (ISH)	Systolic BP 160 mmHg or more despite diastolic BP below 95 mmHg

it is possible to calculate from insurance company data that a man aged 35 with a blood pressure of 160/90 has a shorter life expectancy than a similar man whose blood pressure is 150/100. Although the diastolic blood pressure of the former is lower, his higher systolic blood pressure means that he is a greater risk.

The main reason why elevation of the systolic blood pressure has a greater prognostic value than that of diastolic blood pressure is that systolic pressure rises more sharply with advancing age and this rise may, in part, be caused by the development of thickening of the brachial artery owing to chronically raised intra-arterial pressure. This implies that raised systolic blood pressure may, in some respects, be a reflection of arterial damage. The presence of other evidence of end-organ damage, for example LVH or a previous vascular complication such as a stroke, is, not surprisingly, a powerful prognostic feature in an individual patient. It might be inferred, therefore, that the level of systolic blood pressure would be more closely related to life expectancy than the diastolic blood pressure.

In the elderly, the systolic blood pressure, which is mainly related to a continuing rise in peripheral resistance, rises steadily with advancing age and it continues accurately to predict life expectancy. By contrast, after about the age of 60 years, diastolic blood pressures tend to level off and then fall gradually, possibly due to a decline in cardiac output. This explains, at least in part, why the height of the diastolic blood pressure is less predictive over the age of 60 years.

Blood pressure in populations

An understanding of the epidemiological approach to blood pressure is important to the clinician if he or she is to manage hypertensive patients properly. The epidemiologist sees blood pressure from the point of view of its impact on the health of the whole population rather than of individual patients. Sir George Pickering pointed out that hypertension should be seen as a quantitative rather than a qualitative entity. In the general population, blood pressure is distributed in a roughly normal or Gaussian manner in a bell-shaped curve with a slight skew towards higher readings (Fig. 2.1). There is, therefore, no evidence for any subgroup of hypertensive individuals distinct from normotensives and no dividing line can be identified between normal and raised blood pressure levels.

Pickering also drew attention to the fact that the risk of heart attack or stroke is directly related to the height of blood pressure at all levels. Even people whose blood pressures are average or even below average for their age have a higher cardiovascular risk than those with lower pressures even though they would not be regarded as clinically hypertensive (Fig. 2.2). Again, hypertension appears to be a disease of quantity rather than of quality and the higher the pressure the worse the outlook. Again there is no dividing line between

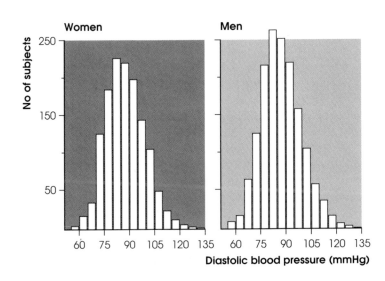

Figure 2.1

The distribution of blood pressure in middle–aged men and women in Renfrew, Scotland.

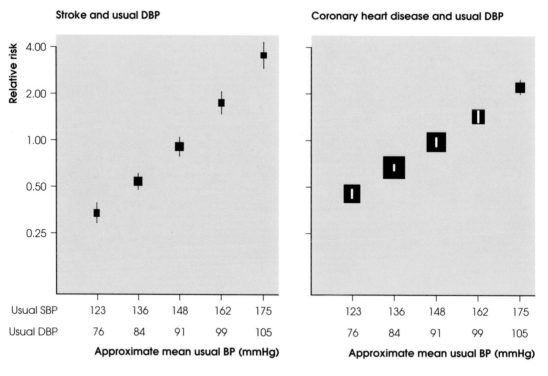

Figure 2.2
The relative risks of stroke and heart attack in relation to systolic and diastolic blood pressures. Pooled data from nine study populations.

pressures that carry a low risk and pressures that are associated with premature death.

It is apparent that, with the exception of hypotension due to autonomic neuropathy or associated with severe generalized illness, Addison's disease or following a heart attack, it is not possible to have too low a blood pressure. Unlike hypertension, which is associated with premature death, low blood pressure on its own is not a diagnosis of any prognostic significance even though there are reports that individuals with low pressures may have a higher frequency of depression and non-specific mild complaints. Despite these symptoms, they tend to live longer.

Blood pressure and age

In Westernized societies, average blood pressures tend to rise with advancing age. This rise starts soon after birth and continues until the age of about 6 weeks. Blood pressures then level off until about the age

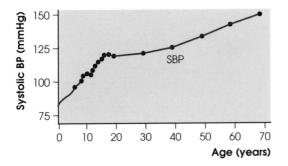

Figure 2.3
Changes in systolic blood pressure with age.

of 4 years when they start to rise again and continue to do so up until the age of about 60 with a particularly sharp rise during the growth spurt of adolescence (Fig. 2.3). This phenomenon of a rise in the average blood pressure with increasing age is not seen in most primitive or rural populations and consequently hypertension and its vascular complications are very rare. Thus, the epidemiologist would prefer to see action taken to prevent this rise in blood pressure with age, as this could lead to effective primary prevention of hypertension, and its cardiovascular complications. The rise in blood pressure with age is not 'normal' or physiological and its avoidance would be beneficial to the health of the nation.

The public health approach

The public health physician considers that 'clinical' hypertension is a disease affecting varying numbers of people who are, epidemiologically speaking, not particularly important or common. Instead, the epidemiologist considers that the blood pressures of the whole population in Westernized societies are too high and that these pressures explain the high incidence of heart attack and stroke. If the average blood pressure of the population could be reduced by as little as 5 mmHg, then there should be a reduction of the heart attack and stroke rates in the whole population by an amount which would be greater than that which could be achieved by the efficient detection and management of all 'clinically' hypertensive patients.

The concept of personal risk versus population risk may, at first, sound mutually exclusive but this is not so. Within the concept of improving primary health care as well as managing those individuals with 'clinical' hypertension, the 'high risk' strategy and the 'whole population' approach can be carried out simultaneously.

Complications of hypertension

High blood pressure has been called the hidden killer as it may be symptomless until an advanced stage. One disastrous definition of hypertension is based solely on the symptoms or complications of the disease. This means that treatment is not started until there is evidence of target organ damage. If this definition alone were to be employed, then the population would suffer even more potentially preventable strokes, heart attacks and other vascular crises than it does at present. Only about 30% of hypertensive patients have evidence of cardiovascular disease when first detected in a primary health care setting. It is far too late to wait for ECG evidence of left ventricular hypertrophy, yet alone clinical evidence of angina, heart attack or stroke.

Malignant hypertension

The term malignant hypertension is now regarded as being synonymous with accelerated hypertension. It implies very high blood pressures in association with retinal haemorrhages, exudates, and cotton wool spots with or without papilloedema. If left untreated, 88% of such cases are dead within two years.

Benign hypertension

Benign hypertension is an unfortunate term which is best avoided. It simply means that the hypertension is not associated with malignant hypertensive retinopathy. However, the prognosis of 'benign' hypertension in its severer forms can hardly be regarded as benign.

Primary or essential hypertension

The term primary hypertension is reserved for about 95% of hypertensives, in which no immediately evident underlying renal or adrenal cause can be found for the raised blood pressure. It is a confusing term as clearly all hypertension does have a cause, even if this is due to complicated inter-relationships between genetic and environmental factors.

Secondary hypertension

In a minority of hypertensives, the raised blood pressure is due to underlying renal or renal artery disease, adrenal cortical or medullary hormone excess, drugs or systemic arteritis.

HOW COMMON IS HYPERTENSION?

In men and women aged 35–65 years of age, severe hypertension with diastolic pressures of 130 mmHg or more is found in about 0.5% of the population (Table 2.2). A small proportion of these patients may have the malignant phase of hypertension. This syndrome is, however, fortunately rare. In a busy district hospital serving a population of around 300,000 people, about five or six new cases of malignant hypertension are seen each year.

Table 2.2
Estimated number of patients who are registered with an average British general practice who haver a single casual blood pressure of 160/95 mm Hg or more. Figures in brackets denote the percentage of people in that age band with hypertension.

Age	Men	Women
0–19	7 (2%)	4 (1%)
20–39	25 (7%)	8 (3%)
40–59	70 (25%)	52 (18%)
60–79	66 (35%)	93 (37%)
80+	10 (50%)	26 (50%)
Total	178	183

Diastolic blood pressures of 110–129 mmHg are found in about 4% of the adult caucasian population and 8–9% of blacks in the UK and the USA. These figures show that the disease has about twice the prevalence of diabetes mellitus.

The combined prevalence of moderate and severe hypertension is, therefore, around 4.5%. In the average primary health care practice, with about 2000 patients of all ages registered with a single practitioner, about 15 patients below the age of 65 will be found to have diastolic blood pressures of 110 mmHg or more.

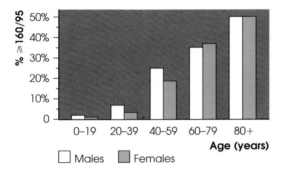

Figure 2.4
Prevalence of hypertension in Westernized populations.

It will be seen from the bell-shaped curve of the distribution of blood pressure that the milder grades of hypertension are the most common. Diastolic blood pressures between 90 and 109 mmHg are found in about 20% of the middle-aged adult population. In younger adults the prevalence is lower and in the elderly the prevalence is correspondingly higher. A casual blood pressure of 160/95 mmHg or more is found in roughly 50% of Western populations aged 70 years or more (Fig. 2.4). It is possible to calculate that in the population of England and Wales (roughly 50 million people), 7,196,000 people (14.5% of the population) of all ages will have a single casual blood pressure reading of this level or above. An average general practitioner should, therefore, expect to have around 300 patients on his list with a single casual blood pressure reading of 160/95 mmHg or more.

Similarly, in the USA, blood pressures exceeding 160/95 have been estimated to be present in 23.2 million people, this representing 15–19% of whites aged 18–74 and 27–29% of blacks. If the criteria for diagnosing hypertension are lowered to include cases with diastolic pressures between 90 and 95 mmHg, then around 40% of the population will be considered hypertensive.

Isolated systolic hypertension (ISH), where systolic pressures exceed 160 mmHg whilst diastolic pressures are below 95 mmHg, is found in around 5% of people aged under 60 years but in around 25% of people aged 75 years. This group of people are known to benefit from antihypertensive therapy.

The above figures, obtained from population screening surveys, are based on single casual blood pressure readings. On rechecking, many of these high blood pressures fall. This is partly due to familiarization of individuals to the screening survey techniques and is also partly due to the statistical trend for initially high values (and initially low values) to move towards the mean of the population on resampling. After measuring blood pressure on three or four occasions, the prevalence of hypertension falls. In one major and recent American study, only 6.9% of the non-elderly population had diastolic blood pressures that were persistently 90 mmHg or over.

All the above statistics were based on population surveys which have employed diastolic blood pressures measured at the disappearance of sounds (fifth phase). A higher prevalence would be found if the muffling of sound (fourth phase) were used, although this technique is now considered obsolete. Variations between different population surveys may be due to this, and also to the number of readings taken, and the age, gender and ethnic distribution of the population under study. Other factors influencing pressures are the manometer cuff size and the position of the arm in relation to the heart, the amount of training of the observers, the time of day and the time of year, the ambient temperature, the anxiety of the subject, and the wait time before the pressure is actually measured (see Chapter 3).

THE RISK OF HYPERTENSION

High blood pressure is the commonest risk factor for the commonest cause of death in Western populations. The two-year survival rate for patients with malignant hypertension, if left untreated, is around 12%. Patients with diastolic blood pressures between 130 and 150 mmHg but with no retinopathy have a 40% two-year survival rate if left untreated (Fig. 2.5).

Moderate hypertensives with diastolic blood pressures between 110 and 129 mmHg have an 80% two-year survival rate. However, these statistics, the only ones available, are based on information obtained 40 years ago before the advent of effective antihypertensive drugs. Such patients now receive drug therapy and their mortality is correspondingly reduced although not normalized.

In the milder grades of hypertension, where diastolic blood pressures are between 95 and 105 mmHg, the annual mortality rate at the age of 45 years is about three times higher than in people whose pressures are nearer the average for the population. While this increased relative risk is marked, the absolute risk, that is, the chance of dying within five years, is fairly small, and many people with mild hypertension survive to a normal life expectancy.

Even people whose blood pressures are just above average for the population have an annual mortality at the age of 40 years of about 4 per 1000 so that, within 10 years, 4% will die of vascular disease attributable to hypertension. By contrast, people whose blood pressures are well below the population average have an annual mortality of about 3 per 1000.

In practical terms, the clinician should be aware that a man aged 35 years with a blood pressure of 150/100 mmHg has an odds-on chance of dying before he reaches the age of 60 years unless active steps are taken to

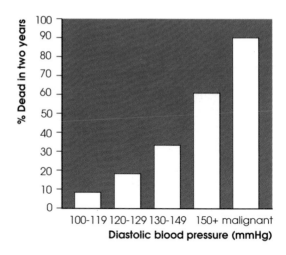

Figure 2.5
Survival rate for untreated patients with high blood pressure.

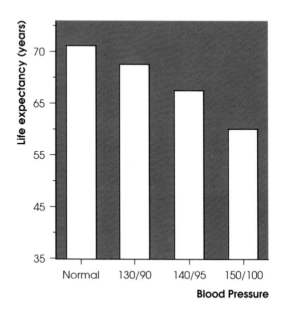

Figure 2.6
Life expectancy in relation to untreated blood pressure in men aged 35 years.

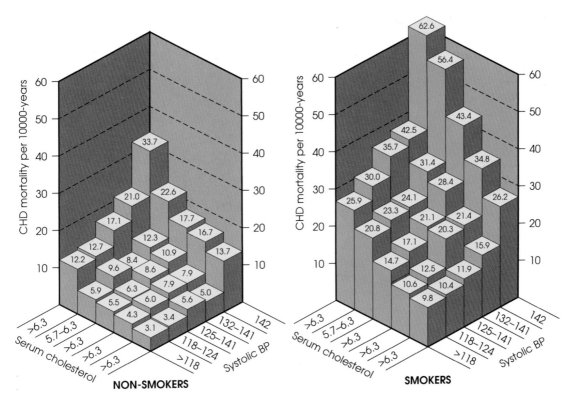

Figure 2.7
Coronary mortality rates in relation to smoking, blood pressure and cholesterol. Data from male examinees screened for the Multiple Risk Factor Intervention Trial (MRFIT).

reduce the pressure (Fig. 2.6). With advancing age, the risk of death for a given level of blood pressure increases. 'Clinical' hypertension represents about the top quintile of the blood pressures of the population aged 45 years and carries a 3% annual death rate. The same pressures at the age of 55 carry a 5% annual mortality and at the age of 65 years, annual mortality rises to 8%.

Multiple risk factors

As stated earlier, there are two other important and reversible cardiovascular risk factors in addition to raised blood pressure. These are cigarette smoking and raised blood lipids (Fig. 2.7). It is important to note that these three factors have a multiplicative or synergistic effect on each other. A person with two risk factors is much worse off than a person with only one. Thus a patient with mild hypertension but no other risk factors is not at a particularly high risk compared with a similar patient who also smokes cigarettes and has an elevated plasma cholesterol.

When assessing the risk for an individual person, all risk factors need to be taken into account, including concurrent glucose

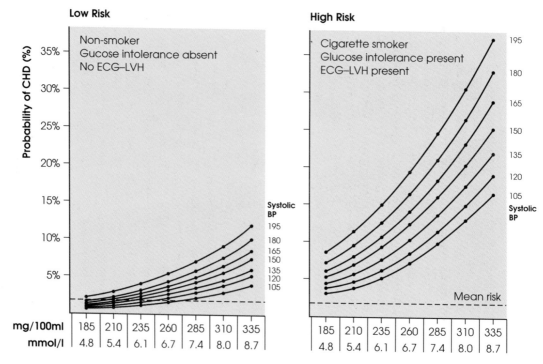

Figure 2.8

High and low risk of heart attacks. Data from the Framingham study.

intolerance and the presence of LVH (Fig. 2.8). It is important then to estimate a patient's absolute risk of premature death. However, other factors which cannot be treated also influence survival rates and the chances of sustaining a heart attack or a stroke. Firstly, as stated earlier, age is an important consideration and, in general, the benefits of managing hypertension in the elderly are greater than in younger people. This is because they have a greater absolute risk of death which may in part be reversible with drug therapy. Women have a lower risk than men at all levels of blood pressure up until the age of about 50 years when their risk steadily rises to the same level as seen in men. As discussed in more detail elsewhere, there are important ethnic and racial differences in the risk of hypertension with stroke being particularly common problem among blacks and coronary heart disease being a major cause of death among South Asians.

Another important factor which must be taken into account is the genetic influence, which exerts its effect independently of the three main cardiovascular risk factors. People with a family history of premature death, heart attack or stroke are at higher risk. This is only partly explained by familial similarities of life-style, diet and smoking habits.

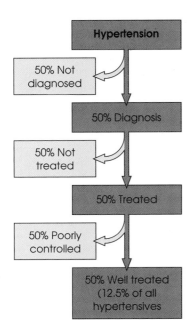

Figure 2.9
The rule of halves.

There is now increasing evidence that a high salt intake and a low potassium intake as well as a high alcohol intake have adverse effects on stroke mortality rates partially via raised blood pressure but also partly due to the direct effect on cerebral vasculature. By contrast, obesity, when it is not associated with hypertension, hyperlipidaemia or glucose intolerance, does not appear to be a major independent risk factor for cardiovascular death.

By any criteria, hypertension is important; it is also neglected. The main consideration in this chapter has been the risk of blood pressure to the individual as well as to the whole population. Most heart attacks and strokes occur in people whose pressures are either only mildly raised or are just above the average for the population. Although the risk

of death from near average blood pressure is small, because this very mild hypertension is so common, the number of vascular complications attributable to hypertension in the community is large. Primary care clinicians need to be concerned not only with blood pressures that are high enough to require antihypertensive drug therapy but also to see a lowering of blood pressures of all their clients. The goal of good medical care should include not only successful management of patients but also the primary prevention which can be achieved with a well organized educational programme.

THE UNDERDIAGNOSIS OF HYPERTENSION

The term 'the rule of halves' was first coined in the early 1970s in the United States and population studies in the UK, Europe and elsewhere have reported similar findings (Fig. 2.9). The rule of halves means that, unless special efforts are made, only half of all the hypertensive people will ever be diagnosed. Furthermore, of those cases that are diagnosed, only about half will receive antihypertensive treatment and, of those, only half will have adequate control of their blood pressure. The end result is that only 10–15% of hypertensives receive adequate medical care, a situation which constitutes a national and international scandal. It has been calculated that in the UK around 300 people die from preventable hypertension-related disease every six weeks. If a fully laden jumbo jet were to crash every six weeks killing all its passengers the mortality figures would be about the same. If such an improbable series of disasters did occur, there would be a public outcry, while these hypertension-related deaths pass almost unnoticed.

Dangerous myths

The climate that has led to the 'rule of halves' is due in part to a series of dangerous myths and misconceptions; doctors, health care administrators, politicians and patients are remarkably ignorant of the true priorities of medical care and the relative importance of chronic diseases like hypertension.

Myth 1 *Cancer is the most important health hazard.* Whilst cancer is seen as more terrifying and a more urgent medical problem, hypertension-related diseases kill more people than all other causes combined, including cancer, in men. Furthermore, hypertension is treatable and, therefore, premature deaths can be avoided. There is, however, scant evidence to show that medical care can favourably influence cancer mortality.

Myth 2 *Severe hypertension is a more important hazard to health than mild hypertension.* Although severe hypertension is a major cause of premature death, it is relatively rare. Mild hypertension with its lower risk, by contrast, is very common and its prevention or cure could lead to a massive reduction in cardiovascular disease and premature death.

Myth 3 *Hypertension is characterized by symptoms including headache and tiredness.* In the past, practically all medical textbooks stated that hypertension causes headache, tiredness and other symptoms. More recent textbooks, however, draw attention to the fact that most people with hypertension are symptomless. There is only a very weak relationship between headache and epitaxis

and the presence of mild to moderate hypertension. This means that hypertension cannot be relied upon to present with diagnostically useful symptoms at an early stage before the development of the severe vascular complications of the disease.

Myth 4 *Mild elevations of blood pressure are often due to some recent psychosocial stress and can be ignored.* Single casual measurements of blood pressure during insurance medical examinations, for example, are very important predictors of risk. A man aged 35 with a single casual diastolic blood pressure of 100 mmHg or more is unlikely to survive until retirement age unless something is done to reduce his pressure. The prognosis of people with transiently elevated blood pressure is uncertain but they cannot be regarded as being without risk. They need careful follow-up.

Myth 5 *Among patients receiving drug therapy, once blood pressure is well controlled, therapy can be stopped.* Many patients hold the mistaken belief that antihypertensive drugs are, like antibiotics, only needed for a short course of treatment. This dangerous misconception is often the fault of the doctor, who has failed to explain the nature of the disease and its treatment to the patient. Very rarely and only under close supervision is it possible to stop therapy in patients with very mild hypertension. It is only feasible if pressures have been under excellent control for some years and where only a single antihypertensive drug was necessary. Even then the majority of patients do require to restart therapy over the ensuing years and, anyway, all patients whose drug therapy has been discontinued need very active and careful follow-up.

Perhaps the biggest single reason for 'the rule of halves' is that the system of primary and secondary health care in most countries is not orientated towards the management of chronic diseases. It could be said that most countries have a national disease service rather than a national health service. Usually the doctor's role is rather like that of a shopkeeper. The patient presents with a symptom and is then given the appropriate treatment, frequently as a commercial trans-action. The onus is on the patient to seek diagnosis, treatment and follow-up. The solution to 'the rule of halves' is to reverse the patient–doctor relationship so that the initiative is in the hands of health care professionals to seek out hypertensive patients and supervise the long-term control of their blood pressure and other risk factors. This is preventative medicine at its best.

Solutions

There are remarkably few diseases for which the mass screening of healthy populations can be justified. The main criteria for well population screening are:

- The disease must be sufficiently common to justify the efforts of examining millions of healthy people.
- The disease must be detectable at an early and presymptomatic stage.
- The disease must be worth treating at an early stage, contributing to prevention of death or disease.
- The screening technique should be cheap, simple and acceptable to healthy people.
- Screening and follow-up must be contin-uous, ongoing and feasible within the existing health care resources.

By all these criteria, hypertension is a suitable case for some form of screening. It affects up to 20% of the adult population, is easily detectable and is worth controlling. The main problem is the organization of detection and follow-up programmes. Chapter 11 shows how this can be managed. This is one of the major contributions that the primary care team can make to the reduction of life-threatening levels of blood pressure in the population.

FURTHER READING

Lever AF, Harrap SB. Essential hypertension: a disorder of growth with origins in child-hood? *J Hypertens* 1992; **10**:101–20.

Hawthorne VM, Greaves DA, Beevers DG. Blood pressure in a Scottish town. *Br Med J* **1974**; 3:600–3.

MacMahon S, Peto R, Cutler J, Collins R, Sorlie P, Neaton J, Abbott R, Godwin J, Dyer A, Stamler J. Blood pressure, stroke, and coronary heart disease. Part 1, prolonged differences in blood pressure: prospective observational studies corrected for the regression dilution bias. *Lancet* 1990; **335**:765–74.

Miall WE, Chinn S. Screening for hyperten-sion: some epidemiological observations. *Br Med J* 1974; **3**:595–600.

Pickering G. Hypertension, definitions, natural histories and consequences. *Am J Med* 1982; **52**:570–83.

Smith WCS, Lee AJ, Crombie IK, Tunstall-Pedoe H. Control of blood pressure in Scotland: the rule of halves. *Br Med J* 1990; **300**:981–3.

3 THE CAUSES OF HYPERTENSION: EPIDEMIOLOGICAL CLUES

BACKGROUND

The epidemiological view of hypertension differs from the clinical view. When seen from the point of view of national mortality and morbidity statistics, hypertension- and hypertension-related deaths assume enormous proportions. This is mainly due to the very large numbers of mildly hypertensive people rather than the relatively small number of people with severe or malignant hypertension. The epidemiologists notice that the average blood pressure in all Western communities is a great deal higher than in rural African populations where hypertension and its vascular complications are almost unheard of. It is important, therefore, to work out why the average blood pressure of the whole population is raised and to investigate the many genetic and environmental factors that affect the blood pressure of the whole community.

Large surveys of population groups with accurate follow-up and notification of fatal and non-fatal cardiovascular events (cohort studies) are able to identify risk factors for hypertension and its related conditions. The object of this chapter is to discuss the information available from these surveys in relation to the cause of hypertension and also its prevention.

BLOOD PRESSURE AND AGE

Western countries

In Western countries, older people tend to have higher blood pressures than young people. Follow-up studies have demonstrated two important trends. Firstly, blood pressures rise with advancing age, and secondly, those individuals whose blood pressures start at a higher level tend to retain their place in the distribution of blood pressure and, therefore, sustain a faster age-related rise in pressure. This phenomenon of tracking is seen in all age groups, including infants. It implies that whatever environmental factors influence blood pressure, they start to exert their effect at a very early age (Fig. 3.1). This is not to deny that genetic factors have a role. It is probable that different populations and groups within populations do have geneti-

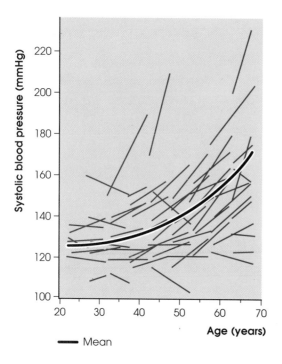

Figure 3.1
Tracking of systolic blood pressure in a follow–up study in the population of Rhondda, South Wales. Initially and on rescreening a decade later.

there may be some sort of vicious cycle effect by which those individuals with higher pressures in early life tend to develop minimal arteriolar damage, which in turn itself causes a further rise, particularly in systolic blood pressure. This rise then causes more vascular damage and further elevation of blood pressure.

Extreme old age

A slightly different picture emerges when examining the distribution of blood pressure in extremely old people (i.e., over age 85 years). Cross-sectional studies have shown that the average diastolic blood pressures of people at this age tend to be lower than those of people aged around 60 years. Longitudinal population surveys have also shown that elderly people genuinely do sustain a fall in diastolic pressure when they become very old. although their systolic blood pressures may continue to rise. This fall in diastolic blood pressure may not necessarily be physiological but may be due to clinical or subclinical cardiac damage leading to a reduction of cardiac output. Other diseases associated with weight loss and general ill-health may also be present which may contribute to a lowering of blood pressure. Another possible factor is that those people with raised blood pressures may have died earlier, leaving mainly the survivors with lower pressures to take part in population surveys. This selective mortality of hypertensive individuals may also explain why over the age of about 85 there is an inverse relationship between the height of the blood pressure and the subsequent mortality and morbidity from heart attacks and strokes so that people with the lowest pressures have the highest mortality.

cally determined differences in susceptibility to environmental influences. In Western societies it has been estimated that about 40% of the variation of blood pressure can be explained from genetic factors and about 40% from environmental factors. The remaining 20% are due to chance associations and errors.

The clear demonstration of a faster rise in blood pressure in people with higher pressures in early age also suggests that

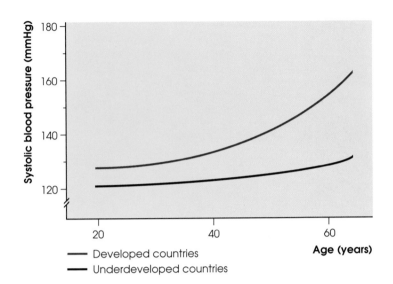

Figure 3.2
Changes in blood pressure
in developed and
developing countries.

Primitive societies

Whatever the mechanisms are that produce
a rise in blood pressure with age, there is
no reason to suppose that they are physiological. Studies of non-Westernized rural
populations have shown that hypertension
is unknown in these groups and blood
pressures show only a tiny rise with advancing age. By contrast in genetically similar
people and even relatives living in urban
communities, particularly in Africa, a
marked rise in blood pressure is seen with
age (Fig. 3.2). A recent detailed migration
study from Kenya has shown that tribesmen
whose pressures are initially low when seen
in rural areas sustain a rapid rise in blood
pressure within months of migration to live

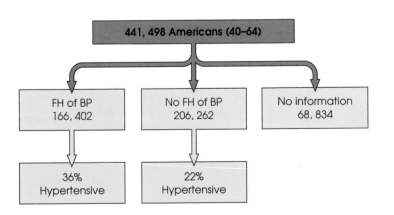

Figure 3.3
Hypertension in relation to
family history.

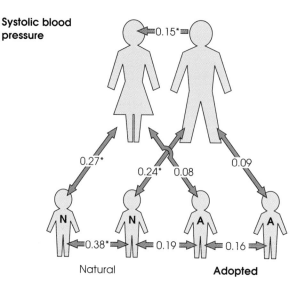

Systolic blood pressure

0.15*

0.27* 0.24* 0.08 0.09

0.38* 0.19 0.16

Natural Adopted

Figure 3.4

Relationships of systolic and diastolic blood pressures between parents and their natural and adopted children.

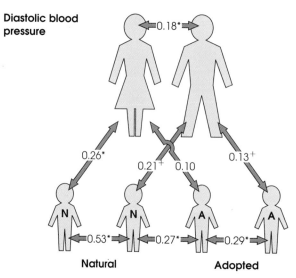

Diastolic blood pressure

0.18*

0.26* 0.21+ 0.10 0.13+

0.53* 0.27* 0.29*

Natural Adopted

*Significant at the 0.001 level of probability

+ Significant at the 0.01 level of probability

in the city. Thus, the rise in blood pressure seen with advancing age in urban societies must primarily be due to some very powerful environmental factors. The likely factors are differences in diet and other socio-economic factors, including environmental stress. However, these influences may be more marked in people with some genetic predisposition to develop hypertension in the first place.

BLOOD PRESSURE AND GENETICS

Family history

High blood pressure tends to run in families (Fig. 3.3). Furthermore, the 'normotensive' children of hypertensive patients tend to have higher blood pressures than age-matched children of people with normal blood pressures. This familial concordance of blood pressure may, in part, be due to shared exposure to environmental influences, including diet and stress, but there remains a large genetic component. This genetic component is well demonstrated by studies of monozygotic and dizygotic twins who were brought up separately and together as well as studies of adopted and non-adopted children, their siblings and their parents (Fig. 3.4).

Genetic susceptibility

The genetic component of the development of high blood pressure may not itself necessarily cause hypertension. Rather there may be a genetic predisposition to develop raised pressure in response to various environmental factors. There is some suggestion, although the data are not impressive, that normotensive relatives of hypertensives may be more susceptible to the pressor effects of high salt intake, environmental noise, isometric exercise, mental arithmetic and even high alcohol intake.

It is possible that the cause of the rise in blood pressure with age and thus the cause of hypertension may be found by investigating children or babies or even neonates. Again it is important to ascertain those influences which are genetic and those which are due to poor social environment. For instance a recent study has shown that babies with a relatively low birth weight (excluding those with intrauterine growth retardation) have a higher prevalence of hypertension in later life. This low birth weight may be related to poor socio-economic and environmental conditions experienced by their mothers during pregnancy.

RACE AND BLOOD PRESSURE

Clues into the aetiology of hypertension may also be obtained from comparison of different racial groups. Most studies of blood pressure in black and white people in the UK and the USA have reported a higher average blood pressure in blacks and, consequently, higher prevalence of hypertension. Hypertension is also common in urban Africa. By contrast, however, blacks living in rural Africa have low blood pressures and no rise with advancing age. The Kenya Luo migration study demonstrated that the marked rise in blood pressure with urbanization occurred in tandem with a sharp rise in sodium intake and a fall in potassium intake. Within Westernized countries, the higher blood pressures in black people are still apparent after correction for socio-economic and dietary factors as well as obesity. While in the UK and the USA, blacks are more likely to be unemployed, poor or stressed and they may also receive inferior medical care, there is every reason to believe that, in part, the hypertension is due to some racially determined factors. Most clinicians are aware that hypertension seems to be rather different in blacks with some differences in responses to antihypertensive drugs. Black hypertensives are less sensitive to beta-blockers and angiotensin-converting enzyme

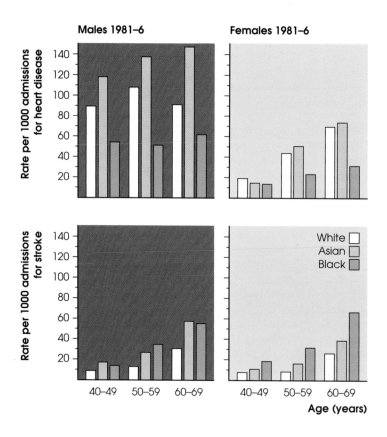

Figure 3.5
Heart attacks and strokes in blacks, whites and Asians.

inhibitors. They also have lower plasma renin levels.

It has been suggested that in the hunter-gatherer societies of rural Africa thousands of years ago, a genetically determined tendency to retain the relatively small amount of salt in the diet conveyed a biological advantage. This tendency, however, became a disadvantage in urbanized societies where salt intake, often from junk food, is high.

While hypertension is definitely commoner in black people in the USA and UK, they have less coronary heart disease than do white people but have considerably more strokes (Fig. 3.5). It remains uncertain, however, whether, for a given level of blood pressure, blacks have a higher risk of death than white people. Most population surveys have shown that black people have lower serum total cholesterol levels and higher HDL cholesterol levels than whites. This may, in part, explain their apparent protection from coronary heart disease. However, it is probable that the differences in coronary heart disease between blacks and whites cannot be entirely explained by differences in the three known coronary risk factors, hypertension, cigarette smoking and hyperlipidaemia.

Other ethnic groups

There are few reliable studies of other ethnic minority groups in Western countries. Hypertension is known to be common among people of Indian and Pakistani origin in the UK and in Trinidad. The relatively small number of studies conducted in the Indian subcontinent suggest the rise in blood pressure with advancing age is more evident in urban than in rural populations. The Asian population in the UK does have higher rates of coronary heart disease than the whites, even though their blood pressures are not higher.

There is considerably more information about hypertension amongst Japanese people. In Japan, high blood pressure is very common and in line with this the stroke incidence is also very high. By contrast, coronary heart disease is rare in Japan. Comparisons with Japanese migrants to Honolulu and the West coast of the USA have shown that with increasing adoption of American life-styles and diet, there is a reduction in hypertension and stroke incidence but a marked rise in coronary heart disease. The Japanese migrant studies, therefore, also confirm a very powerful effect of environmental factors on hypertension and its complications.

BLOOD PRESSURE AND GENDER

Below the age of about 45, women tend to have slightly lower blood pressures than men. They also have less coronary heart disease and strokes. These differences in early life may be due to endocrinological events associated with the childbearing years (Fig. 3.6). High blood pressure remains a

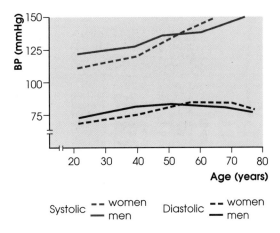

Figure 3.6
Changes in blood pressure with age in men and women.

risk factor for heart attacks and strokes in premenopausal women but the gradient of blood pressure and risk is less steep than in men.

Blood pressure and pregnancy

There is a weak tendency for women who have had pre-eclampsia in the past to develop high blood pressure in later life. The topic of hypertension in pregnancy is covered in more detail in Chapter 16.

Blood pressure and the menopause

After the age of about 50 years, blood pressures rise in women to become similar to those seen in men. At the same time, heart attack and stroke rates increase. The

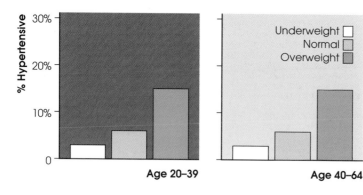

Figure 3.7
Prevalence of hypertension in relation to weight.

relative absence of hypertension in cardio-vascular disease in women before the menopause raised the possibility that endogenous oestrogens are in some way protective. However, high doses of synthetic oestrogens as are used in the oral contra-ceptive pill certainly confer no benefit and occasionally themselves cause hypertension. In postmenopausal women who have low endogenous oestrogen levels, replacement with low-dose natural oestrogens does not appear to cause any rise in blood pressure and may be protective against coronary heart disease and strokes (see also Chapter 14).

SOCIOLOGICAL AND DIETARY FACTORS

Weight

Fat people have higher blood pressures than thin people (Fig. 3.7). There is, however, an important confounding factor to be taken into account. There is a greater error when measuring blood pressure in obese arms, particularly if the blood pressure cuffs are too small. There is a tendency to overestimate blood pressure in people with fat arms and the fatter the arm, the greater the overestima-tion. After correction for arm circumference, there still remains a positive relationship between body mass index and both systolic and diastolic blood pressure. Recent statistical analysis suggests that body mass index exerts its effects mainly on diastolic blood pressure with little independent effect on the systolic pressure, which is mainly related to age. The mechanism by which obese people have a high blood pressure is uncertain. It is proba-ble that obese people eat more sodium and less potassium and, therefore, may develop a rise of blood pressure due to dietary factors. It is probable also that high blood pressure is more closely correlated with central obesity rather than with high body mass index alone. More recently it has been suggested that obese people are relatively resistant to insulin whilst undergoing intravenous glucose toler-ance tests. This concept of insulin resistance is now the subject of a great deal of research. It has been postulated that insulin resistance leads to a rise in intracellular sodium concentration and to renal retention

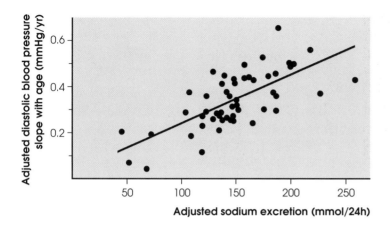

Figure 3.8
Relationship between sodium excretion and the rise of blood pressure with age. Data from INTERSALT project.

of salt and water. Thus, insulin itself may possibly play some role in the aetiology of essential hypertension, particularly in obese individuals.

Since obesity is itself associated with high blood lipid levels, glucose intolerance and high blood pressure, fat people are more prone to coronary heart disease. It is possible, however, that after allowing for these factors, a high body mass index alone may not itself be an independent cardiovascular risk factor. This is only a theoretical consideration as obese people do tend to have the other cardiovascular risk factors and thus have a high risk of death. When people lose weight, their blood pressures tend to fall.

Salt

The first suggestion that a high salt intake gives rise to high blood pressure goes back four thousand years to the ancient Chinese Yellow Emperor, Huang Ti. He suggested that people who ate too much salt developed harder pulses. More recent epidemiological evidence is impressive so that the salt hypothesis can no longer be considered controversial.

As stated earlier, primitive rural societies in Africa and also in the South Pacific islands consume very little salt (below 50 mmol per day) and have hardly any hypertension and no rise in blood pressure with age. Conversely, European, American and Japanese populations consume a lot of salt (200–300 mmol/day) and have high average blood pressures. The very high incidence of strokes amongst the northern Japanese may well be related to their very high salt intake and the recent impressive reduction in stroke rates may well be attributable to the reduction in salt intake that has occurred over the last 20 years. The INTERSALT project was a major international collaborative study in which directly comparable data were obtained from 52 different populations in 30 countries. All the important confounding differences between urban or Westernized populations and primitive groups were taken into account. The INTERSALT study showed unequivocally that the rise in blood pressure seen with advancing age in urban but not rural populations was due to the amount of salt in the diet (Fig. 3.8).

Similarly a recent overview or meta-analysis of all the reliable individual population surveys of blood pressure in relation to salt intake confirmed a close relationship between salt intake and the height of the blood pressure.

There is good evidence that over the last 50 years, dietary salt consumption in the USA and Europe has fallen and this has been paralleled by a fall in stroke incidence. The fall in stroke incidence since the Second World War is only partly due to the more frequent use of antihypertensive medication in hypertensive people. There is now evidence that high salt intake may cause strokes partly through a direct effect on cerebral vessels and partly by a concomitant high prevalence of hypertension.

It used to be said that while international comparisons support the salt story, individual national studies do not. However, in the INTERSALT project, a positive relationship was found between salt intake and systolic blood pressure in 39 of the 52 populations examined and this association was statistically significant in 15 populations.

The salt hypothesis receives further confirmation from observations that extreme salt loading can cause a rise in blood pressure and that modest salt restriction causes a significant fall in blood pressure in hypertensive and normotensive people.

Taking all these facts into account, it is our opinion that the salt hypothesis should no longer be regarded as a controversial hypothesis but more as a confirmed mechanism.

Potassium

The role of potassium in lowering blood pressure has received less attention until recently. International comparisons of blood pressure and potassium intake, and notably the INTERSALT project, have shown that a higher potassium intake appears to be associated with a lower prevalence of hypertension. It is also probable that a low potassium intake has an independent effect on stroke mortality which is separate from that of the blood pressure. Sodium and potassium cannot be easily considered separately and when assessing their effects, it is probably best to examine dietary or urinary sodium/potassium ratios.

It is interesting to note that in the USA, where hypertension is common in blacks, there are virtually no differences in sodium intake or urinary sodium excretion between blacks and whites but there are marked differences in potassium intake and excretion. Black people tend to consume lower quantities of potassium-rich foods, which are usually of high quality and expensive. This may partly explain some of the social and economic factors causing racial differences in blood pressure.

Alcohol

Most epidemiological studies have shown a close positive relationship between alcohol consumption and blood pressure. This was particularly evident in the INTERSALT project. There is also evidence for a correlation between a high alcohol intake and stroke mortality and morbidity in both community and clinical studies. There is a trend, however, for the lowest blood pressures to be recorded in those people who regularly consume small amounts of alcohol when compared with people who drink no alcohol at all. Strangely, 'teetotallers' seem to have slightly higher blood pressures than moderate drinkers (Fig. 3.9). This is probably due to the fact that some

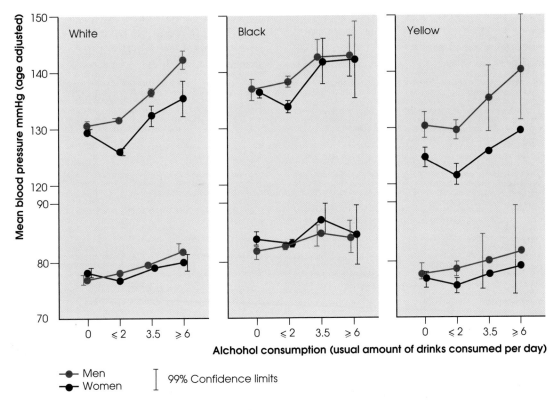

Figure 3.9
Relationship between alcohol intake and blood pressure. Data from Kaiser Permanente Health Insurance Program.

people who claim that they do not drink have, in fact, stopped drinking for medical reasons or they may have deceived their enquirers. Alternatively, teetotallers may genuinely have slightly higher blood pressures. This would imply that small amounts of alcohol lower blood pressure but large amounts of alcohol raise it. In heavy drinkers, hypertension is common and the more they drink, the higher their blood pressures are. Hypertensive patients have a higher frequency of raised liver

enzymes (gamma glutamyltransferase) and higher mean erythrocyte cell volumes (MCV). It has been estimated that about 10% of hypertensives have alcohol-induced hypertension.

The alcohol–hypertension relationship remains the subject of future research, particularly as no convincing mechanism can yet be identified. However, in view of the reversibility of the link between alcohol and blood pressure, it is important that clinicians attempt to moderate the amount of alcohol their patients consume, where possible avoiding antihypertensive drugs.

The mechanism by which alcohol raises blood pressure remains unknown. It is possible that amongst very heavy drinkers, the height of the blood pressure is more closely related to the symptoms and signs of alcohol withdrawal rather than to the alcohol itself. During alcohol withdrawal, many patients develop sympathetic over-activity and very high plasma noradrenaline levels have been reported.

In contrast, acute alcohol loading studies conducted amongst hypertensives and normotensive volunteers have shown that alcohol causes a rapid rise in blood pressure and a rapid fall afterwards, and that this relationship closely follows the blood alcohol levels. This acute rise in blood pressure in response to alcohol may be due to the direct effect of alcohol on vascular smooth muscle.

Population surveys also tend to support a relatively acute affect on alcohol and blood pressure. Examinees in such surveys who have drunk heavily in the days prior to screening tend to have high blood pressures. By contrast, people who drank heavily more than three days before being examined but have drunk nothing in the three days immediately prior to screening have lower blood pressures.

The findings of the acute rises and falls of blood pressure in response to alcohol has led to the hypothesis that alcohol does not so much cause hypertension but causes transient elevations in blood pressure which are detectable in clinical practice and lead to the individual being labelled as hypertensive.

Coffee and blood pressure

A great many studies have shown that there is a positive link between coffee consumption and coronary heart disease. This may be partly explained by the confounding effect of concomitant cigarette smoking and a high-cholesterol diet. There is also some evidence that coffee consumption causes an acute but reversible rise in blood pressure. Recently, a long-term study has shown that continued abstinence from coffee over a period of several weeks may slightly reduce blood pressure. It has been claimed that instant coffee has a greater pressor effect than 'real' coffee, as long as it is not made with boiling water.

Animal fats

In general, vegetarians have lower blood pressures than non-vegetarians but it is uncertain why this difference occurs. After correction for the effects of the associated salt content of non-vegetarian meals, this effect seems to persist. This has led to the hypothesis that a high animal fat diet itself may be related to hypertension. It is possible also that the high fibre content of the vegetarian diet may explain its protective action against hypertension.

Calcium

Some population studies have reported a positive correlation between blood pressure and serum total calcium concentrations. There is, however, little convincing evidence that high blood pressure is related either to a low or to a high calcium intake in the diet. It has been suggested that a low-calcium diet may contribute to raised blood pressure in some populations but these data remain controversial. More recently, an overview of all the studies of calcium loading has shown that this manoeuvre has a negligible effect on blood pressure.

Smoking

After one or two cigarettes have been smoked, blood pressure may rise sharply. Despite this acute effect, epidemiological studies have shown no relationship or even a negative correlation between blood pressure and cigarette smoking. Non-smokers have a slightly higher blood pressure than smokers and people who stop smoking sometimes sustain a small rise in blood pressure. These differences may be due to changes in body weight. Heavy smokers are thinner, iller and more breath-less and when they stop smoking, they eat more and gain weight. Although smoking is not related closely to blood pressure, it is of course a potent independent risk factor for cardiac death. Hypertensive patients who are also smokers have a much higher risk of death.

There is one rare but interesting excep-tion to the rule that cigarette smoking and blood pressure are negatively associated. Several studies have shown that the preva-lence of cigarette smoking is high amongst malignant hypertensives compared with non-malignant hypertensives and when compared with the general population. Cigarette smoking is also closely associated with atheromatous renal artery stenosis.

Blood pressures and social class

In Western countries, blood pressures as well as coronary heart disease and stroke rates tend to be lower in people from higher social classes. It is probable that these differ-ences can be explained by differences in salt intake, alcohol consumption and body mass index. More recently, it has been suggested that intrauterine undernutrition, which is also related to poverty, may be a factor in the aetiology of hypertension in later life. It remains uncertain, however, whether the social class differences in blood pressure can all be explained on the basis of other concomitant environmental factors. In the USA, it has been demonstrated that the highest social class blacks still have higher blood pressures than the lowest social class whites (Fig. 3.10). It is important to note that in the developing countries of Africa, the social class/hypertension relationship is the reverse of that seen in Europe. Strokes and hypertension are commoner in people who are in the executive and managerial classes in West Africa, and these are the most economically active. The situation in Africa now resembles that seen in the UK before the 1939–45 war. Nutritional factors must explain these trends and this will be the basis of a new major international study to be conducted during the mid-1990s.

Stress

Hypertension being a disease of Westernized, and particularly of urban, societies (although large urban/rural differ-ences are not seen much in Europe and the USA), it is tempting to attribute high blood pressure to stress and modern living. Certainly, acutely stressful stimuli raise blood pressure and may be more pressor in subjects who have familial hypertension. However, there remains considerable doubt as to whether chronic stress raises blood pressure. Investigation of environmental

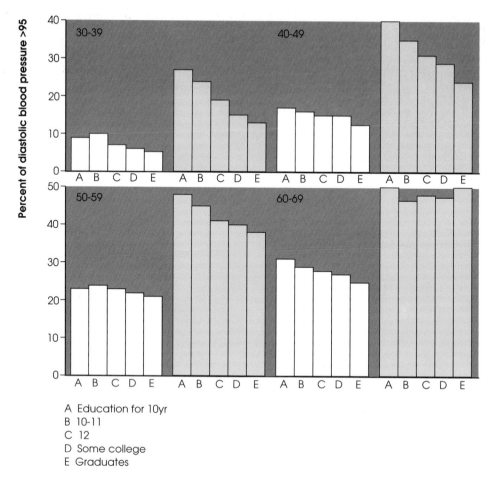

A Education for 10yr
B 10-11
C 12
D Some college
E Graduates

Figure 3.10
Hypertension in relation to the duration of education in blacks and whites.

stress and high blood pressure in population surveys is confounded by other social factors, including poverty, dietary fats, calorie, electrolyte and alcohol intake and cigarette smoking. Studies of various psychosocial indices, including aggression, neuroticism and introversion, have produced conflicting results. Many reliable studies have found no clear-cut effect. In individu-als, there is some evidence of a relationship between stress and hypertension. The type A/type B classification of personality has demonstrated, with many exceptions, that type A (stressed) people have higher blood pressures and a relatively higher risk of death than type B people. However, hyper-tensives may develop higher stress levels once they have been diagnosed and made

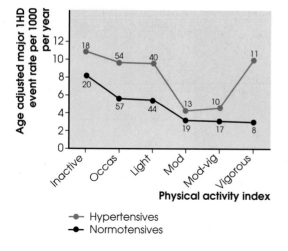

Figure 3.11
Exercise and coronary heart disease.

More recently, a study of the effects of different levels of exercise in a randomized controlled trial have demonstrated that increasing exercise lowers blood pressure independently from any other dietary manoeuvres.

Trace metals

It has been claimed that both cadmium and lead, which are environmental pollutants, may cause high blood pressure. Many of these associations have not been confirmed by detailed studies which have taken concurrent alcohol intake into account. The main source of cadmium to the human body is cigarette smoke. The evidence for the trace metal hypertension hypothesis must now be regarded as very fragile. Conversely, however, there is fairly good evidence that blood pressures are lower in areas where the drinking water is hard (i.e. has a higher calcium content). The mechanisms for this association are unknown.

to worry about their health. The term 'hypertensive personality' is misleading and may only be an accurate description of people who are being called frequently to the blood pressure clinic.

Exercise

Dynamic exercise raises blood pressure and isometric exercise raises it a lot. Despite this, there is good evidence that people who take regular exercise are healthier and have lower blood pressures than those who take none. There is evidence that regular exercise decreases coronary heart disease in normotensives and hypertensives (Fig. 3.11). This may be partly because they are thinner and tend to have more sensible dietary, drinking and smoking habits.

Ambient temperature

There is a fairly close relationship between blood pressure and ambient temperature. In the northern hemisphere, blood pressures settle in the summer when it is warmer. There is less variation in blood pressure in areas where there is less seasonal variation in temperature. In Britain, blood pressures tend to be higher in the winter and similarly stroke mortality is also high at this time. This may be due to a direct pressor effect of cold weather. Conversely, in warm weather people may be more cheerful, may lose more sodium in sweat and may be relatively vasodilated. This effect of ambient temperature on blood pressure is of little clinical importance but is an important confounding variable to be taken into account in population surveys.

CONCLUSIONS

The epidemiologist's view of hypertension has led to the identification of a series of risk factors which are relevant to clinical practice. It is also true that reversal of those environmental factors in populations could have a greater impact on mortality and morbidity from hypertension-related disease than the efficient care only of those individuals with high pressures.

Even after taking into account all the environmental and genetic influences discussed in this chapter, a large amount of variation of blood pressure between populations remains unexplained. For this reason, epidemiological research must be continued and novel possible risk factors investigated.

FURTHER READING

Havlik RJ, Feinleib M. Epidemiology and genetics of hypertension. *Hypertension* 1982; 4 (Suppl 3):121–7.

The HDFP Cooperative Group. Race, education and prevalence of hypertension. *Am J Epidiol* 1977; **106**:351–61.

Intersalt Cooperative Research Group. Intersalt: an international study of electrolyte excretion and blood pressure. Results for 24 hour urinary sodium and potassium excretion. *Br Med J* 1988; **297**:319–28.

Klatsky A, Friedman GD, Siegelaub MS, et al. Alcohol consumption and blood pressure. Kaiser-Permanente multiphasic health examination data. *N Engl J Med* 1977; **296**:1194–200.

Perry IJ, Whincup PH, Shapter AG. Environmental factors in the development of essential hypertension hypertension. *Br Med Bull* 1994; **50**:246–59.

Stamler R, Stamler J, Riedlinger WF, et al. Family (parental) history and prevalence of hypertension. *JAMA* 1979; **241**:43–6.

4 FACTORS CONTROLLING BLOOD PRESSURE

BACKGROUND

This chapter discusses the mechanisms that are known to control blood pressure in normal people and those factors that may raise it both in patients with essential hypertension and in the small minority of patients with an underlying cause. Studies in the community and also in general practice have shown that less than 2% of patients with high blood pressure have an identifiable underlying cause. Even in hospital practice less than 10% of cases have a renal or an adrenal disease underlying their hypertension. Hence in the majority of people with raised blood pressure the cause is not known. Rather than call this 'hypertension of unknown cause' it is usually labelled 'primary hypertension' or, more commonly, 'essential hypertension'. A great deal of research has been centred on the mechanisms underlying essential hypertension. An understanding of these mechanisms might help prevent high blood pressure developing. This is preferable to having to treat the blood pressure at a relatively late stage in the course of the disease.

MECHANISMS FOR MAINTAINING NORMAL BLOOD PRESSURE

The height of the blood pressure is determined by the amount of blood that is pumped out by the heart and by the resistance to flow in the peripheral arterial tree. Surprisingly the major resistance to flow is not in the large arteries or in the capillaries but in the small arterioles of the vascular system. These arterioles are highly contractile and at all times constricted to some degree. The amount of narrowing for a given cardiac output determines the height of the blood pressure. Variations in the degree of constriction from one area to another also regulate regional blood flow.

There are many complex systems regulating the degree of resistance of the arterioles as well as the cardiac output. For example, during exercise there is an increase in cardiac output but a large reduction in peripheral vascular resistance in the arterioles supplying the voluntary muscles. Blood pressure therefore tends to remain relatively constant.

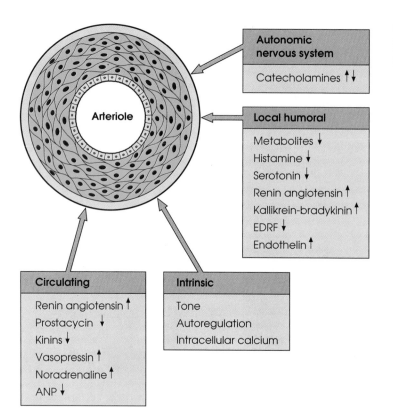

Figure 4.1
Factors affecting arteriolar tone.

Labels within the figure:

Arteriole

Autonomic nervous system
Catecholamines ↑↓

Local humoral
Metabolites ↓
Histamine ↓
Serotonin ↓
Renin angiotensin ↑
Kallikrein-bradykinin ↑
EDRF ↓
Endothelin ↑

Circulating
Renin angiotensin ↑
Prostacycin ↓
Kinins ↓
Vasopressin ↑
Noradrenaline ↑
ANP ↓

Intrinsic
Tone
Autoregulation
Intracellular calcium

Cardiac output

In patients with established hypertension, cardiac output is normal and the elevated blood pressure is due to a raised peripheral resistance. In very severe hypertension when the heart is under strain, cardiac output may fall and left ventricular failure may supervene, particularly where there is associated coronary artery disease. It has been suggested that in the early phase of the development of essential hypertension, cardiac output is raised and peripheral resistance is normal and that, as blood pressure rises over the ensuing years, peripheral resistance rises and cardiac output returns to normal. However, evidence for this is not convincing. These subjects with so-called 'borderline hypertension' were likely to be more anxious and thereby have increased cardiac output when first examined.

Left ventricular hypertrophy

Due to the increased resistance to blood flow the left ventricle has to pump harder and enlarges. This maintains cardiac output but in the longer term may lead to heart failure and an increased incidence of cardiac arrythmias.

Peripheral resistance

The walls of the small arterioles contain smooth muscle cells which respond to both local and circulating hormonal influences and to neural input through the autonomic nervous system. The degree of contraction of smooth muscle cells is thought to be determined by their intracellular free calcium content. Calcium is normally found in very low concentrations in these cells compared with plasma so that in order to maintain this gradient calcium pumps on the cell membrane extrude calcium from within the cell to the outside. There are also mechanisms within the cell controlling intracellular calcium. Several lines of evidence now suggest that the increased tone in the arteriolar smooth muscle cells of patients with high blood pressure may well be related to an increase in intracellular calcium within the arteriolar smooth muscle cell.

There is also evidence that the increased pressure within the arterioles leads to the development of structural changes within the vessels. The vessels become thicker so that the lumen is further reduced and this may lead to further increases in peripheral resistance and blood pressure. This vascular hypertrophy or remodelling may possibly occur independently of the rise in blood pressure and may be due to vascular growth factors either within the arteriolar smooth muscle or circulating.

Regulation of peripheral resistance

The degree of constriction of the arterioles is controlled by many factors (Fig. 4.1). Nearly all arterioles have the intrinsic ability to regulate flow so that if flow is increased, the arterioles constrict to reduce the flow and, if flow is reduced, the arterioles dilate.

This so-called 'autoregulation' may be dependent on local metabolites but increasing evidence suggests that it may be related to local hormones released by the endothelium. One of these that has been recently characterized is the endothelial-derived relaxant factor, or nitric oxide.

The autonomic nervous system

The autonomic nervous system, particularly the sympathetic, can cause both constriction and dilation of arteriolar smooth muscle. Under normal circumstances the circulating amounts of noradrenaline (norepinephrine) and adrenaline (epinephrine) play only a small role in determining the degree of contraction of arterioles. Most circulating noradrenaline is derived from peripheral sympathetic ganglia or nerve endings where it is a neurotransmitter. Relatively little is derived from secretion by the adrenal gland so that the major effect of the sympathetic nervous system to the arterioles is through the nerves that directly supply the small arterioles. Drugs which block the sympathetic system, including the alpha- and beta-blockers, lower blood pressure in both normotensive and hypertensive subjects, clearly illustrating the important role that the autonomic nervous system has in maintaining peripheral resistance and thereby blood pressure in both hypertensive and normotensive subjects.

Overactivity of the sympathetic nervous system has been suggested as a possible cause of essential hypertension. Early papers appeared to show a relationship between plasma noradrenaline levels and blood pressure but these did not take into account the rise in plasma noradrenaline levels that occurs with age. Furthermore, assessing the activity of the sympathetic nervous system is

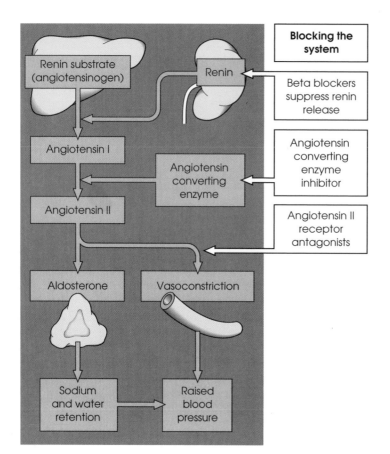

Figure 4.2
The renin angiotensin system and site of action of drugs that block the system.

extremely difficult. Plasma levels of noradrenaline and adrenaline reflect sympathetic activity rather poorly and in particular do not reflect regional differences in sympathetic outflow. Therefore, at present, there is little evidence that increased sympathetic activity causes high blood pressure. On the other hand, the sympathetic nervous system has a very important role in the short-term variations in blood pressure, particularly in response to stress, exercise and changes in posture.

The renin–angiotensin–aldosterone system

The renin–angiotensin–aldosterone system, like the sympathetic nervous system, is an important mechanism which maintains normal blood pressure, and both systems are closely integrated. The various components of the renin system can be easily measured and therefore assessment of the activity of the system is more easy than that of the sympathetic nervous system. Renin is an enzyme secreted by the juxtaglomerular cells in the cortex of the kidney. In the plasma it cleaves off a small peptide, angiotensin I, from a large circulating protein (renin substrate or angiotensinogen) which is made in the liver. The small peptide, angiotensin I, has no physiological action but is immediately converted to the peptide, angiotensin II, by the so-called angiotensin-converting enzyme inhibitor (ACE).

Angiotensin II is one of the most potent vasoconstrictors known, causing contraction of both the small arterioles and veins. It can also stimulate the sympathetic nervous system by a direct effect on the brain and also indirectly by increasing peripheral neurotransmission.

Angiotensin II is an important stimulus for the secretion of aldosterone from the adrenal gland. Both aldosterone and angiotensin II are directly important in the regulation of sodium and water balance, causing retention of sodium. The activity of the renin–angiotensin system is closely related to the concurrent dietary salt intake; as more salt is consumed, the amount of circulating angiotensin II decreases. If salt intake is reduced .there is a large rise in renin and angiotensin II levels. Other stimuli for the release of renin are the sympathetic nervous system and the baroreceptors within the renal arterioles which directly respond to a fall in pressure by increasing renin release.

Various inhibitors of the system have been developed. Beta-blockers cause a fall in renin release by about 50%. There are also direct renin inhibitors but as yet the only oral one available is short-acting and poorly absorbed. More important are the converting enzyme inhibitors that directly block the enzyme that converts angiotensin I to angiotensin II. They are widely used in the treatment of high blood pressure and heart failure. Recently, direct competitive antagonists of angiotensin II at receptor sites which can be taken orally have been developed and they are likely to become another major way of blocking the system. Studies with these different inhibitors have clearly shown that the renin–angiotensin system is an important buffer system that regulates blood pressure under normal conditions and tries to maintain blood pressure under different volume conditions at the same level (e.g. alteration of salt intake).

In view of the important role of the renin system in regulating normal blood pressure it is not surprising that it also plays an important role in regulating blood pressure in essential hypertension. However, whether it is involved in the cause of the high blood pressure is much more debatable. In general, patients with essential hypertension have lower circulating levels of renin and angiotensin II than normotensive individuals of the same age. Only in renovascular hypertension, where the renal artery is narrowed and the perfusion pressure of the glomeruli drops, and in malignant or accelerated hypertension, where there is direct damage to the afferent arterioles, again leading to a fall in glomerular pressure, are large amounts of renin secreted. In these few patients the raised levels of angiotensin II is the immediate direct cause of their high blood pressure.

Aldosterone is a potent sodium-retaining mineralocorticoid hormone secreted by the adrenal cortex. Its main action is on the distal renal tubules, increasing the exchange of sodium for potassium, thereby causing sodium retention at the expense of potassium loss (Fig. 4.3). In man, aldosterone release is mainly under the control of angiotensin II.

Atrial natriuretic peptide

The atria of the heart secrete peptides that play an important role in regulating the sodium balance by a direct effect of increasing sodium

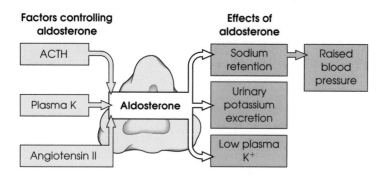

Figure 4.3
Aldosterone.

Factors controlling aldosterone: ACTH, Plasma K, Angiotensin II → Aldosterone

Effects of aldosterone: Sodium retention → Raised blood pressure; Urinary potassium excretion; Low plasma K+

excretion from the renal tubules as well as indirectly by suppressing renin release (Fig. 4.4). The plasma levels of atrial natriuretic peptides are raised in many patients with essential hypertension. Drugs which block the breakdown of atrial natriuretic peptides have been developed; these atriopeptidase inhibitors raise the endogenous levels of atrial peptides two-to-three-fold. These drugs may have a role in the treatment of hypertension and heart failure in the future.

Vasopressin

Vasopressin (antidiuretic hormone) is secreted by the posterior pituitary gland and plays an important role in controlling water balance. Despite its name it probably has little to do with blood pressure control under normal circumstances. This is due to the fact that its vasoconstrictor actions are buffered by the baroreceptors which cause reflex changes in cardiac output so that there is little change in blood pressure.

Cortisol

Cortisol is secreted by the adrenal gland and appears to have a direct pressor effect on

vascular tissues as well as an indirect effect through its slight mineralocorticoid action on the kidney. At the same time high cortisol levels may cause a rise in circulating renin and, thereby, angiotensin II. Unsurprisingly, therefore, patients with excess cortisol secretion (Cushing's disease) have an increase in blood pressure. By contrast when the adrenals fail, as occurs in Addison's disease, both cortisol and aldosterone levels are low and patients present with gross sodium and water depletion, low blood pressure and postural falls in blood pressure.

Local vasoactive hormones

Prostaglandins

Prostaglandins are local tissue hormones that may play an important role in determining local arteriolar tone. When given by intravenous infusion most prostaglandins cause vasodilatation. This is particularly so for prostacyclin. However, there is no evidence to suggest that there is any abnormality of prostaglandin metabolism in patients with high blood pressure, but indomethacin, an inhibitor of prostaglandin production, does block some of the blood pressure-lowering

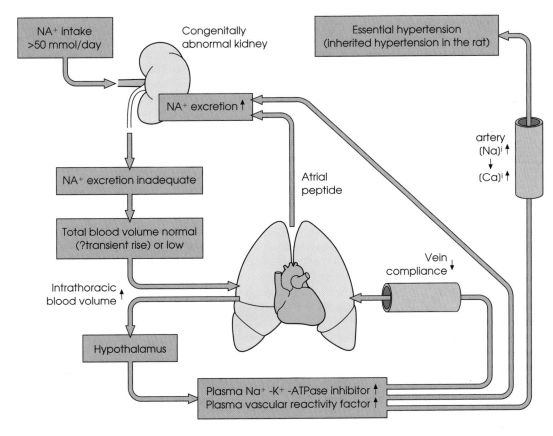

Figure 4.4
Suggested mechanism whereby salt causes high blood pressure.

drugs. In other words, the blood pressure-lowering drug may in part work through this local hormonal system.

Kallikrein–kinin system

The kallikrein-kinin system is a cascade system which produces bradykinin, a local tissue vasodilator, that could possibly lower blood pressure. Bradykinin is partly degraded by the same converting enzyme (ACE) which is responsible for the genera-

tion of angiotensin II. Thus ACE inhibitors could work both by reducing plasma angiotensin II production and by increasing bradykinin levels although it is probable that the fall in plasma angiotensin II is the main mode of action.

Serotonin (5-hydroxytryptamine)

A vasoconstrictor serotonin is released by platelets but in this role its action on peripheral resistance is debatable. It also plays an important independent role as a neurotransmitter.

Endothelial relaxant factor (nitric oxide)

A powerful local vasodilator, the endothelial relaxant factor, secreted by endothelial cells lining the arterioles, is now known to be nitric oxide. Studies with inhibitors of the system have shown that it plays an important role in maintaining resting vascular tone and some evidence suggests that in damaged arterioles, particularly in patients with atheroma, its release may be impaired, causing further vasoconstriction.

Endothelin

Endothelin is a peptide which is also secreted by endothelial cells and is the most powerful vasoconstrictor known. However, it has a long half-life and circulates at very low plasma levels. Its physiological role outside a local response to tissue injury is not at present clear.

Baroreceptor reflexes

The baroreceptors in the carotid sinus and aortic arch are sensitive buffers smoothing out variations in heart rate, blood pressure and cardiac output. In patients with high blood pressure there is some resetting of these baroreceptors so that higher pressures are needed to activate the baroreceptor reflex, but there is no evidence that abnormal baroreceptor tone is responsible for the high blood pressure. The abnormalities described to date are more likely to be a consequence of the chronically raised blood pressure.

The kidney

Despite our knowledge of the various mechanisms that maintain normal blood pressure, studies of these systems have so far shed little light on the mechanism underlying essential hypertension. In the early 1960s it was suggested that in essential hypertension there might be a primary abnormality of the kidney causing sodium and water retention. This would cause an increase in extracellular volume and a consequent rise in plasma volume and therefore a rise in cardiac output. The hypothesis suggested that this then caused an increase in peripheral resistance by autoregulation. Blood pressure then increased with a subsequent return of cardiac output to normal. The increase in blood pressure then caused further structural thickening of the small arterioles, giving rise to further vasoconstriction and the development of high blood pressure. This idea, whilst implicating the kidney as the main cause of hypertension, has not received much support as it has been difficult to demonstrate any evidence of plasma or extracellular volume expansion in the early phase of hypertension.

However, the concept that the kidney plays an important role in the development of hypertension has been illustrated by elegant kidney cross-transplantation experiments in rats with genetically determined hypertension. If the kidney from the genetic bred hypertensive rat is transplanted into a control animal, that animal then develops high blood pressure. If the reverse is done, that is a kidney from a normotensive rat is put into the kidney of the genetically hypertensive rat, that rat no longer develops high blood pressure. These experiments clearly demonstrate, at least in these rat models of hypertension, that the kidney is the primary cause of the high blood pressure. Much circumstantial evidence also suggests in human essential hypertension that the kidney is also the underlying cause. For instance, human renal transplant recipients who receive a kidney from a donor with a family history of hypertension have been shown to have higher blood pressure than those receiving a kidney from a donor with a negative family history. Patients have also been described who develop renal failure secondary to essential hypertension who when their own kidneys are removed and have a successful renal transplant, their blood pressure becomes normal. These two findings support the concept that the kidney may possibly carry the underlying abnormality that causes essential hypertension in man. Experiments in rats suggest that the genetic abnormality in the kidney expresses itself as a difficulty in excreting sodium; it is also possible that this may underly the cause of essential hypertension in man.

Natriuretic hormones

This concept can be taken further in that if the kidney is responsible for the development of high blood pressure and the abnormality in the kidney is related to a difficulty in excreting sodium, then subjects who inherit this abnormality will, on a high-salt diet, tend to retain more sodium and thereby stimulate greater compensatory mechanisms to get rid of the extra sodium and water. These compensatory mechanisms would include the atrial natriuretic peptides, which have been found to be raised in many patients with essential hypertension, and may involve other sodium excreting mechanisms which in themselves could, in the longer term, cause a rise in arteriolar tone and peripheral resistance. One potential mechanism whereby this could occur is

through an increase in a sodium transport inhibitor that slows down the sodium–potassium pump lining cell membranes. This will give rise to an increase in intracellular sodium which, by the mechanisms Blaustein has demonstrated, could cause an increase in intracellular calcium and thereby an increase in peripheral resistance. This hypothesis, however, requires further substantiation as there is considerable debate about the nature and actions of sodium transport inhibitors. Recently, a substance very similar to ouabain has been isolated from human plasma but whether this plays an important role in essential hypertension is not known. Nevertheless, the overall concept does help to explain how a high salt intake could cause high blood pressure.

SECONDARY HYPERTENSION

The nature and investigation of underlying renal or adrenal causes that are major causes of secondary hypertension are discussed in detail in Chapter 8. In most the exact mechanisms whereby the high blood pressure is raised are not fully understood. However, excess circulating levels of some of the hormones previously described may directly cause the high blood pressure.

Excess aldosterone (primary aldosteronism)

This is due to the autonomous oversecretion of the adrenal mineralocorticoid aldosterone, usually from a benign adrenal tumour (adenoma) or from bilateral enlargement of both adrenals. The excess aldosterone causes sodium retention and potassium loss. In this condition plasma levels of renin activity and angiotensin II will be very low and plasma aldosterone levels will be high, particularly when compared to the low levels of plasma renin activity. After removal of the adrenal adenoma or blockade of aldosterone by the specific antagonist, spironolactone, blood pressure returns to near normal in some but not all patients.

Excess renin

High blood pressure due to excess renin secretion can occur both in renovascular hypertension and malignant hypertension or accelerated hypertension. This is due to a reduction in perfusion pressure of the glomeruli, thereby causing an inappropriate secretion of excess renin and angiotensin II for the total amount of sodium in the body. Very rare tumours have been described that secrete renin. These occur in the kidney and lead to very high circulating levels of angiotensin II. If the tumour is removed the blood pressure returns to normal.

In some forms of renal disease and in patients with polycystic kidney disease, there may be a subtle abnormalities of the renin level in relation to the degree of sodium balance. In other words, the plasma level of angiotensin II may be inappropriately raised for the degree of sodium balance. These two factors in combination could be responsible for the high blood pressure. However, in most forms of renal disease, the high blood pressure is due to sodium retention.

Excess adrenaline or noradrenaline

Excess levels of these hormones are produced by phaeochromocytomas and other neuroendocrine tumours. Classically the tumour causes an intermittent release of noradrenaline and adrenaline, causing palpitations, headaches, sweating attacks, anxiety and very high blood pressures, which are directly due to the very high levels of these hormones.

FURTHER READING

Ching GWK, Beevers DG. Hypertension. *Postgrad Med J* 1991; **67**:230–46.

De Wardener HE, MacGregor GA. The relation of a circulating sodium transport inhibitor (the natriuretic hormone?) to hypertension. *Medicine* 1983; **62**:310–26.

Folkow B. Cardiovascular structural adaptation; its role in the initiation and maintenance of primary hypertension. *Clin Sci* 1978; **55**:3s-22s.

Laragh JH. Vasoconstriction-volume analysis for understanding and treating hypertension: the use of renin and aldosterone profiles. *Am J Med* 1973; **55**:261–74.

Moncada S, Palmer RMJ, Higgs EA. Nitric oxide: physiology, pathophysiology, and pharmacology. *Pharmacol Rev* 1991; **43**:109–42.

Sagnella GA, MacGregor GA. Atrial natriuretic peptides. *Quart J Med* 1990; **77**:1001–7.

5 DRUG-INDUCED HYPERTENSION

BACKGROUND

There are many drugs that have been shown to cause or aggravate hypertension. Others interfere with the response to some antihypertensive agents. Patients receiving any of these drugs should be monitored regularly for changes in blood pressure.

MINERALOCORTICOID HYPERTENSION

Oral contraceptives

All women who take combined oral contraceptives sustain a rise in blood pressure but this is usually within the normal range and is not considered of clinical importance (Fig. 5.1). However, about 5% of women, particularly those who take the high-dose oestrogen pill, develop diastolic blood pressures above 90 mmHg. In the majority of these women, however, blood pressure was already in the upper range of normal before starting the pill. More severe hypertension and malignant hypertension has been reported occasionally in some patients. Apart from the height of the blood pressure before starting the pill there do not seem to be any obvious criteria which would predict a greater rise in blood pressure. In particular, hypertension induced by previous pregnancy or pre-eclampsia does not appear to be an important risk factor and in those women who gain weight on the pill, there does not seem to be any close relationship to the rise in pressure.

The increase in pressure is associated with changes in the renin–angiotensin system with

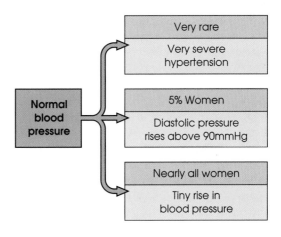

Figure 5.1
Changes in blood pressure in women taking oral contraceptive pills.

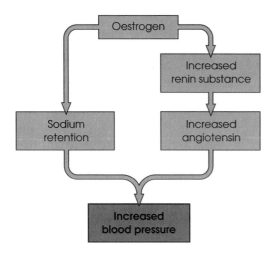

Figure 5.2
Mechanism of the rise in blood pressure associated with oral contraceptive pill.

a rise in the level of plasma renin substrate and in the amount of circulating angiotensin II. There is also some evidence that there is volume expansion and the combination of a raised plasma angiotensin II and increased circulating volume may be the mechanism of the high blood pressure (Fig. 5.2). The lower dose oestrogen pills that are now more commonly used also raise blood pressure although possibly to a lesser extent. Some women who develop hypertension on the high-dose oestrogen may sustain a fall in pressure when the oestrogen content is reduced. There remains some doubt whether the progesterone-only contraceptive raises blood pressure but it is probably preferable in those women who start with blood pressures in the upper range of normal, although it is a less secure form of contraception than the combined pill. If hypertension does develop on the pill, they should be advised to stop the combined pill and

either change to a progesterone-only pill or change to alternative methods of birth control. However, there are some occasions when the cardiovascular or social risk from an unwanted pregnancy is so great that oral contraceptives have to be continued and blood pressure-lowering drugs are given concurrently. All patients on the pill should have regular checks on their blood pressure. The cardiovascular risk from the oral contraceptive is substantially worse in cigarette smokers, and in older women.

Hormone replacement therapy (HRT)

The effects of HRT on blood pressure are controversial, but the majority of studies now indicate that there is little change in blood pressure (Fig. 5.3). Indeed, in some hypertensive patients there may be a fall. Blood pressure should be checked regularly and, if there is a rise, it may be necessary to discontinue HRT. However, the presence of mild to moderate hypertension before the start of HRT is not a contra-indication to it. Some evidence suggests that women who are on HRT have a lower overall cardiovascular risk profile than those who are not taking it, so that women who have treated high blood pressure or blood pressure in the upper normal range should not be denied the benefits of HRT.

Carbenoxolone/liquorice

Carbenoxolone is a liquorice-based drug that was used for the treatment of peptic ulcers. It blocks the action of the enzyme that protects mineralocorticoid receptors, thus allowing the normal levels of circulating

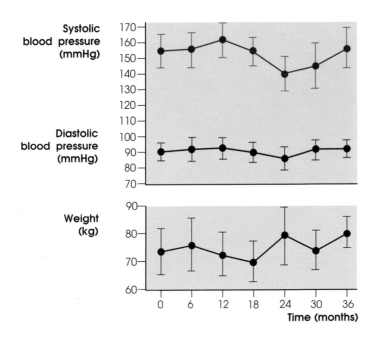

Systolic blood pressure (mmHg)

Diastolic blood pressure (mmHg)

Weight (kg)

Time (months)

Figure 5.3
Sequential changes in blood pressure and weight in 75 hypertensive women taking hormone replacement therapy (HRT).

cortisol to have a pronounced mineralocorticoid effect. This causes an identical syndrome to primary aldosteronism. The drug has now been replaced by the histamine antagonists (e.g. cimetidine etc.) and proton pump stimulators. Liquorice has an identical action to carbenoxolone and when eaten in excess can cause high blood pressure, hypokalaemia and oedema. Thiazide diuretics when used to reduce the oedema will cause further falls in plasma potassium and may cause muscle weakness and even paralysis. In some parts of Europe, particularly Holland, combined liquorice and salt tablets are eaten as sweets, which frequently causes high blood pressure. The combination of these sweets (Dubbel Zoote Drop) with the oral contraceptive is particularly dangerous.

Oral corticosteroids

High-dose oral corticosteroid therapy raises blood pressure. This is, in part, due to the mineralocorticoid action of these high doses causing sodium retention, but also there is an increase in plasma renin substrate and, thereby, increased levels of angiotensin II. Whether chronic low-dose steroid therapy with prednisolone in the treatment of rheumatoid arthritis or asthma causes an increase in blood pressure is more controversial. Nevertheless, all patients receiving prednisolone or other steroids need to have regular checks on their blood pressure. There are reports of hypertension developing with the use of high-dose topical steroid preparations for skin, ear and eye conditions. Some topical steroids have marked mineralocorticoid properties, causing sodium and water retention with hypokalaemia mimicking primary aldosteronism. Several lines of evidence do suggest that steroids do have an adverse effect on cardiovascular risk profile, not necessarily through high blood pressure, but probably as a result of a greater tendency to thrombosis. This needs to be borne in mind in patients on long-term steroids, particularly those who already have an adverse cardiovascular risk profile.

PURGATIVES

Purgatives do not cause hypertension but they may induce hypokalaemia, which may suggest the presence of either renal or adrenal disease. Unexplained hypokalaemia in a hypertensive patient can occasionally be due to purgative abuse and/or surreptitious vomiting. Diuretics remain the commonest cause of hypokalaemia.

COLD CURES AND ANORECTICS

Many remedies for coughs and colds and also some slimming pills contain sympathomimetic amines that can put up blood pressure. The phenylamine group (ephedrine, pseudoephedrine, phenylephrine and phenylpropanolamine) all cause vasoconstriction and hypertension has been reported in some patients. The imidazoline antifungal derivatives resemble clonidine in their chemical structure and both hypertension and hypotension have been reported.

NEPHROTOXINS

Any drug that damages the kidney may cause a rise in blood pressure. For instance, some antibiotics can cause renal failure, particularly the aminoglycocides (e.g. gentamicin) and some cephalosporins. This usually only occurs when they are given in high doses to patients who already have renal failure or are acutely ill. Phenacetin (an obsolete anti-inflammatory drug), when taken chronically, can cause renal papillary necrosis and eventually renal impairment. Because the damage is mainly in the medulla of the kidney, there is usually sodium loss. In general, patients with phenacetin nephropathy therefore have a low rather than a high blood pressure.

CYCLOSPORIN

Cyclospirin is a fungal metabolite that is a potent immunosuppressant and is being increasingly used in patients with heart or kidney transplants either in conjunction with the steroids or with other immunosuppressants, or on its own. However, it can cause both hepatic and renal impairment. Often mild renal impairment has to be accepted as a price to be paid for the better immunosuppression. The dose of the drug has to be very carefully monitored. Almost invariably, cyclosporin causes a rise in blood pressure. This is, in part, related to the renal impairment and also seems to be related to sodium and water retention that may occur. Blood pressure in all of these patients needs to be carefully monitored and appropriate treatment given if the blood pressure does rise. It is claimed that the calcium antagonists may be particularly effective in lowering blood pressure in cyclosporin-induced hypertension, but these drugs may also cause an increase in plasma cyclosporin levels.

ERYTHROPOETIN

Used in the treatment of the anaemia of chronic renal failure, erythropoetin leads to a significant rise in blood pressure of 30–35% of patients. The mechanisms of this pressure response are uncertain but may be related to a rise in haematocrit and increased total blood viscosity. In addition, erythropoetin may alter renal blood flow and stimulate renin release. Patients with chronic renal failure should not be denied the benefits of erythropoetin, but careful monitoring of blood pressure is mandatory, together where necessary with an increase in antihypertensive medication (see Chapter 14).

HYDRALAZINE

This drug can cause a drug-induced lupus syndrome, which is usually reversible. Hydralazine-induced lupus is less common in fast metabolic acetylators and is rare if the total daily dose of the drug is below 100 mg. Hydralazine is now rarely used for the treatment of high blood pressure.

METHYSERGIDE

Fibrosis of the retroperitoneal tissues can occur with methysergide therapy for migraine. The ureters become obstructed and bilateral hydronephrosis and renal failure develop. The early beta-blocker practolol may also have caused retroperitoneal fibrosis, but there is no evidence that this is a problem with any beta-blocker available today.

PSYCHOTROPIC DRUGS

Monoamine oxidase (MAO) inhibitors

These powerful antidepressant drugs are not now widely used, but all of them may cause a sudden and occasionally disastrous rise in blood pressure if amines such as tyramine in cheese and yeast extract are eaten, or decongestant 'cold cures' are taken.

Tricyclic antidepressants

These do not cause hypertension, but do interfere with the antihypertensive effects of some obsolete adrenergic neurone blocking drugs, such as bethanidine and guanethidine. They may also cause serious arrhythmias and their use in hypertensive patients should be discouraged, particularly if they have evidence of ischaemic heart disease.

LITHIUM

This agent is used on a long-term basis in manic depression and bi-polar depression. The concurrent use of thiazide diuretics may increase the risk of lithium toxicity, so regular measurements of plasma lithium need to be made.

NON-STEROIDAL ANTI-INFLAMMATORY DRUGS (NSAIDS)

Indomethacin and all other non-steroidal anti-inflammatory drugs relieve painful inflammation by blocking prostaglandin synthesis. They can also cause fluid retention and a rise in blood pressure. They block the antihypertensive action of the thiazide diuretics as well as part of the action of beta-blockers, some vasodilators and ACE inhibitors, but they do not seem to affect the blood pressure-lowering capability of calcium antagonists.

CLONIDINE WITHDRAWAL

Clonidine, a centrally acting alpha-stimulating drug, reduces blood pressure, but when clonidine is suddenly discontinued, a rebound rise in blood pressure occurs which may be very severe and mimic a phaeochromocytoma crisis. Occasional rebound hypertension has also been reported with other centrally acting drugs such as methyldopa. In our opinion, clonidine has no place in the treatment of hypertension.

TRACE METALS

Gold therapy can cause glomerulonephritis and hypertension. Both lead and cadmium as environmental pollutants have been implicated in causing hypertension. Recent evidence suggests that this is unlikely in the case of cadmium but there is still debate about lead as a cause of raised blood pressure. Both metals can cause renal damage when ingested in high doses as occurs in most occupationally exposed workers.

NARCOTIC ADDICTION

During narcotic withdrawal blood pressure rises to high levels. This is very similar to that seen in alcohol withdrawal. Marijuana will increase the heart rate but usually lowers the blood pressure. Cocaine can cause significant transient hypertension.

DRUG-INDUCED HYPOTENSION

Apart from the antihypertensive drugs discussed in Chapter 11, some other drugs may cause unwanted falls in blood pressure and some, particularly in overdosage, cause circulatory collapse. All tranquillizers and sedatives, particularly chlorpromazine derivatives and many opiate analgesics, may cause idiosyncratic or dose-related hypotension.

FURTHER READING

Lip GYH, Beevers M, Churchill D, Beevers DG. Hormone replacement therapy and blood pressure in hypertensive women. *J Hum Hypertens* 1994; **8**:491–4.

Masserli FH, Frohlich ED. High blood pressure. A side effect of drugs, poisons and food. *Arch Intern Med* 1979; **139**:682–7.

Porter GA, Bennett WM, Sheps SG. Cyclosporine-associated hypertension. *Arch Intern Med* 1990; **150**:280–3.

Raine AEG. Hypertension, blood viscosity, and cardiovascular morbidity in renal failure: implication for erythropoietin therapy. *Lancet* 1988; **1**:97–9.

2

Section Two

6 BLOOD PRESSURE MEASUREMENT

BACKGROUND

The height of the blood pressure is such an accurate predictor of an individual's future morbidity and mortality from cardiovascular disease that its measurement is the most important observation ever made in clinical practice. As blood pressure measurement is simple and carries no hazard, it should be regarded as a routine check to be carried out in everyone.

Despite the importance of high blood pressure, there remains considerable confusion over the correct methods of measurement. Insufficient care is often taken with the technique, defective apparatus is often used and documentation is haphazard.

HISTORY

The ancient Chinese Emperor Huang Ti, (2000 B.C.) is credited with the first observation that people with full volume pulses develop strokes and he also noted that people who eat a lot of salt have full volume pulses. He can, therefore, be regarded as the first person to appreciate the importance of estimating the blood pressure within the circulation although he did this by palpating the pulse and noting its character. In 1827, Richard Bright inferred that the blood pressure must be high when he observed that people dying of renal failure often had large hearts but he had no blood pressure measurements to rely on.

The first recorded measurement of blood pressure was in 1730 by The Reverend Steven Hales, a distinguished biologist and curate of Teddington, England. He introduced a cannula into an artery in the neck of a horse and measured the height of the column of blood rising up a glass tube. He observed that when the horse struggled, the blood pressure rose. This intra-arterial method of measuring blood pressure was perfected later by Sir George Pickering in humans and has considerable research potential but no clinical value.

The indirect measuring of blood pressure was invented in 1898 by Scipione Riva Rocci. Using a mercury manometer, he was able to measure the pressure needed to occlude the brachial artery and obliterate the radial pulse. Riva Rocci's original apparatus subsequently underwent several modifications but the basic principle remains the same to this day. The idea of listening below the occluded artery rather than just palpating it dates from 1905 when Nicolai Korotkov, a Russian army surgeon, wrote a thesis on the sounds that were audible as the mercury manometer was deflated. In honour of him, the blood pressure sounds are called the Korotkov sounds.

The oscillometric method of measuring blood pressure was introduced in 1890 by Michel Pachon. This technique relies on measuring the fluctuation in pressure within the air-filled cuff. The systolic and mean arterial pressures are thus measured accurately and the diastolic blood pressure is then calculated.

The advent of electronics has made possible the production of a great many automatic devices with varying degrees of accuracy. Some rely on the auditory technique of Korotkov and some on the oscillometric principles of Pachon. In normal practice, however, the mercury manometer remains the standard method and is attractive if only because of its simplicity and robustness.

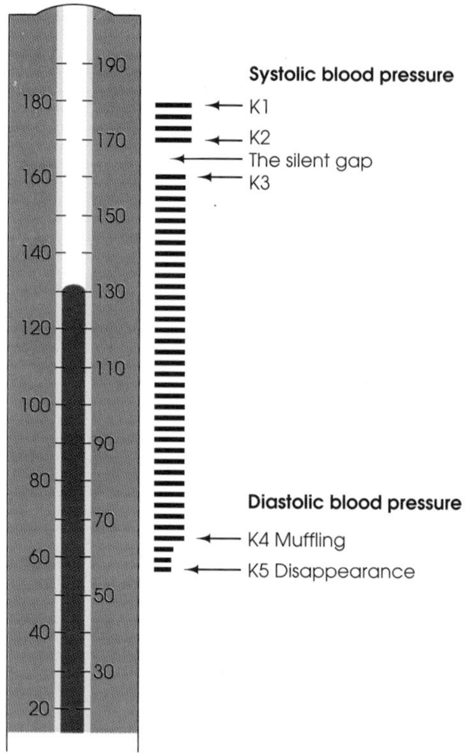

Figure 6.1
The Korotkov sounds.

THE KOROTKOV SOUNDS

After the cuff is inflated to the level that produces complete occlusion of the brachial artery, the column of mercury is allowed to be deflated at the rate of 2 mmHg/s. As the column falls, the various phases are heard through a stethoscope applied over the brachial artery. The exact physiological significance of the sounds heard is unclear and their prognostic importance is unreli-

able. The Korotkov sounds are not transmitted heart sounds but are related to turbulence induced by constriction of the brachial artery (Fig. 6.1).

Phase 1 The first appearance of sounds
The systolic blood pressure is usually recorded when the second beat is heard on the grounds that the first beat might have been due to some form of extraneous noise.

Phase 2 The softening or disappearance of sounds The silent gap is usually no more than 5 mmHg and is frequently not present. When it is present it may lead to an underestimation of systolic blood pressure. It is thus very important to inflate the mercury column to 30 mmHg above that pressure needed to occlude the brachial pulse.

Phase 3 The reappearance of sounds These sounds are sometimes difficult to hear at first but they become louder after 2 mmHg and assume a distinct tapping character.

Phase 4 Muffling of sounds The muffling of sounds phase used to be taken as the level of diastolic blood pressure. Usually it is not possible to identify this distinct muffling phase compared with phase 5.

Phase 5 The final disappearance of sounds Now regarded the best measurement of diastolic blood pressure, the final disappearance of sounds is closer to the intra-arterial diastolic blood pressure.

In some patients with hyperdynamic circulation (for example in pregnancy, thyrotoxicosis, after exercise and in children), sounds may not completely disappear but may continue to be audible down to 0 mmHg. Sometimes this persistence of sound is caused by tight clothing causing partial occlusion of the brachial artery above the cuff. More often than not, however, phase 4 and phase 5 diastolic blood pressures coincide and a difference of more than 5 mmHg is unusual, even in pregnancy.

Brachial artery bruits

In some elderly patients, atheromatous narrowing of the brachial arteries means that there is a bruit over the artery even when there is no compression applied by the cuff. Under these circumstances, it is necessary to record the phase 4 diastolic blood pressures. It is worth, however, measuring the blood pressure in the contralateral arm where there may be no bruit. Also in these circumstances, automatic oscillometric blood pressure measurement may be useful.

The SI units of blood pressure measurement (kilopascals) have no place in the field of hypertension.

BLOOD PRESSURE MEASUREMENT

Systolic or diastolic pressures

Most clinical research and randomized controlled trials have concentrated on the diastolic blood pressure rather than the systolic blood pressure. There is really no good reason for this. Epidemiologists demonstrated 40–50 years ago that both systolic and diastolic blood pressure are potent producers of risk. Furthermore, over the age of 45 years, the height of the systolic blood pressure predicts future morbidity and mortality more accurately than the diastolic blood pressure.

Since 1991, several clinical trials in the elderly have demonstrated that the drug treatment of raised systolic blood pressure is of great clinical benefit even where the diastolic blood pressure is not raised.

It is possible, therefore, that over the next 10 years clinicians will increasingly concentrate their attention on the height of the systolic blood pressure. However, further research is necessary before confident recommendations on the value of systolic versus diastolic blood pressures can be made in the non-elderly population.

Korotkov phase 4 or phase 5

Both phase 4 and phase 5 can be regarded as candidates for the best estimation of diastolic blood pressure. Neither represents true diastolic blood pressure, which can only be measured by using an intra-arterial cannula and blood pressure transducer. The indirect diastolic blood pressures are usually higher than the intra-arterial pressures and so it follows that phase 5 is closer to the true intra-arterial diastolic blood pressures. In clinical practice, diastolic blood pressures should normally be taken at phase 5, the disappearance of sounds. The reasons for this are:

- Most epidemiological studies of populations and cardiovascular risk have employed phase 5.
- All the recent clinical trials on the treatment of hypertension have employed phase 5.
- The inter-observer variation is less when diastolic blood pressure is measured at phase 5.
- The assessment of when blood pressure sounds start to muffle is more subjective than when blood pressure sounds disappear completely.

Lying, sitting or standing

Normally, the diastolic blood pressure rises a little on standing whilst the systolic blood pressure may fall by a few mmHg. Postural hypertension may occur in diabetics with autonomic neuropathy and occasionally it is seen in elderly patients. The obsolete adrenergic neurone-blocking drugs and the centrally acting alpha agonist, methyldopa, cause larger falls in standing as opposed to seated blood pressures.

It is probably wise, therefore, to measure blood pressure in the standing position at least once when assessing a new patient. If no postural drop is detected, lying or seated pressures can be employed thereafter. In diabetics, where there is a high risk of postural hypotension, blood pressure should routinely be measured in the standing and seated position.

All of the large-scale epidemiological studies and almost all of the randomized therapeutic controlled trials have employed seated diastolic blood pressure measurements. This is the most convenient position for routine clinical practice and it is suggested, therefore, that lying blood pressures should not be measured as a routine.

Mean arterial pressure

Mean arterial pressure can be calculated from the sum of the diastolic blood pressure plus one-third of the pulse pressure (systolic pressure minus diastolic pressure). Mean arterial blood pressure, therefore, takes into account both systolic and diastolic components of pressure. This calculated mean arterial pressure is closely related to the measured mean intra-arterial blood pressure. There is no reason to believe that mean arterial pressure has any greater physiological or pathological significance than either the systolic or diastolic blood pressures and for this reason the mean arterial pressure measurements have no role in clinical practice.

Resting, casual or basal pressure

All blood pressures vary from minute to minute, day to day and season to season. There is a tendency for blood pressure variability to be greater in people with higher blood pressures. Data available from insurance companies and from long-term observation surveys based on single casual blood pressure measurements show that these measurements are very accurate predictors of future risk. When people relax in a quiet room, their blood pressures almost invariably fall and even very high blood pressures associated with end-organ damage may settle considerably. Epidemiological studies have not been able to show that the basal blood pressure is of any greater or lesser prognostic significance than the casual blood pressure and the variability of blood pressure appears to have little significance at all.

However, recent studies employing 24-hour ambulatory blood pressure measurement tend to lend support to the idea that the lower blood pressures measured away from the clinical environment may be more predictive of risk than casual readings obtained during screening surveys or in clinical practice. No reliable long-term population surveys have yet tested out this relationship but there is now fairly good evidence that the lower blood pressures away from the home environment are more clearly related to left ventricular size as assessed by echocardiography.

White coat hypertension

This term applies to patients whose blood pressure can be demonstrated to be raised only in the presence of a doctor. If reliable evidence from 24-hour ambulatory blood pressure measurement can unequivocally confirm that the blood pressure is completely normal at all stages except during a clinical consultation, then a diagnosis of white coat hypertension is made. However, patients whose blood pressures are elevated in a clinical environment but normal while at home do require very careful observation and they cannot be regarded as 'normotensive'.

If mild hypertensives are assessed properly, they should have their blood pressures measured at least twice on four consecutive occasions. Many patients' blood pressures settle if this is done. It is uncertain as to whether blood pressures measured frequently in a clinical environment as suggested above provide any more or less information than a 24-hour ambulatory blood pressure measurement.

Blood pressure load

Recently, the concept of blood pressure load has been advanced. This implies that the number of raised blood pressure readings over a 24-hour period may be of prognostic significance. Thus, patients whose blood pressures settle at night ('dippers') have a lower 24-hour blood pressure load and may be at lower risk than patients classified as non-dippers.

BLOOD PRESSURE MEASUREMENT

Sources of error

Whilst blood pressure measurement is easy, it is also easy to make serious errors. These may lead to inappropriate diagnosis of hypertension or the inappropriate reassurance of patients who have got genuinely raised blood pressures. We support the

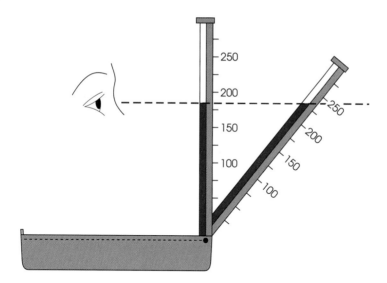

Figure 6.2
Blood pressure overestimation owing to faulty hinges.

aphorism 'if you cannot measure something accurately, then measure it often'.

Errors due to the manometer

- Insufficient or too much mercury in the manometer so that at rest the mercury column does not read 0 mmHg.
- The mercury column slopes away from the vertical owing to damaged hinges on the manometer box (Fig. 6.2). This causes falsely elevated blood pressure readings. (Some manometers are manufactured with a built-in tilt and in these a correction is made with a slightly longer glass column.)
- The mercury column becomes dirty; as air is freely in contact with the mercury, mercuric oxide can form on the inside of the glass tubing so that the mercury meniscus can no longer be seen (Fig. 6.3). All glass tubing should be cleaned about once per year.

- If the rubber tubing is perished and leaky, this will cause over-rapid and uncontrolled deflation of the cuff and may lead to falsely low blood pressure readings.

Errors caused by the cuff

Cuff size too small When the rubber bladder inside the cuff is too small, there is inadequate compression of the brachial artery. The cuff itself should be a minimum of 25 cm longer than the internal rubber bladder with a tail of over 60 cm. Velcro cuffs have shorter tails and are convenient but they may tend to lose their grip unless they are cleaned regularly.

The rubber bladder inside the cuff should encircle about 80% of the arm circumference and preferably more. Bladders that are too small cause over-reading of the blood pressure. Most commercially available blood pressure cuffs have bladders that are too small.

Figure 6.3
A dirty manometer tube (photographed when reading 0 mmHg) in a hospital casualty department.

The 'large adult' cuff does encircle a sufficient part of the circumference of the arm but unfortunately its width (15 cm) means that it is often not possible to apply one's stethoscope over the brachial artery unless the patient is very tall as well as being obese.

In routine clinical practice, we now strongly recommend that the 'alternative adult' cuff should be used (Fig. 6.4). This has a rubber bladder which measures 12.5–13 cm × 33–35 cm. If this cuff is used

in routine practice, then it will only very rarely be necessary to employ a large adult cuff. The conventional adult cuff of 12.5 × 23 cm should now be phased out as it is unsuitable for measurement of blood pressure where the arm circumference exceeds 33 cm. A recent survey demonstrated that 7.5% of the general population and 15% of hypertensive patients have arm circumferences that exceed 33 cm so that the standard adult cuff would not provide accurate readings.

The alternative adult cuff is now available through most manufacturers and is recommended for routine practice by the British Hypertension Society and is now also routinely used in Sweden.

There is some bacteriological hazard from the continued use of dirty blood pressure cuffs in hospital wards.

The cuff is not at the same level as the heart Whilst it does not matter where the mercury manometer is in relation to the heart (it should be as near as possible to the observer's eye), it is very important that the forearm cuff is at the same level as the heart. If the arm is raised, falsely low readings are obtained and if the cuff is below heart level, falsely high readings are obtained (Fig. 6.5). It is also very important that the arm is supported as the isometric exercise of holding the arm up can cause a rise in blood pressure.

Faulty or blocked inflation/deflation devices If the inflation/deflation device is faulty, it is very difficult to control the column of mercury as it falls and this may lead to overestimation of blood pressure. Chromium-plated inflation/deflation devices are more reliable than the more modern plastic-coated equipment.

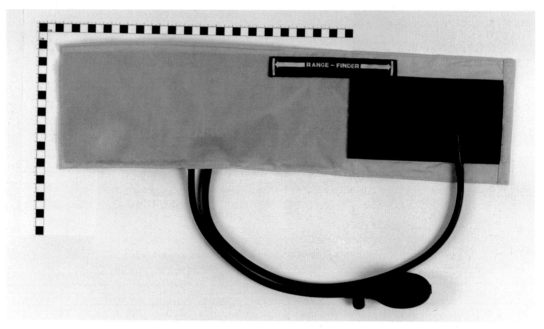

(a)

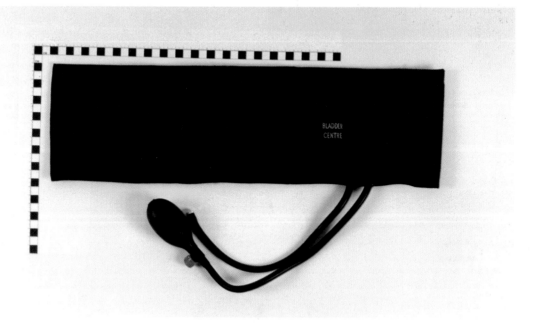

(b)

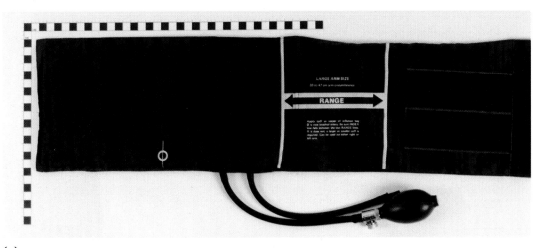

(c)

Figure 6.4
(a) The 'alternative adult' cuff with rubber bladder (13 x 35cm); highly recommended use. (b) The 'normal adult' cuff with rubber bladder (13 x 23cm); only suitable if arm circumference is less than 33cm. (c) The 'large arm size' cuff with rubber bladder (15 x 30cm); useful if arm cirmcumference exceeds 33cm; however, it tends to extend into antiorbital fossa unless the patient has long arms.

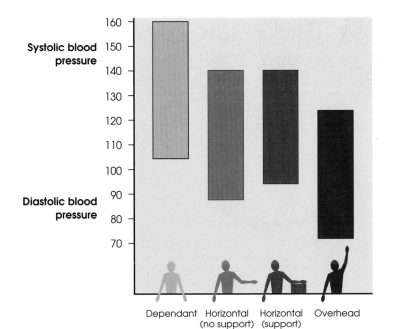

Figure 6.5
Effect of arm position on blood pressure.

Observer errors

Faulty technique If the blood pressure cuff is not inflated high enough to occlude the brachial artery, systolic blood pressure is seriously underestimated. The clinician may falsely conclude that phase 3, reappearance of systolic sounds, is the systolic blood pressure rather than phase 1.

Parallax error If the mercury column is not level with the observer's eye, a parallax error of up to 2 mmHg may occur.

Terminal digit preference This occurs when the observer reads either up or down to the nearest 5 or 10 mmHg. As the markings on the glass tubings are in 2 mm intervals, it is not logical to measure blood pressure to the nearest odd number. This problem may not appear to matter too much in individual cases with severe

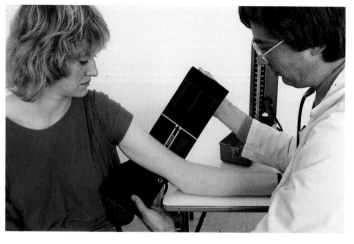

Figure 6.6
The correct technique for measuring blood pressure. (i) Ensure the mercury meniscus reads zero before use. The observer's eye must be level with the top of the meniscus to avoid parallax error.

(ii) The Φ mark must be over the brachial artery.

hypertension but it is very important when assessing mild hypertensives and it is also important in randomized controlled trials or population surveys. Systematic differences may be obtained between observers if one observer has a tendency to read up to the nearest 10 mmHg and another observer has a tendency to read down to the nearest 10 mmHg. In view of the enormous importance of blood pressure in predicting individual survival, a very accurate blood pressure reading should be obtained. The blood pressure should, therefore, be measured to the nearest 2 mmHg.

Observer bias If the observer is aware that the patient is receiving treatment, he may tend to bias readings to be lower to fulfil his preconceived notions. Observer bias must be abolished or minimized in randomized controlled trials and in population surveys.

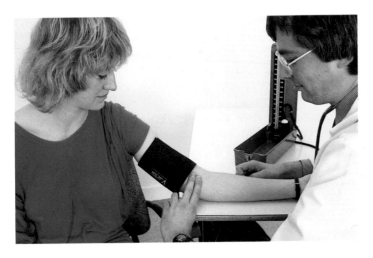

(iii) Ensure that there is enough space below the cuff sot that the stethoscope does not come into contact with the cuff.

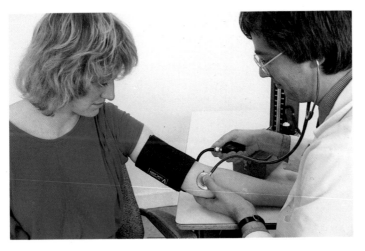

(iv) Use a stethoscope diaphragm to listen over the brachial artery.

Hearing impairment Hearing impairment will cause the observer to underestimate the systolic blood pressure and overestimate the diastolic blood pressure.

Male and female connectors To avoid confusion and aid total interchangeability of cuffs and manometers, it is conventional for the manometer to have the male connection and the cuff to have the female connection. It is sensible for the clinician to have some spare connectors readily available.

Correct technique for measuring blood pressure (Fig. 6.6)

(1) Ensure the patient is seated comfortably leaning on the back of his chair and is neither too hot nor cold. Blood pressures are lower in a warmer environment, and rise when it is cold. Try to avoid exertion and stressful discussions immediately before pressures are being measured. If this is the patient's first ever test, it is wise to explain that there will be some slight discomfort as the cuff is inflated. Try to position the patient so that he is unable to see the mercury column.

(2) Apply the forearm cuff neatly, with the zero mark over the brachial pulse. Many modern cuffs have the 33 cm circumference marked out. If the arm circumference exceeds this range, a larger cuff should be used.

(3) Ensure that the manometer column is vertical and connect it to the cuff.

(4) Ensure the forearm is supported, preferably resting on a desk, slightly extended and externally rotated.

(5) Inflate the cuff at a slow steady rate to 30 mmHg above the level needed to occlude the pulse.

(6) Place the diaphragm of the stethoscope over the brachial artery. Do not press too hard. It does not matter if the diaphragm is partly underneath the edge of the cuff, although this can cause creaking noises which may confuse the observer.

(7) The observer's eyes should be at the same level as the top of the column of mercury.

(8) Deflate the manometer cuff at the rate of 2 to 3 mmHg per second.

(9) Record the systolic blood pressure (phase 1) when the blood pressure sounds are first heard.

(10) Record the diastolic pressure at phase 5 (disappearance of sounds). If sounds can still be heard, even when the manometer reads 30 mmHg or less, then diastolic pressures should be taken at the muffling of sounds (phase 4).

(11) Blood pressures should be measured to the nearest 2 mmHg.

(12) Write down all the readings immediately.

(13) At first consultation check the blood pressure in both arms to ensure there is no discrepancy. If pressures differ significantly there may be atheromatous narrowing of the subclavian artery causing falsely low pressure readings. In this case the arm with the higher pressure should be used thereafter.

(14) Measure the blood pressure at least twice at all consultations. The second reading is the one on which decisions are usually made.

Special situations

Atrial fibrillation Due to coronary heart disease, alcoholic cardiomyopathy, thyroid disease or rheumatic heart disease, atrial fibrillation renders blood pressure difficult.

At least three readings should be taken on each occasion.

Pregnancy It has been argued that when measuring blood pressure in pregnant women, it is 'common' to be unable to identify the fifth phase as, due to hyperdynamic circulation of pregnancy, sounds are audible over the brachial artery even when there is no arm compression. However, recently, a comparison of pregnant versus non-pregnant women has shown that there is little difference in the gap between muffling and disappearance of diastolic sounds in relation to pregnancy. This and other observations mean that now diastolic blood pressures in pregnancy should also be measured at the fifth phase and not at the fourth phase. A recent survey demonstrated considerable confusion amongst obstetricians, half of whom employed phase 4 and half phase 5.

It should be remembered that in obstetrical practice, automatic blood pressure machines are often employed and these, whether oscillometric or auditory, all measure diastolic blood pressure at the fifth phase. It is reasonable, therefore, for clinicians to adopt the same technique as the machinery they employ and the same practice as clinicians in all other branches of medicine.

Aortic coarctation There is evidence that aortic coarctation is being underdiagnosed. Where the foot pulses are either unobtainable, weak or delayed, routine measurement of blood pressure in the legs is strongly advocated. This is a simple technique. The patient, if male, must remove his trousers and lie prone. An appropriate thigh cuff is applied and the stethoscope placed in the popliteal fossa. Readings are then taken in the same way as in the arms.

Children The measurement of blood pressure should be an integral part of the assessment of a paediatric case. The principles are no different from those used in adults. In children over the age of two, a conventional mercury manometer is used and the Korotkov sounds auscultated. If the Korotkov sounds prove inaudible, the systolic pressure can be measured by palpation alone. In infants, in whom conventional measurements are impossible, Doppler blood pressure measuring devices should be used.

Anaeroid sphygmomanometers

Anaeroid sphygmomanometers are useful, and when new they are usually accurate although it is sometimes difficult to obtain a reliable reading when the needle flickers. They tend to deteriorate after two or three years, however, and there is no way of telling whether they are accurate except by checking them against a mercury manometer, with a Y-tube connection to a cuff wrapped around a bottle.

It is, therefore, best not to use anaeroid sphygmomanometers in hospitals or in clinics and health centres, where the mercury manometer is preferable. Anaeroid manometers are, however, more portable and so are useful for home visits.

The random-zero sphygmomanometer

The Hawksley random sphygmomanometer is based on the same principle as the conventional manometer but is designed to minimize at least some systematic error and abolish observer bias. This equipment has been used in many population surveys and in most randomized controlled trials of drug therapy. The system relies on a mercury reservoir which is of variable size so the clinician is unaware of the level of mercury that is zero at the time when he is measuring the pressure. After the manometer is disconnected from the cuff, the column mercury falls to a figure which is meant to be randomly distributed between 0 and 60 mmHg (0–20 mmHg in the USA). Recent evidence has suggested that the random zero is not randomly distributed although it remains unpredictable.

London School of Hygiene Sphygmomanometer

Heavy, expensive but reliable, the London School of Hygiene Sphygmomanometer is powered by cylinders of carbon dioxide. It did provide accurate measures of blood pressure in a totally unbiased manner, but it is now hardly every used.

Automated manometers

A great many automatic electronic blood pressure measuring devices are now available. In general, the clinician armed with a well-maintained conventional mercury manometer has no need for other more expensive equipment. Many electronic devices are marketed but, with some exceptions, most are inaccurate. Unless there are published data available on a particular manometer demonstrating that readings are closely matched to those of a mercury mercuromanometer, the clinician should avoid these types of equipment.

If patients are keen to measure their blood pressures at home, they should be encouraged to bring their automated device to the clinic so that its accuracy can be assessed in relation to concurrent measurements using the conventional manometer.

Unfortunately, a great many automated blood pressure systems are marketed where no attempt has been made to produce any form of standardization or accuracy testing. For this reason, the cheaper automatic manometers should be regarded with suspicion.

Automatic manometers can be employed to measure blood pressure repeatedly at intervals of between 30 seconds and one hour. These instruments are expensive but if they are reliable, they are useful during infusion studies and after test doses of drugs, like the ACE inhibitors, in patients with severe hypertension or heart failure. Similarly they are useful as an alternative to 24-hour ambulatory blood pressure measurements. A patient who may have 'white coat hypertension' may benefit from being left in a quiet room with an automatic machine and blood pressure measured every half an hour for 2–3 hours. Very often, the blood pressure will settle as the patient relaxes away from the formal clinical environment.

Intra-arterial blood pressure

This invasive technique for measuring blood pressure is mainly used in research units, and cannot be applied generally. All the prognostic and therapeutic information available on high blood pressure and its treatment is based on the indirect cuff method and the prognostic significance of the lower ambulatory intra-arterial pressure is uncertain. The technique is also not without hazard.

Non-invasive ambulatory and home blood pressure measurements

There is increasing interest in the assessment of blood pressure away from the stressful environment of the clinic or hospital. In general, home blood pressures are lower than clinic readings. Many ambulatory automated non-invasive manometers are now coming into use. However, the fact remains that accurate but 'casual' pressure readings obtained by a doctor are a very reliable guide to prognosis and the meaning of lower readings obtained at other times is uncertain.

The 24-hour ambulatory technique has, however, drawn attention to the so-called 'white coat hypertension'. This occurs in patients whose blood pressures are only elevated when the doctor or nurse is present and is completely normal for the remainder of the 24-hour period. It is uncertain whether the 24-hour ambulatory blood pressure measurement provides any more reliable assessment than the careful re-measuring of blood pressure on four separate occasions. The main problem is that there has as yet been no formal epidemiological assessment of the prognostic significance of ambulatory blood pressure measurement compared with accurate 'clinical' recordings. One long-term, follow-up study suggests that the ambulatory readings predict survival better than conventional clinical (office) blood pressure measurements but the blood pressure measurement techniques used are no longer generally available. There is some cross-sectional evidence that the 24-hour ambulatory blood pressure recording is more closely related to the degree of left ventricular hypertrophy as measured by echocardiography. The main problem faced by the clinician is that patients whose pressures are persistently elevated in the clinical environment cannot be regarded as being without risk simply because their pressures are 'normal' when at home. However, ambulatory blood pressure measurement does have a role in assessing some mild hypertensives who have absolutely no evidence of end-organ damage and who appear agitated or distressed, particularly at hospital attendance.

Whatever happens, however, patients with 'white coat hypertension' need careful long-term follow-up even though they may not immediately require antihypertensive drug therapy.

Training of observers

Both medical and nursing students are taught blood pressure measurement at an early stage of their careers and they are often taught by non-clinicians in physiology classes and thereafter there is no re-training. Many surveys have shown a disastrous state of confusion on the correct method of measuring blood pressure and the assessment of the diastolic pressure (muffling versus disappearance of sounds).

It is essential, therefore, that all junior doctors and trained nursing staff should be re-trained on blood pressure measurement using the methods described here. When major national or international surveys or trials are contemplated, again the re-training and certification of trainees is mandatory if systematic errors or biases are to be avoided.

Several video-cassette recordings are now available which emphasize the correct techniques, and display a series of falling columns of mercury, together with the Korotkov sounds. They are highly recommended, and should be standard equipment in every school of medicine or nursing, primary health care teams and specialist blood pressure groups.

FURTHER READING

British Hypertension Society. British Hypertension Society recommendations on blood pressure measurement. *Br Med J* 1986; **293**:611.

O'Brien E, O'Malley K. Blood pressure measurement. In *Handbook of Hypertension*. Vol 14. Ed. by WH Birkenhäger and JL Reid. Amsterdam: Elsevir, 1991.

Pickering TG, Harshfield GA, Devereux RB, Laragh JH. What is the role of ambulatory blood pressure monitoring in the management of hypertensive patients? *Hypertension* 1985; **7**:171–7.

7 THE ASSESSMENT OF A NEW PATIENT

BACKGROUND

Most often a new hypertensive patient is detected during the course of a routine medical examination for employment or insurance or during some sort of case detection programme or screening survey. Many are diagnosed at consultation for an unrelated condition or when they sustain one of the vascular complications of hypertension, for example, a heart attack or a stroke. This is unfortunate, as early detection and management should prevent many of these vascular complications. In women hypertension may be detected by obstetricians during pregnancy or while following up patients receiving the oral contraceptive. It is logical, however, to check the pressure of patients seeking any form of medical aid as this simple measurement has such important preventive implications. All subjects who either have a diastolic pressure greater than 90 mmHg or a systolic pressure greater than 160 mmHg should undergo further assessment.

CLINICAL HISTORY

Patients from screening programmes or who are examined during routine consultation

In the absence of vascular complications these patients are usually symptomless. Symptoms due to the raised blood pressure itself are rare but there is a common misconception among patients and relatives that blood pressure causes symptoms. In the majority it is a risk factor for premature cardiovascular disease. Once diagnosed patients can sometimes develop symptoms owing to the anxiety created by the act of diagnosis. All patients should be asked whether they have ever had their blood pressure measured before and if they can remember the level.

Patients with symptoms

Headache Headaches do occur in very severe hypertension and in those with malignant phase hypertension due to the raised intracranial pressure. Otherwise, migraine and tension headaches, whilst troublesome, are not related to the high blood pressure.

Breathlessness Left ventricular failure with orthopnoea and paroxysmal nocturnal dyspnoea may occasionally be due to severe hypertension alone, particularly in accelerated hypertension, but is more likely to be a complicating factor with co-existent coronary heart disease. Asthma and chronic obstructive airways disease are common but not associated with hypertension. When present these diagnoses are important as they influence the choice of antihypertensive drugs. Patients with heart failure or asthma should not receive beta-blockers, so converting enzyme inhibitors, calcium antagonists or diuretics should be used (see Chapter 14).

Precordial pain Precordial pain may be due to angina or heart attack, both of which are complications of hypertension.

Palpitations A history of recurrent episodes of tachycardia raises the possibility of phaeochromocytoma although it may be due to intrinsic cardiac disease, anxiety or thyrotoxicosis. Alcohol excess can cause arrhythmias and raised blood pressure.

Intermittent claudication Aortic or femoral atheroma are complications of hypertension and when present beta-adrenoceptor blockers are contraindicated. Furthermore, patients with arterial disease may also have undiagnosed atheromatous renal artery stenosis, particularly if they are also cigarette smokers.

Polyuria and nocturia Polyuria and nocturia can occur with intrinsic renal disease which may, itself, cause hypertension or may follow renal damage secondary to the raised blood pressure. Nocturia also occurs in men with advancing age due to prostatic hypertrophy. The calcium-entry antagonists themselves, particularly the dihydropyridines such as nifedipine and amlodipine, can cause nocturia and it is important not to confuse this with prostatic hypertrophy. Alpha-blockers can cause stress incontinence in women, or aggravate this symptom.

Diabetes mellitus Patients with diabetes are more prone to hypertension and its vascular complications. The presence of diabetes substantially influences the management (see Chapter 14); in particular, diuretics should be avoided in diabetics as they may cause or aggravate glucose intolerance.

Visual symptoms Visual loss only occurs in hypertension if there are retinal haemorrhages or exudates due to accelerated hypertension. The relatively rare syndromes of central or branch retinal vein thrombosis and retinal artery occlusion are strongly associated with hypertension as well as cigarette smoking. Amaurosis fugax may result from embolus formation from carotid artery stenosis. There may also be visual disturbance due to transient cerebral ischaemia or strokes.

Neurological symptoms Transient or persistent hemiplegia may be due to cerebral haemorrhage or infarction, both of which are complications of hypertension. Hypertensive patients are particularly prone to subarachnoid haemorrhages, particularly if they have polycystic disease or are smokers.

PAST HISTORY

It is important to take an accurate history, particularly seeking for past renal disease or evidence of previous vascular complications of raised pressure. In women a detailed obstetric history is necessary. Previous pre-eclampsia or pregnancy-induced hypertension or raised pressure whilst receiving the oral contraceptive are important. There is an association between pregnancy-induced hypertension and raised blood pressure in later life.

FAMILY HISTORY

Frequently patients do not know whether their parents or siblings had hypertension but useful indicators in the family history are premature death, heart attack or stroke. Essential hypertension does run in families as does polycystic kidney disease which is inherited as a mendelian dominant condition. This should be particularly considered where there is a strong family history of hypertension, subarachnoid haemorrhage or renal failure.

Diabetes mellitus Diabetes, particularly maturity onset diabetes, does appear to be partly familial, and is strongly associated with hypertension.

Relatives of hypertensive patients Patients should always be advised to tell their relatives to have their blood pressures checked.

THE SOCIAL HISTORY

The epidemiology of hypertension is discussed in Chapter 3. Some aspects are especially relevant to the individual case.

Occupation Hypertension is slightly more common in people of lower socio-economic groups, but is not associated with any particular occupational groups and is not necessarily associated with stressful jobs. The social class link may be explained by the higher prevalence of obesity and a higher intake of alcohol and salt. Some hypertensive patients show a very marked pressor response to stress at home or at work and detailed questioning may reveal this. The evidence that psycho-social stress causes chronic elevation of blood pressure is poor and reliable studies have demonstrated no association.

High alcohol intake Closely related to high blood pressure, the effect of heavy drinking is independent of age, sex, personality, cigarette smoking, obesity or salt consumption. Alcoholics and heavy drinkers are frequently hypertensive and their blood pressure settles without drugs if they stop drinking. Detailed questioning on drinking habits is necessary in all hypertensive patients.

Salt intake Patients should be asked whether they consume much salt and particularly if they add it at the table or in the cooking. Many processed foods have a high salt content and patients who eat out or eat fast food are likely to have quite high salt intakes. However, many patients underestimate their salt intake, particularly when 24-hour urine collections are done to measure it.

Fat intake The amount of saturated animal and vegetable fat in the diet is an important determinant of cholesterol level, which is one of the three major risk factors for cardiovascular disease. It is important therefore to question all patients about the amount of fat in their diet.

Calorie intake Many patients with high blood pressure are overweight and it is important to try to get some idea of their calorie intake in order to advise them how best to lose further weight.

Cigarette smoking An independent cardiovascular risk factor, cigarette smoking is not related to high blood pressure, but when these two independent risk factors are present together, the degree of risk is compounded. Patients who smoke are more likely to develop peripheral vascular disease and, in particular, renal artery stenosis and malignant hypertension.

DRUG HISTORY

Antihypertensive drugs Often hypertensives are receiving unnecessarily complicated drug combinations. Many patients do not know what their tablets are or what they are for. At a clinical assessment where the previous drug history is not known, patients should be asked to bring all their tablets with them. There is often an alarming difference between the treatment the doctor thinks the patient is receiving and the tablets the patient actually takes. Patients should be given special cards or booklets which list drug names and doses as well as blood pressure measurements. These can be written in by any doctor or nurse who manages the patient and this information, in particular, improves liaison between the family and hospital doctors.

Other medication Some drugs, notably the oral contraceptives and carbenoxolone, can cause hypertension. Some psychotropic

drugs and non-steroidal analgesics interreact with antihypertensive drugs (see Chapters 5 and 11).

EXAMINATION

Breathlessness, distress and anxiety may be present in hypertensive patients who are unwell. The following features suggest specific diagnoses relevant to raised blood pressure:

Plethoric appearance A plethoric appearance suggests polycythaemia which itself is associated with raised blood pressure. It also occurs in patients with excessive alcohol intake and Cushing's syndrome.

Cushingoid appearance Cushing's syndrome may cause hypertension (see chapter 8) as does corticosteroid therapy. More commonly, the alcoholic pseudo-Cushing's syndrome is present and other stigmata of liver disease should be looked for (Fig. 7.1).

Sweating, tremor, restlessness and anxiety These symptoms raise the possibility of hyperthyroidism in which case the systolic pressure may be raised. Phaeochromocytoma or simple anxiety itself can also cause these symptoms.

Blanching and pallor Together with weight loss, sweating and tachycardia, blanching and pallor raise the possibility of phaeochromocytoma. Most cases are persis-

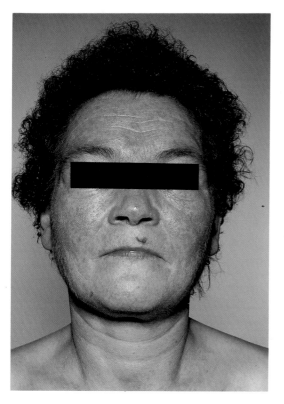

Figure 7.1
Patient with alcoholic pseudo–Cushing's syndrome.

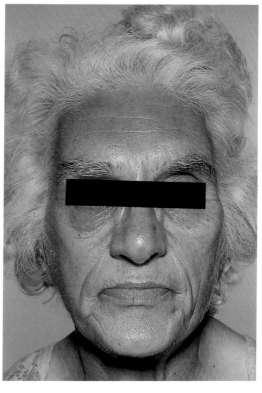

Figure 7.2
Patient with acromegaly and hypertension.

tently hypertensive but with great fluctuations in pressure.

Obesity Obesity is associated with raised blood pressure which is compounded by a tendency to overestimate the blood pressure in obese arms when an inappropriately small cuff is used (see Chapter 6). Body weight should be checked as well as height. In obese patients it is useful to plot weight in relation to height. Perhaps it is better to calculate the body mass index, which is the weight in kilograms divided by the height in metres squared.

BMI >30   obese
BMI 25–29 overweight
BMI <25   acceptable

However, body mass index does not take into account central obesity, which in men may be a more powerful predictor of cardiovascular risk.

Acromegaly About 50% of patients with acromegaly are hypertensive (Fig. 7.2).

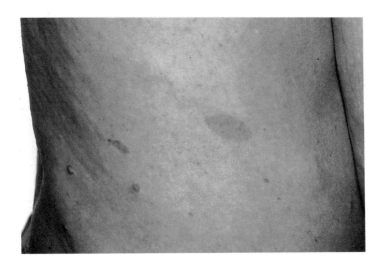

Figure 7.3
Patient with von Recklinghausen's neurofibromatosis.

Neurofibromatosis (von Recklinghausen's disease) Multiple neurofibromata and *cafe au lait* spots suggest neurofibromatosis which is associated with phaeochromocytoma and renal artery stenosis (Fig. 7.3).

Examination of the cardiovascular system

Blood pressure The correct technique for measuring blood pressure is covered in chapter 6. Pressures should be measured at least once in both arms. Seated blood pressures are best employed when assessing patients but pressures should also be measured standing if the patient complains of postural dizziness. This may particularly occur in the elderly and in hypertensive patients with phaeochromocytoma and in those patients receiving the outdated adrenergic blocking drugs. Atrial fibrillation renders blood pressure measurement difficult due to the fact that blood pressure will vary from beat to beat. Several readings should be taken. Atrial fibrillation may be due to coronary heart disease, alcoholic cardiomyopathy, thyroid disease or rheumatic heart disease.

The pulse Classically in hypertension the pulse has a large volume but this is not a reliable sign. Tachycardia suggests anxiety, thyrotoxicosis and, very rarely, phaeochromocytoma. Bradycardia is most commonly due to beta-blockers. In untreated cases it may be due to myxoedema or to heart block and an ECG should be obtained before any drugs are given (beta-blockers and verapamil drugs may make heart block worse). All peripheral pulses should be checked and the carotid and femoral pulses auscultated for bruits. The femoral pulse should always be checked once against the brachial or radial pulse to detect radial–femoral delay or a disparity in volume suggesting coarctation of the aorta or severe aortic atheroma.

Cardiac apex The position of the cardiac apex should be measured and the presence of a left ventricular heave noted. The presence of left ventricular hypertrophy is a potent predictor of risk in hypertension patients.

Heart sounds In patients with raised blood pressure the aortic component of the second heart sound is loud. If there is clinical or subclinical left ventricular failure, a third sound or even a combined third and fourth sound (gallop rhythm) may be heard.

Cardiac murmurs are assessed in the conventional manner; hypertension can exist with mitral valve disease and with aortic stenosis with or without regurgitation.

Aortic systolic murmurs of no haemodynamic significance are common in hypertension. If, however, the aortic component of the second heart sound is quiet, aortic stenosis should be considered, particularly if there is evidence of disproportionate left ventricular hypertrophy.

Coarctation of the aorta is usually associated with loud systolic murmurs over most of the left precordium into the left scapula region.

The respiratory system

The presence of basal pulmonary crepitations suggestive of left ventricular failure, or of rhonchi suggesting obstructive airways disease, strongly influences the choice of antihypertensive drugs. With airway obstruction, beta-blockers are absolutely contraindicated (see Chapter 11).

The abdomen

The presence of hepatomegaly raises the possibility of liver disease caused by alcohol abuse, although in decompensated cirrhosis with jaundice or ascites, hypertension is rare. It is, however, seen in cases with compensated cirrhosis.

Bimanual palpation may reveal unilateral or bilateral renal enlargement so polycystic kidney disease must be considered. Renal bruits suggestive of renal artery stenosis may be heard 10 cm lateral and 5 cm above the umbilicus, although they are often better heard by listening in the back.

The central nervous system

Examination may reveal evidence of neurological defect due to cerebrovascular disease.

The optic fundi

Ophthalmoscopy is an integral part of the assessment of every hypertensive patient with a diastolic blood pressure greater than 110 mmHg, diabetes mellitus and renal failure. A good view must be obtained, if necessary in a darkened room, with dilatation of the pupils by tropicamide eye drops.

The most frequent findings in hypertensives are:

Increased arterial tortuosity This physical sign is as much related to the age of the patient as to the height of the blood pressure.

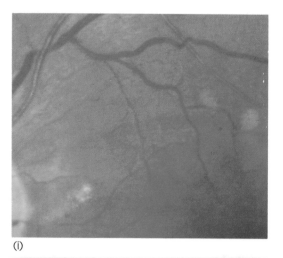

(i)

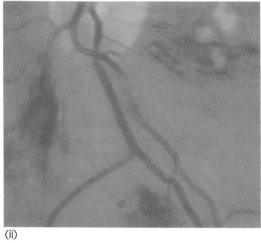

(ii)

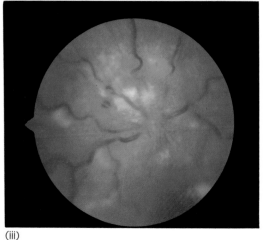

(iii)

Figure 7.4
Optic changes in hypertension. (i) Cotton wool spots and arteriovenous nipping. (ii) Cotton wool spots and flame–shaped haemorrhages. (iii) Retinal haemorrhages, exudates and papilloedema.

Silver wire changes In the retinal arteries a silver wire change suggests arteriolar wall thickening. It is seen in hypertensives but also occurs with advancing age.

Arteriovenous nipping or nicking Arteriovenous nipping occurs when the retinal veins appear to be occluded as they pass under the thickened retinal arteries.

However, all of these changes can occur in many normotensive subjects, particularly as they become older. The important findings in the retina which suggest severe hypertension which requires immediate action are shown in Fig. 7.4.

Retinal flame-shaped haemorrhages These are related to malignant hypertension and retinal vein occlusion.

Soft fluffy exudates or cotton wool spots
These are now know to be retinal infarcts.

Hard shiny exudates These ae lipid-laden retinal infarcts which frequently radiate from the macula (macula star).

Papilloedema Swelling of the optic disc. This is usually associated with raised intra-cranial pressure or ischaemic optic neuropathy.

If the above are seen, this is a medical emergency and blood pressure must be treated immediately.

The Keith Wagener classification of hypertensive retinopathy is out of date and is misleading in that Grades III and IV are changes that occur in accelerated or malignant phase hypertension and there is no point in differentiating between them as they have the same implications and prognosis.

- **Grade I** Minor vessel change only.
- **Grade II** Silver wire vessel change, arterial tortuosity and arteriovenous nipping.
- **Grade III** Retinal haemorrhages and/or cotton wool spots and/or shiny hard exudates.
- **Grade IV** Retinal haemorrhages, exudates and papilloedema.

The classification is frequently referred to in some medical journals and textbooks but it is better to describe the actual features seen.

Other types of retinopathy Diabetic retinopathy may be present in hypertensive diabetics. It is particularly associated with poor control of blood pressure, inadequate control of blood sugar, longstanding diabetes and possibly cigarette smoking. If

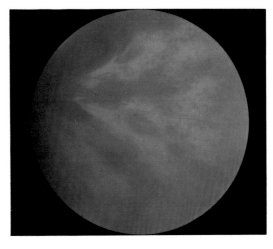

Figure 7.5
Central retinal vein thrombosis.

there is evidence of new vessel formation, i.e. proliferative retinopathy, patients should be referred immediately to an ophthalmologist for laser therapy.

Unilateral retinal vein thrombosis or branch vein thrombosis with multiple haemorrhages occurs more commonly in hypertensive patients (Fig. 7.5). Retinal artery occlusion with ischaemic pallor and empty arteries is also associated with hypertension and can be precipitated in accelerated hypertension by too rapid lowering of the blood pressure.

INVESTIGATIONS

Urinalysis The urine should be tested with dipsticks at least once in all newly diagnosed hypertensive patients and thereafter at least annually. Severe hypertensives with renal disease and patients receiving thiazide diruretics should have their urine tested at each visit to the outpatient clinic.

Proteinuria Proteinuria can occur both in malignant hypertension where it is due to fibrinoid necrosis and in the non-malignant phase due to hypertensive nephrosclerosis. If proteinuria is heavy, however, it suggests intrinsic renal disease, for example, glomerulonephritis or nephrotic syndrome. Dipstick tests for urinary protein are now very sensitive, becoming positive when urinary protein is above 300 mg/l. If proteinuria is persistent this should be further investigated by a 24-hour urine collection.

Haematuria This occurs in many intrinsic renal conditions associated with hypertension, including cancer, glomerulonephritis or pyelonephritis, as well as in various urological conditions, all of which need thorough investigation. Haematuria is common in malignant hypertension.

Glycosuria Glycosuria suggests the diagnosis of diabetes mellitus (see Chapter 14). Furthermore, diuretics (particularly thiazides) used in treating hypertension are diabetogenic.

Urine microscopy and culture This is not a useful routine investigation; urine microscopy and culture should be reserved for patients who have urinary symptoms or in whom urine dipsticks have revealed an abnormality. Reliable contaminant-free midstream specimens of urine are hard to obtain and are time-consuming for bacteriological laboratories. Bacterial growth without leucocytes is not an indicator of urinary infection.

However, the presence of leucocytes in the urine without bacterial growth (sterile pyuria) is an important finding and is most often due to partially treated urine infection but it also occurs in renal tuberculosis or renal tumours.

All patients who are to receive blood pressure-lowering drugs should also undergo routine biochemical and haematological profiling, although in most cases no abnormalities will be found.

Haematology

Polycythaemia Mild polycythaemia commonly occurs in essential hypertension. Frank polycythaemia occurs in some renal tumours. In population studies, haemoglobin levels and blood pressure are weakly correlated. A raised haemoglobin level should raise the possibility of Cushing's syndrome, alcohol excess and chronic chest disease.

Anaemia In the presence of chronic renal failure, there is usually a normochromic normocytic anaemia. This is due to deficient erythropoietin, mild marrow aplasia due to uraemia, mild haemolysis and sometimes intestinal blood loss.

Microangiopathic haemolytic anaemia Seen in some cases of glomerulonephritis, microangiopathic haemolytic anaemia is also noted in malignant hypertension.

Macrocytosis A raised MCV is a moderately reliable indicator of excessive alcohol intake. Hypertensive patients who have MCVs greater than 92 fl should be carefully questioned about their drinking habits.

Biochemistry

Plasma sodium   Plasma sodium is high or high/normal in primary hyperaldosteronism (142–150 mmol/l) and returns to normal with treatment with spironolactone or with surgery.

In renal or malignant hypertension, with or without chronic renal failure, there may be secondary hyperaldosteronism but in this situation serum sodium is low or low/normal (125–138 mmol/l). Diuretics can also cause a lowering of plasma sodium.

Plasma potassium   The commonest cause of hypokalaemia is diuretic therapy. In the absence of diuretic therapy, the presence of hypokalaemia with a serum potassium of 3.5 mmol/1 or less is a strong indicator of either primary or secondary aldosterone excess and always requires further investigation.

Hyperkalaemia occurs in acute renal failure but it may also occur if potassium-sparing diuretics are given to patients with renal failure and particularly if given with potassium supplementation. Hypokalaemia may develop when potassium sparing diuretics are given with ACE inhibitors.

Plasma bicarbonate   Hypokalaemia, due to excess aldosterone, causes a metabolic alkalosis with a high plasma bicarbonate. A metabolic acidosis with low serum bicarbonate in association with hypokalaemia suggests congenital or acquired renal tubular disease, particularly renal tubular acidosis.

Blood urea or creatinine   Plasma creatinine is a less labile index of renal function than blood urea. Patients should have their renal function monitored regularly and at least once a year, even if previous results are normal. In cases with chronic renal failure, the reciprocal of the serum creatinine

when regularly checked may be a good index of the rate of deterioration of renal function and may predict when dialysis will become necessary (Fig. 7.6). Estimations of creatinine clearance are not particularly useful in routine clinical practice.

Plasma creatinine should be checked routinely within a few weeks of starting ACE inhibitor therapy. If the creatinine rises significantly then a diagnosis of renal artery stenosis should be considered.

Serum calcium   Hypertension is present in up to 60% of cases of primary hyperthyroidism. Thiazide diuretics can also cause mild rises in plasma calcium and may reveal covert primary hyperparathyroidism.

Serum phosphate   A raised serum phosphate occurs in chronic renal failure whereas in primary hyperparathyroidism low levels are seen.

Plasma uric acid   Hyperuricaemia is found in about 40% of untreated patients with essential hypertension even when renal function is normal. It is more common when hypertension is associated with renal damage. Hyperuricaemia is also common in people consuming excess alcohol. Diuretic therapy causes serum uric acid to be raised in 60% of cases even though clinical gout is seen much less commonly (about 2%).

Serum lipids   Hyperlipidaemia is an important risk factor for coronary heart disease independent of raised blood pressure (see Chapter 2). There is also an association between hypercholesterolaemia and hypertension. All hypertensive patients should have a random cholesterol measurement. If this is raised, fasting cholesterol and

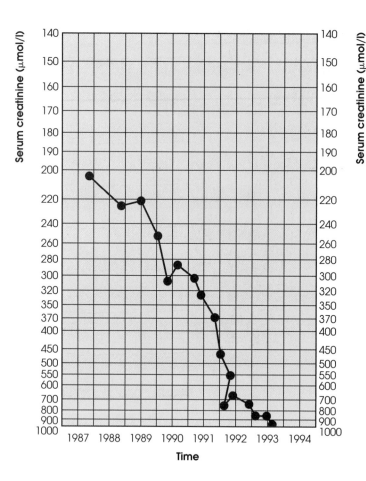

Figure 7.6
Example of a reciprocal creatinine chart in a patient with progressive chronic renal failure.

triglyceride levels should be measured together with measurement of either LDL cholesterol or HDL cholesterol.

Gamma glutamyl transferase (GGT) or aspartate aminotransferase (AST) The GGT and AST enzymes are useful indicators of liver damage and particularly indicate alcohol excess.

Thyroid Many women may develop sub-clinical myxoedema and T4 and TSH levels should be measured in women over the age of 50 where there is any suspicion of thyroid disease.

Chest x-ray Radiological assessment of cardiac size is not reliable as variations occur depending on the depth of inspiration. For this reason a chest x-ray may be omitted unless specifically indicated. It is necessary if there is concurrent chest disease or left ventricular failure. The cardiothoracic ratio (CTR) should be recorded each time a chest x-ray is taken and should be asked for on the request form.

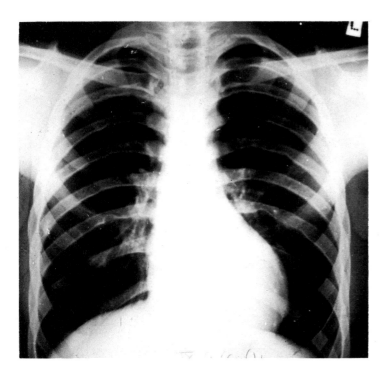

Figure 7.7
X–ray of a patient with aortic coarctation showing notching of the inferior surfaces of the third to seventh rib.

The presence of fractured ribs should raise the possibility of alcohol excess.

In coarctation of the aorta there is notching of the inferior edge of the second to sixth ribs owing to the dilated intercostal arteries. Also there may be sharp indentation of the lateral border of the initial portion of the descending aorta (Fig. 7.7).

Electrocardiogram All hypertensive patients requiring antihypertensive drugs should have an ECG. It is particularly useful as a reference if the patient subsequently develops symptoms of coronary heart disease. Ideally the ECG should be checked annually in all severe hypertensives. It may reveal evidence of myocardial infarction or left ventricular hypertrophy. The ECG abnormalities in left ventricular hypertrophy are:

(*a*) Biphasic p wave in leads V1 and V2 indicating left atrial dilatation. This is not a very specific ECG sign.

(*b*) Tall R waves (more than 12 mmHg) in a lead aVF.

(*c*) Chest lead criteria: The summation of the R wave in V5 or V6 with that of the S wave in V1 when greater than 35 mm strongly suggests the presence of left ventricular hypertrophy.

(*d*) ST depression and T wave inversion in leads V5 and V6 indicates relative ischaemia due to a hypertrophied left ventricle (the so-called strain pattern).

The ECG criteria of left ventricular hypertrophy are relatively crude and may miss many patients who have hypertrophy. Echocardiography is better but not readily available (see chapter 8). Nevertheless, if

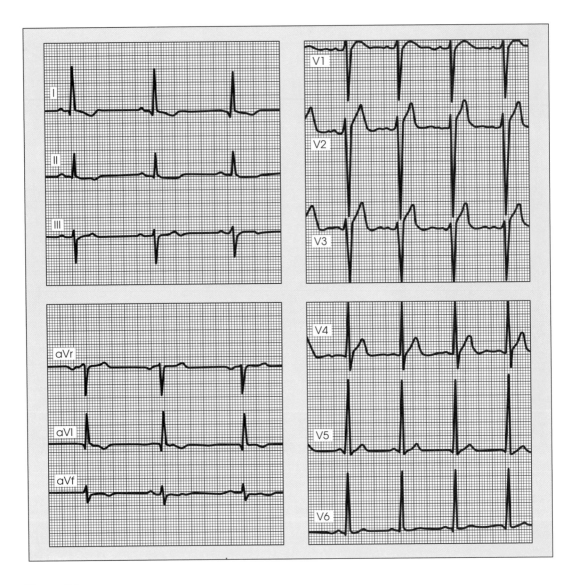

Figure 7.8
ECG of a patient with left ventricular hypertrophy.

present, left ventricular hypertrophy does indicate that the hypertension is sustained and should be treated assiduously as the risk of death for a given level of blood pressure is three times greater (Fig. 7.8).

Twenty-four-hour urinary sodium With the increasing awareness of the value of sodium restriction in the treatment of hypertension, there is a good case for measuring 24-hour urinary sodium at the stage of the first assessment and thereafter monitoring the reduction of salt intake in the diet. Many patients claim not to be eating large amounts of salt and are often surprised by the amounts of sodium excreted in their 24-hour urine collections.

INVESTIGATION OF HYPERTENSION IN PRIMARY CARE

The investigation of hypertension in primary care is discussed in Chapter 13. For the primary care practitioner, a reasonable rule is to investigate all patients in whom drug treatment is thought necessary. The investigations needed are a urine test, a full blood count, a biochemical profile including cholesterol and an ECG. In the majority of patients, however, no abnormalities will be found but when abnormalities are found, they are usually important. More detailed investigation, possibly with referral to a unit with a special interest in high blood pressure, should be reserved for those who fulfil the following criteria:

1. Clinical suspicion of secondary cause.
2. Moderate to severe hypertension.
3. Young (less than 35 years old).
4. Raised plasma creatinine.
5. Blood, protein or cells in the urine.
6. Low plasma potassium.
7. Variable blood pressure.
8. Failure to respond to treatment.
9. A large postural drop in blood pressure.

FURTHER INVESTIGATION

The more detailed investigations to be conducted in these cases are discussed in Chapter 8. In a large primary health care group there may be one physician who specializes in hypertension who may choose to investigate further without hospital referral.

In hospital practice there are still too few clinics with a specific interest in investigation and better treatment of patients with blood pressure. Patients often end up distributed between cardiologists, nephrologists and general physicians and clinical care can become very unsystematic. There is a need for specialized blood pressure clinics who, in close liaison with primary medical care, can investigate hypertensives more logically and manage them more efficiently with the long-term aim of a better control of their blood pressure.

FURTHER READING

Berglund C, Anderson O, Wilhelmsen L. Prevalence of primary and secondary hypertension: studies in a random population sample. *Br Med J* 1977; **2**:554.

Gifford RW, Kirkendall W, O'Connor DT, Weidman W. Office evaluation of hypertension: a statement for health professionals by a writing group of the Council for High Blood Pressure Research, American Heart Association. *Hypertension* 1989; **13**:283–93.

Lip GYH, Beevers M, Beevers DG. The failure of malignant hypertension to decline. A survey of 24 years experience in multiracial population in England. *J Hypertens* 1994; **12**:1297–1305.

Semple PF. ABC of blood pressure management. Investigation. *Br Med J* 1981; **282**:1306–9.

8 FURTHER INVESTIGATION OF HYPERTENSION

BACKGROUND

Hypertension is very common with approximately 10% of the population having persistently raised blood pressure on repeated measurement. The majority of these people have essential hypertension and patients with underlying causes of hypertension, because they are relatively rare, and have been felt to be not worth looking for. However, this attitude is changing with greater diagnostic ability and more sophisticated treatment. Many patients with secondary hypertension can now be cured, or treated more appropriately. Therefore, it is very important in treating hypertension to always bear in mind the possibility of an underlying cause, and this chapter oulines the types of tests that can be done and the more important causes of secondary hypertension.

HOW FAR TO INVESTIGATE

Certain routine investigations such as haematological and biochemical profiles and urine tests which are done on all patients may point to a renal or adrenal cause. Investigating for the rare causes of hypertension such as a phaeochromocytoma or renal artery stenosis that will not be picked up on these routine tests is a difficult decision. The dilemma therefore is how far to investigate patients to be sure of not missing a rare but curable form of high blood pressure. In general, patients whose blood pressure is severe or resistant to conventional treatment should be investigated further.

BRIEF DESCRIPTION OF FURTHER TESTS

Renal ultrasound

A simple non-invasive test, renal ultrasound is very useful for looking at renal size, cysts in the kidney and ureteric obstruction. It may also pick up adrenal masses as well as other abnormalities in the abdomen but it does not exclude them and although in renovascular hypertension it may show a difference in renal size it does not exclude renal artery stenosis.

Plain x-ray of the abdomen

This is rarely done but a plain x-ray of the abdomen may reveal unsuspected renal or vascular calcification, renal stones or occasionally a difference in kidney size. Phaeochromocytomas may occasionally be seen as a soft tissue shadow above one kidney.

Intravenous urography

Once a routine investigation in patients referred to hospital with high blood pressure, intravenous urography (IVU) is time-consuming and occasionally may produce life-threatening allergic reactions. It has fallen out of favour, particularly with the advent of angiography using much smaller catheters and digital subtraction techniques. An IVU should only be done if there is some reason to suspect an underlying kidney disease, that is, when there is heavy proteinuria, red cells or casts in the urine, or increased serum urea or creatinine concentrations. However, the IVU is the best test for the investigation of pylonephritis with or without reflux uropathy. In our view it should not be used as a screening test for renovascular hypertension.

Renal angiogram

The renal angiogram is the only test that can exclude renal artery stenosis and with modern techniques and digital subtraction the procedure can be done on a day-patient basis and has no greater incidence of problems than the IVU. Very clear anatomical pictures of the renal arteries are obtained.

In patients with renal impairment, even the much smaller amounts of contrast which are now given may cause a deterioration in renal function. It is extremely important that the patients are well-hydrated before the angiogram.

Radioisotope imaging

Radioisotope renograms are used in the diagnosis of renal artery stenosis, often with and without an angiotensin-converting enzyme inhibitor, usually captopril. There is considerable controversy about their ability to exclude renal artery stenosis but they may possibly indicate functional changes in blood flow better than the arteriogram. They are certainly useful as follow-up procedures in patients with renal artery stenosis following angioplasty or surgery.

A radio-labelled analogue of guanethidine, metaiodobenzyl guanadine (MIBG), is concentrated in some phaeochromocytomas and this is a useful test in conjunction with CT scanning, particularly when there are multiple or extra-adrenal tumours. However, some tumours do not take up the isotope and too much reliance should not be placed on the test, particularly when it is negative.

Selenium cholesterol scans of the adrenal gland have also been used to try and pick up adrenal adenomas, as cholesterol is taken up into some adenomas. However, our experience is that the test is not that helpful and may be misleading. It is much better to rely on CT or MRI scans (see primary aldosteronism later in the chapter).

CT scans

CT scans have revolutionized the investigation of adrenal causes of hypertension and are particularly useful in localizing phaeochromocytomas and adrenal adenomas secreting aldosterone. However, CT scans are expensive and do involve a considerable amount of radiation to the patient. They should only be carried out if there is biochemical evidence of aldosterone or catecholamine excess, or some other indication.

MRI scans

For diagnosing adrenal tumours at the present state of knowledge, MRI is no better than a CT scan.

Echocardiography

Echocardiography is a more accurate method of assessing left ventricular size and wall thickness than the ECG. Where available, it is a useful test, particularly in assessing patients with borderline hypertension or who are suspected to have 'white coat hypertension' where the finding of left ventricular hypertrophy may indicate that the blood pressure level is more sustained. It may also be useful in the follow-up of patients who have enlargement of the left ventricle to see whether hypertrophy regresses as the blood pressure is controlled.

Twenty-four-hour urine collections

The accurate collection of 24-hour urine is vital to avoid misleading results, particularly for catecholamine collections. It is therefore very important that the correct procedure is explained to the patient and that a large enough bottle or three 1 litre bottles are provided together with a non-transparent carrier bag. Best of all is to give printed instructions to the patients or have the instructions stuck on the bottle, but in our experience it is vital that a nurse goes through the instructions in detail as often there are difficulties in understanding exactly what is required (Table 8.1).

Sodium and potassium

Nearly all of the sodium and most of the potassium we eat comes out in the urine so that a 24-hour collection is a good guide to intake. The test is therefore useful in trying to find out how much salt the patients are eating and in particular whether they are complying with advice about reduction of salt intake.

Catecholamine excretions

The routine measurement of urinary metabolites of adrenaline (epinephrine) and noradrenaline (norepinephrine) or their metabolites is the best test for the rare but curable phaeochromocytoma. Depending on the local laboratory, different metabolites of catecholamines are measured. Urinary metanephrines and vanillylmandelic acid (VMA) are the most commonly assayed. However, probably the best measurement, where available, is the excretion of urinary noradrenaline and adrenaline itself. It is very important for these hormonal measurements that the urine collection is an exact one and contains sufficient hydrochloric or boric acid in order to preserve the catecholamine.

Creatinine excretion

Measurement of creatinine excretion is useful to assess the completeness of a 24-hour urine collection as the average creatinine excretion is around 1 gram per day. It will be more in men and particularly those with a large muscle bulk. If plasma creatinine is measured concurrently, a creatinine clearance can be calculated and this may be useful in patients with renal impairment although probably the best assessment of the rate of deterioration of renal disease is to plot the reciprocal of serial measurements of the plasma creatinine (Chapter 7).

Urinary protein

If dipstick tests show more than a trace of proteinuria, a 24-hour collection should be carried out to measure total urinary protein loss. Dipsticks are only positive if the concentration of protein in the urine exceeds 0.3 grams per litre, which is ten times the upper limit of normal.

For the Guidance of Patients

Table 8.1

24-HOUR URINE COLLECTION

1. It is *IMPORTANT* to collect all urine that your kidneys make during a 24 hour period.
2. The collection should start in the morning between 6.00 a.m. and 10.00 a.m. The exact time you start should be written down.
3. For example, if you start on Sunday at 6.00 a.m. then you should finish your collection at 6.00 a.m. on Monday.
4. When you start the collection, empty your bladder and discard the urine.
5. All urine produced for the next 24 hours should be put in the bottle provided.
6. Exactly 24 hours after starting a collection, empty bladder whether you need to or not, but this time into the bottle.

If you forget or spill some of your urine during this period the collection is no good. Discard the urine and collect a new bottle from the laboratory or the Out-Patients Department.

HINTS

1. Put the bottle in the toilet so that you do not forget to use it.
2. Ladies may find it easier to pass urine into a jug and then put it into a bottle.
3. When you find the need to open your bowels, make sure you pass urine into the bottle first.

IMPORTANT
The 24-hour specimen of urine must be brought into the hospital on the same day it is completed.

BLOOD HORMONE MEASUREMENTS

Blood hormone measurements are only done in selected patients and some of them are not generally available, which is ten times the upper limit of normal.

Measurement of the activity of the renin–angiotensin system

All the components of the renin–angiotensin system can be measured but the commonest and easiest measurement is plasma renin activity. This gives the rate of formation of angiotensin I in plasma which has been shown to correlate very closely with the prevailing level of plasma angiotensin II. Plasma aldosterone can also be measured by radioimmunoassay. The tests are indicated where there is suspected renal artery stenosis or a renin-secreting tumour, where renin levels may be high, and where primary aldosteronism is suspected, where plasma renin activity is low and plasma aldosterone will be high due to the autonomous secretion of aldosterone from the adrenal gland. In secondary aldosteronism due to renal disease the high level of renin and angiotensin II is the cause of the raised aldosterone.

Plasma catecholamines

Measurement of plasma adrenaline and noradrenaline levels are also helpful in the diagnosis of phaeochromocytoma, particularly during an 'attack' when there is a sudden rise in blood pressure, possibly with tachycardia and blanching. These assays are only available in a few specialist centres.

Plasma cortisol

Routine estimation of plasma cortisol is indicated where Cushing's syndrome is suspected. It is of limited use because of the diurnal variation of plasma cortisol. However, if a random plasma cortisol is normal, Cushing's syndrome is very unlikely. If plasma cortisol is raised then further investigations are indicated, in particular, dexamethasone suppression test. The 24-hour urine collections for cortisol are also used to exclude Cushing's disease.

ADRENAL CAUSES OF HIGH BLOOD PRESSURE

Primary aldosteronism

This syndrome is due to excessive secretion of aldosterone by the adrenal gland. This causes sodium and water retention which will suppress the renin system leading to low levels of plasma renin activity. There are two major causes of primary aldosteronism. One is a small 0.5–2 cm benign adenoma of the adrenal cortex which is directly responsible for the high levels of aldosterone. Therefore, when the adenoma is removed the condition is usually cured. The other cause of primary aldosteronism is bilateral adrenal hyperplasia, where both adrenal glands oversecrete aldosterone due to mechanisms which are not fully understood. Again there is sodium and water retention and suppression of the renin–angiotensin system. These patients present with an identical clinical and biochemical picture with sodium and water retention, moderately raised plasma sodium, high blood pressure, reduced plasma potassium, and inappropriately high potassium excretion. These two conditions need to be distinguished from secondary aldosteronism, where aldosterone is elevated due to an increase in renin release and angiotensin II formation. This occurs in conditions where angiotensin II is high, such as malignant hypertension, renal artery stenosis and where there is sodium and water depletion usually caused by a diuretic. In this situation, plasma potassium will also be low but it is relatively easy to distinguish primary and secondary aldosterone because the plasma renin activity will be high in secondary aldosteronism, and low in primary aldosteronism. It is vital, therefore, when measuring plasma aldosterone to also measure plasma renin activity.

Clinical features

Most patients with primary aldosteronism have high blood pressure and low plasma potassium levels although in the early stages and particularly if patients restrict salt intake, plasma potassium may not be low. In some patients, particularly when on a high salt intake, potassium levels may be very low and they may present with muscle weakness, tiredness and arrhythmias. This is particularly likely to happen if thiazide diuretics are given, as this causes a further fall in plasma potassium. Patients with primary aldosteronism can, contrary to some reports, develop malignant or accelerated hypertension.

Biochemical features

The hallmark of primary aldosteronism is a low plasma potassium, i.e. below 3.4 mmol/l, a raised plasma sodium usually to between 140 and 150 mmol/l with a metabolic alkalosis, i.e. an increase in plasma bicarbonate. The 24-hour excretion

of potassium will also be inappropriately high for the low plasma potassium. Measurement of plasma aldosterone will be high with a low plasma renin activity. Ideally these measurements should be done when patients are not receiving drug treatment with a concomitant 24-hour urine collection to assess salt intake. However, in many patients this may be unnecessary as the ratio of plasma aldosterone to plasma renin activity is a good index of whether aldosterone secretion is excessive. More complicated tests used to be done to try and distinguish between adenomas and bilateral hyperplasia. In general, patients with adenomas have a loss of diurnal variation of plasma aldosterone and suppression does not occur after salt loading or fludrocortisone. These tests are now rarely done. The advent of CT scanning has largely replaced them.

CT scans

CT scanning has revolutionized the investigation of primary aldosteronism. Most adenomas can be picked up if they are greater than 0.5 cm in diameter by good quality high resolution CT scans (Fig. 8.1).

Adrenal venography and adrenal vein sampling

Before CT scanning became available, adrenal venography and adrenal vein sampling were necessary to locate adrenal adenomas. These investigations are hazardous in that they may lead to adrenal infarction. The only indication at present is where there is some doubt as to whether there is an adenoma. Even here, in our view, it is better in patients with a negative CT scan to treat their blood pressure with drugs and repeat the CT scan at 2–3 year

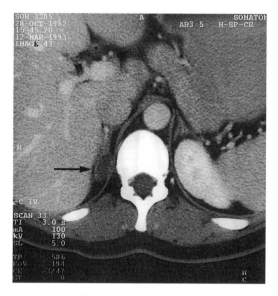

Figure 8.1
CT scan showing a large right adrenal tumour (arrow), which was an aldosternone secreting adenoma.

intervals. If they have an adenoma it will eventually become larger and will then be seen on the CT scan.

Treatment

Once the adrenal adenoma has been localized it is usual to remove it (Fig. 8.2). Conventionally, this required a major abdominal operation; but it is now possible to remove the adrenal by 'laparoscopic' techniques. Now that surgery is less hazardous, more patients can benefit from the procedure. It is now even more important that these diagnoses are not missed. In cases where surgery is not feasible, the aldosterone antagonist, spironolactone, may be given. Conventionally, high doses were given (100–300 mg/day). These usually caused side effects. Lower doses of spironolactone are effective, particularly when combined with other drugs. With removal of the adenoma, plasma potassium invariably returns to normal; however, the blood pressure does not necessarily return to normal. It is important that this is explained to patients prior to operation as they may be disappointed subsequently to find they still need some drug therapy. In rare cases, carcinoma of the adrenal may secrete excessive aldosterone and it is important to bear this in mind when assessing the need for surgery.

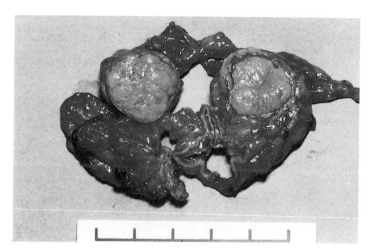

Figure 8.2
Typical adrenal adenoma causing primary aldosteronism.

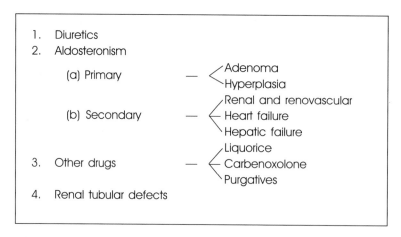

Table 8.2
Causes of hypokalaemia with high blood pressure.

1. Diuretics
2. Aldosteronism

   (a) Primary — Adenoma / Hyperplasia

   (b) Secondary — Renal and renovascular / Heart failure / Hepatic failure

3. Other drugs — Liquorice / Carbenoxolone / Purgatives

4. Renal tubular defects

Bilateral hyperplasia

The biochemical features of bilateral hyperplasia are similar to those of adenoma but no tumour is found. Both the adrenal glands are usually hypertrophied and as yet there is no specific treatment for this condition. Blood pressure may be resistant to treatment. Usually a potassium-conserving diuretic such as spironolactone or amiloride will correct the hypokalaemia. Calcium antagonists may be effective when combined with a diuretic. Salt restriction is particularly useful in controlling blood pressure as well as in correcting hypokalaemia in these patients. It should always be borne in mind in these patients that they may not have bilateral adrenal hyperplasia but may actually have a very small adenoma. Reassessment every few years is justified as there is now good evidence that some patients with bilateral hyperplasia may subsequently develop adenomas. Rarely, a familial form of hyperaldosteronism may be controlled by the use of dexamethasone and patients with any suggestion of a family history of aldosteronism should be referred for further investigation.

Other causes of hypokalaemia

The finding of a low plasma potassium in hypertensives is relatively common and it is important to exclude other causes before assuming that it is due to primary aldosteronism (Table 8.2). The commonest cause of hypokalaemia is the use of diuretic therapy and potassium levels may remain low for up to four to six weeks after treatment has been stopped. A low plasma potassium also occurs with intestinal potassium loss, particularly where there is chronic vomiting, usually surreptitious, or chronic diarrhoea often due to laxative addiction.

Carbenoxolone therapy and liquorice ingestion cause an identical electrolyte picture as occurs in primary aldosteronism (see Chapter 5) and it is important to question patients about their liquorice intake. Very high levels of renin that may occur in malignant/accelerated hypertension and renovascular hypertension may present with a low plasma potassium. Often in these situations and with diuretic therapy, plasma potassium will be low but plasma sodium will also be low. Secondary aldosterone excess can also occur in severe heart failure and in hepatic disease. Renal tubular defects can, in rare cases, cause excessive loss of urinary potassium. This is often associated with failure to acidify the urine and a metabolic acidosis, but blood pressure is usually normal.

Cushing's syndrome

Cushing's syndrome results from excessive secretion of cortisol, which may be either due to autonomous oversecretion by the adrenal gland or to raised ACTH levels from a pituitary tumour. Cushing's syndrome is usually suspected on the basis of the clinical appearance and estimation of plasma cortisol levels or 24-hour excretion of urinary free cortisol. Diagnosis is confirmed by dexamethazone suppression test. Some lung tumours may secrete ACTH and cause excess cortisol and aldosterone secretion. These patients often present with a low potassium/high blood pressure not unlike primary aldosteronism. Further investigations to distinguish between ACTH-secreting tumours and excessive cortisol secretion by adrenal tumours or hyperplasia involve using a variety of specialized endocrine tests. Alcoholism may cause a clinical and biochemical picture similar to Cushing's and it is well worthwhile checking liver enzymes, particularly gamma glutamyl transferase in patients with suspected Cushing's syndrome.

Adrenal enzyme deficiencies

Various congenital deficiencies of the enzymes responsible for the synthesis of adrenal steroids from the precursor cholesterol have been described. Most of these enzyme deficiencies present early in childhood, the commonest one presenting with virilization. Only two of them are associated with high blood pressure, that is the 11- and 17-hydroxylase deficiency. This is due to the fact that they also cause the production of large amounts of mineralocorticoid hormones.

Occasionally there may be partial defects which may mean that they will not be picked up until later in adulthood. Whether more subtle alterations in adrenal enzyme activity may be responsible for the elevation of blood pressure in some patients with essential hypertension remains a matter of controversy.

Phaeochromocytoma

These chromaffin cell tumours produce the most dramatic form of secondary hypertension. They are usually found in the adrenal medulla but may occur in the sympathetic chain of ganglia, particularly in the retroperitoneal space. They have also been described in the thoracic sympathetic chain and in many other parts of the body. They are characterized by intermittent or continuous oversecretion of noradrenaline and adrenaline. The excess secretion of these hormones causes the symptoms of tachycardia, blanching, sweating and sudden rises in blood pressure. They may present at any age and are not uncommon in children. Most patients have severe hypertension, often in the accelerated or malignant phase. However, in some patients, blood pressure may be only mildly raised and there may be

Table 8.3

Phaeochromocytoma

Blood pressure

Hypertensive 98%	– intermittent	30%
	– sustained	50%
	– paroxysmal	20%
	– malignant phase	40%
Normotensive 2%		

Site

Abdominal	98%
– adrenal	70%
– extra-adrenal	10%
– multiple	20%
– bilateral	10%
Thoracic	2%
Neck	<1%
Familial	10%
Malignant tumour	10%

Symptoms

Headache	80%
Sweating	70%
Palpitations	60%
Nervousness	40%
Nausea	40%
Weight loss	40%

intermittent surges of high blood pressure with the release of the catecholamines. Some patients may present with postural hypotension (Table 8.3).

Diagnosis

While phaeochromocytomas are relatively rare, the outlook for a patient with a phaeochromocytoma is extremely poor as fatal hypertensive crises can occur during anaesthesia, pregnancy and other stresses. Most patients, when not recognized, die of their tumour. The only way of definitively diagnosing them is by the measurement of urinary metabolites and/or plasma noradrenaline and adrenaline levels. In most practices it may not be feasible to screen all hypertensive patients with these measurements. Clinical acumen has to be used in selecting patients for further investigations. The following symptoms in patients with high blood pressure suggest the need for measurement of catecholamines:

- A story of intermittent high blood pressure, sweating attacks and palpitation.
- Patients presenting with weight loss and high blood pressure, particularly if there is an associated postural drop in blood pressure.
- All patients with resistant or accelerated malignant phase hypertension.
- Hypertensives diagnosed below age 35 years.

Investigation

The simplest and best investigation is 24-hour urine collection for measurement of catecholamines themselves or cate-cholamine metabolites, for example vanyllil-mandelic acid (VMA) or metanephrines. However, some tumours do not cause excess excretion of VMA or metanephrines in the urine and will be missed. The measurement of urinary noradrenaline and adrenaline may be a better method of screening patients if available. Plasma noradrenaline and adrenaline are raised in most phaeochromocytomas but may be missed, particularly if there are intermittent surges of release of noradrenaline and

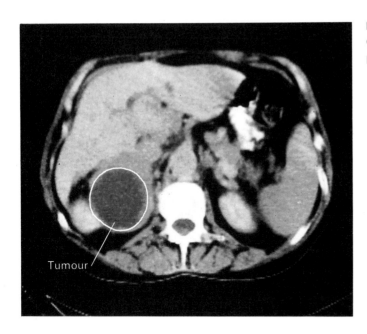

Tumour

Figure 8.3
CT scan of a large right adrenal phaeochromyocytoma.

adrenaline. If the urinary catecholamines are raised or the plasma levels are raised, abdominal ultrasound may locate some of these tumours but CT scanning is the most accurate technique (Fig. 8.3). The majority of the tumours are in the adrenal glands but they may be bilateral or extra-adrenal and are occasionally multiple. Some tumours, whilst histologically identical to others, may spread locally and eventually metastasize, particularly into the bones and the vertebrae. Scanning with a radioisotope MIBG that is taken up in some phaeochromocytomas is useful, particularly in localizing extra-adrenal tumours. In patients where there is difficulty in locating the tumour, venous sampling may be necessary.

Treatment

All patients with phaeochromocytomas must have them removed (Fig. 8.4). Prior to surgery it is very important that their blood pressure is controlled. During surgery dangerous rises in blood pressure may occur, particularly during induction of anaesthesia and when the tumour is being mobilized prior to removal. It is vital that all patients are very carefully prepared preoperatively and that the removal of the tumour is done by an expert anaesthetic/surgical team.

Before operation all patients should be treated medically. Acute paroxysms of high blood pressure can be controlled with the

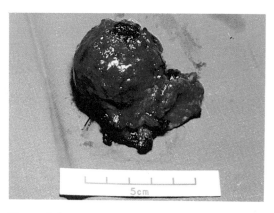 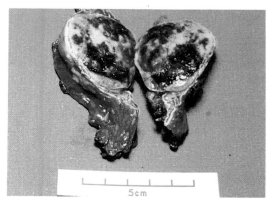

Figure 8.4
A typical phaeochromocytoma.

alpha-blocker phentolamine, 2–5 mg being given intravenously or as an infusion. However, this is a short acting alpha-blocker lasting for only a few minutes. The oral drug of choice is phenoxybenzamine, a longer-acting alpha-blocker that can be given once or twice daily. The dose should be started at 5 or 10 mg twice daily and increased until the blood pressure is controlled. Often these patients are volume-depleted and with the control of blood pressure there may be postural hypotension. In this situation it is important to correct the deficit in sodium balance by giving extra sodium and water either orally or by intravenous infusion. A beta-blocker such as propranolol should also be used in small doses to control the heart rate but should not be started until the alpha-blocker has been established as beta-blockade alone can sometimes cause dangerous rises in blood pressure or precipitate heart failure. Other drugs such as prazosin and labetolol have been claimed to

be of use but in our experience are not as good as the combination of phenoxybenzamine and beta-blocker. It is very important that all patients are adequately alpha-blocked. Indeed, if anything, they should be slightly overtreated to overcome the intense vasoconstriction. During induction of anaesthesia and when the tumour is mobilized, profound fluctuations in blood pressure can occur. For these reasons intra-arterial blood pressure must be monitored and if blood pressure is not controlled by the previous phenoxybenzamine, either phentolamine or sodium nitroprusside should be used to control it. Pulse rate can be controlled by an intravenous beta-blocker. At the time that the blood supply is tied off to the tumour, large amounts of blood and saline may need to be given to overcome profound hypotension.

While most patients have a single adrenal tumour and removal cures them, phaeochromocytomas can recur and all patients should be followed up carefully with annual checking of blood or urinary catecholamines.

Rare familial varieties of phaeochromocytoma also occur particularly in association with other endocrine tumours, particularly parathyroid adenomas and medullary cell carcinoma of the thyroid (Sipple syndrome). Phaeochromocytomas are also associated with Von Recklinghausen's neurofibromatosis and carotid body tumours. Occasionally they may occur around the renal artery, mimicking renal artery stenosis. A family history must always be obtained, and relatives should be screened

Other neural crest tumours

Neuroblastomas and ganglioneuromas can cause hypertension and abdominal tumours. This usually only occurs in children.

Parathyroid

Many patients with primary hyperparathyroidism have high blood pressure. The mechanism of the high blood pressure is not known and removal of the parathyroid adenoma does not usually correct the high blood pressure. Hyperparathyroidism is usually discovered on routine measurement of plasma calcium which should be measured in all patients with high blood pressure. High blood pressure itself is not necessarily an indication for parathyroidectomy unless there is renal damage, metabolic bone disease or other symptoms. Thiazide diuretics themselves can cause an increase in plasma calcium and this may reveal some patients with mild hyperparathyroidism.

Thyroid disease

Patients with overactive thyroids often have a widened pulse pressure and an increase in systolic pressure. Control of the thyrotoxicosis often results in the systolic blood pressure falling. Patients with myxoedema may also have increased blood pressure. The mechanisms for this are not known.

Acromegaly

Hypertension occurs commonly in patients with acromegaly and cardiovascular complications are the commonest cause of death.

Coarctation

Usually in coarctation there is constriction of the aorta just beyond the origin of the left subclavian artery. Severe cases usually present in childhood but less severe defects may not present until adult life. Elevated blood pressure is found above the constriction with a low blood pressure below. The mechanism of the high blood pressure would appear, at least in part, to be due to a diminished perfusion pressure to the kidneys causing excess renin secretion and retention of sodium and water in an attempt to maintain renal perfusion pressure. This leads to the blood pressure in the upper part of the body. The diagnosis is usually made from the simultaneous palpation of radial and femoral or radial and anterior tibial arteries. There will be considerable diminution in the strength of the pulse and delay of the pulse in the legs. If the diagnosis of coarctation is considered likely, blood pressures should be measured in the legs. A chest x-ray may confirm the diagnosis with enlarge-

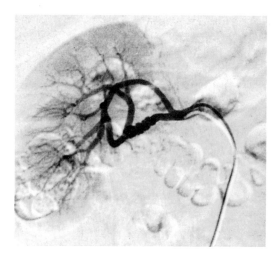

Figure 8.5
Fibromuscular hyperplasia in lower branch of renal artery.

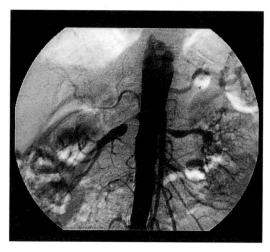

Figure 8.6
Atheromatous bilateral renal artery stenosis with post–stenotic dilatation.

ment of the heart, dilatation of the aorta round the constriction and notching of the ribs by collateral vessels. Echocardiography, CT scanning and, if necessary, aortography can all be used to localize the lesion. Surgery is usually performed, depending on the circumstances, but recently balloon angioplasty has also been used.

RENAL CAUSES OF HIGH BLOOD PRESSURE

High blood pressure secondary to kidney disease may be due to the underlying kidney damage causing sodium retention or an inappropriate release of renin, with inappropriately raised levels of angiotensin II. Usually hypertension in parenchymal

renal disease is due to a combination of both these factors, but it may involve other less well understood factors.

Renal artery stenosis

Of all the causes of hypertension, renal artery stenosis has attracted the most attention because good animal models were developed, but initially it appeared to be a rare cause of hypertension. However, it is now clear that it is by far the most common cause of secondary hypertension.

Cause

The renal arterial narrowing in patients below the age of 40, particularly in women, is usually due to fibromuscular hyperplasia of the renal or intra-renal arteries (Fig. 8.5). In older patients the narrowed arteries are much more likely to be due to premature vascular disease (atheroma) (Fig. 8.6). Very rarely there may be extra-arterial compression by retroperitoneal tumours. When there is a narrowing of one artery to the kidney, the reduced renal blood flow causes increased secretion of renin and high circulating levels of plasma angiotensin II. This can then directly cause the blood pressure to increase. However, in reality, the situation is often more complicated because the other kidney may be damaged and there may therefore be secondary retention of sodium with the combination of inappropriately high renin level for the degree of sodium balance.

Diagnosis

There are no particular clinical features of renal artery stenosis but in general patients tend to have more resistant hypertension and may present in the accelerated or malignant phase. Renal bruits are audible in about 40% of patients. All patients, therefore, with malignant or accelerated hypertension or blood pressure that is resistant to conventional therapy should be thoroughly investigated for renal artery stenosis. Renal artery stenosis is particularly common in patients with peripheral vascular disease and this is particularly so in heavy cigarette smokers.

Investigations

Renal angiogram The renal angiogram is the only reliable test for renal artery stenosis. It requires catherization of the femoral artery followed by an injection of dye into the aorta and renal arteries. In experienced hands and with digital subtraction so that very little contrast medium is given, complications are rare and most patients can be done as day cases with very clear pictures of both renal arteries and the peripheral intra-renal arteries. In patients where other renal disease is being looked for, it is possible to get good nephrogram pictures from the arteriogram, making an additional intravenous pyelogram unnecessary.

Intravenous urography With the advent of much more simple and better angiography, intravenous urography as a screening test for renal artery stenosis is rarely used. Criteria on IVU for diagnosis of renal artery stenosis are that one kidney is smaller than the other, with a smooth renal outline with delay in the appearance of the dye on the immediate film on the affected side. Subsequently there is hyperconcentration of the dye in the affected kidney.

Renograms Renograms with and without captopril have been claimed to be a good screening test for renovascular hypertension. Our experience is that it depends on the excellence of the local nuclear medicine department and some patients with renal artery stenosis that is treatable can be missed. In our view therefore it is important that in all patients where there is a strong suspicion of renal artery stenosis should undergo renal angiopathy.

Measurements of plasma renin Plasma renin activity levels are often high in renal artery stenosis and there is hyper-responsiveness to various manoeuvres to renin release. However, in many patients plasma renin activity levels may be normal or even low, particularly where there is bilateral

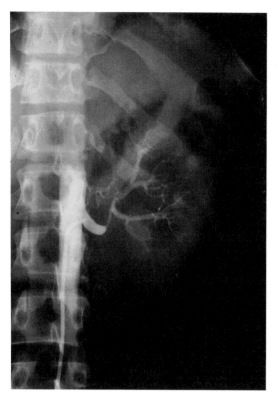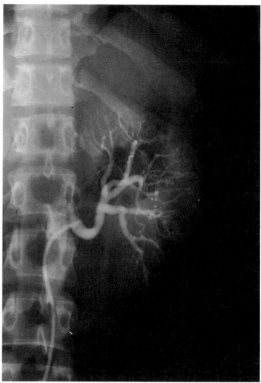

Figure 8.7
Balloon dilatation in a young woman with unilateral renal artery stenosis before (left) and after (right) dilatation.

renal artery stenosis or a unilateral narrowing of one artery and a blocked artery on the other side.

Renal vein measurements Measuring the concentration of plasma renin activity in renal veins was a widely used procedure before the advent of angioplasty. It involves catheterizing both renal veins from the femoral vein, which is relatively easy in experienced hands. Various criteria have been suggested to predict the outcome of surgery or balloon dilatation of the renal

arteries. In particular, it has been claimed that if the renal vein renin levels are at least 1.5 times higher on the affected side compared to the other kidney this was a strong indication that there was a functionally significant narrowing of the renal artery. However, where there is severe renal artery stenosis, blood flow to the affected kidney will be reduced and although the kidney may be secreting very little renin, the amount of renin in the blood draining the kidney may be high because of the very reduced blood flow. When these tests are done it is important therefore to measure the concentration of plasma renin activity both below the kidneys and above the kidneys in the inferior vena cava. A correction can then be made for a diminished blood flow from the affected kidney. Nevertheless, there is now little need to do these measurements. Where lesions can easily be angioplastied it is probably better to do this immediately and see the effect on blood pressure rather than measuring the renin level.

Treatment The advent of balloon angioplasty has changed the treatment of renal artery stenosis over the last few years (Fig. 8.7). Renal artery reconstruction is technically difficult and whether it provides any benefit over good blood pressure control with drugs remains controversial. Balloon angioplasty is a much less traumatic technique which can be very successful in well-selected cases. Complications such as dissection of the artery, damage to the artery or haemorrhage from the artery are rare. However, in many patients with atheromatous lesions, these may recur and frequent angioplasties may be necessary. In patients with more proximal stenosis of the renal arteries, particularly at the origin of the renal artery, an angioplasty may be technically difficult and it may be necessary to put a stent into the renal artery. Well controlled studies comparing angioplasty to medical treatment have not been done. However, there are many reasons why more detailed investigations for renal artery stenosis are now justified and angioplasty is indicated for other reasons than blood pressure control alone (Fig. 8.6).

- Surgery or balloon dilatation in reliable hands can produce excellent results, particularly in younger patients, thus avoiding lifelong drug therapy.

- Even if blood pressure is not normalized, control with drugs may be rendered easier.
- If the arterial supply to the kidney is seriously embarrassed, dilatation or operation may help to preserve renal function.
- Both fibromuscular hyperplasia and atheroma are progressive diseases and might recur either in the same renal artery or on the other side. Some patients with hypertension and heart failure may have unsuspected renal artery stenosis.

Atheromatous renovascular disease is always associated with vascular disease elsewhere. Often patients are heavy cigarette smokers and they should be persuaded to stop. Other steps should be taken to try and prevent the development of further progressive vascular damage. In particular, patients should make every effort to reduce their cholesterol levels as much as possible. Regression of some of these lesions may be possible provided patients are prepared to reduce their fat intake sufficiently and/or take cholesterol-lowering drugs. Furthermore, accurate blood pressure is mandatory.

Renin secreting tumours

Very rare tumours of the renal juxtaglomerular cells (haemangiopericytomas) can secrete excess renin directly causing high blood pressure. They usually occur in children or young adults and present with accelerated/malignant hypertension with high levels of renin and angiotensin II and hypokalaemia secondary to the excess aldosterone. Diagnosis involves differentiating these tumours from other causes of high renin secretion such as accelerated/malignant hypertension itself or renal artery stenosis. Renal vein renin levels will show excess renin secretion from the affected side. The tumours may be seen as blushes on renal angiograms. If the tumour can be localized and removed, the patient can be cured. Hypertension may also occur in children with juvenile renal tumours (Wilms' tumours) as well as in adenocarcinoma of the kidney in adulthood.

Other causes of renal hypertension

Most forms of renal disease cause high blood pressure. The only renal diseases not complicated by raised blood pressure are those affecting the renal medulla alone, where there may be loss of sodium and water and therefore low blood pressure.

Glomerulonephritis

Both acute and chronic glomerulonephritis are associated with high blood pressure. Particularly severe hypertension may occur in patients with IgA nephropathy, very often with raised plasma renin activity. Many of these patients develop the accelerated malignant phase of hypertension with acute deterioration in renal function requiring dialysis and transplantation. Further investigation is outside the scope of this book but involves microscopy of the urine, intravenous urography, exclusion of tuberculosis by early morning cultures and, if indicated, renal biopsy. Control of blood pressure in these patients is particularly important as there is increasing evidence that this in itself may slow down the progression of many renal diseases. There is now evidence that the ACE inhibitors can slow the deterioration of renal function in non-diabetic patients with renal disease.

Pyelonephritis

Features suggestive of radiological pyelonephritis with calyceal clubbing and areas of renal cortical thinning are sometimes seen in hypertensives. There remains some doubt as to whether this form of kidney damage causes hypertension unless there is associated chronic renal failure. Similarly, there is controversy about possible associations between hypertension and chronic urinary infection. Patients with radiological evidence of pylonephritis need detailed urological assessment to exclude obstruction to urine flow due to prostatic enlargement, pelviureteric junction (PUJ) obstruction, or pelvic tumours.

Polycystic kidney disease

A mendelian dominant condition, polycystic kidney disease causes bilateral renal cysts, berry aneurysms of the circle of Willis and sometimes hepatic and pancreatic cysts. Often it is not diagnosed until middle age. The presenting features are hypertension, subarachnoid haemorrhage, abdominal pain, haematuria and, more commonly, the insidious development of renal failure. Increasing evidence suggests that good control of blood pressure may prevent or delay the onset of renal failure and in particular may prevent subarachnoid haemorrhages. With the increasing use of ultrasound, many patients are now being picked up through screening of families and it is important to screen all relatives of patients with polycystic kidney disease. On renal ultrasound the cysts can easily be seen and there is no need now to do intravenous urograms (Fig. 8.8). CT scans will also clearly demonstrate the renal cysts (Fig. 8.9). Patients who are known to have polycystic kidney disease should have regular checks on their blood pressure and even mildly elevated degrees of blood pressure should be treated.

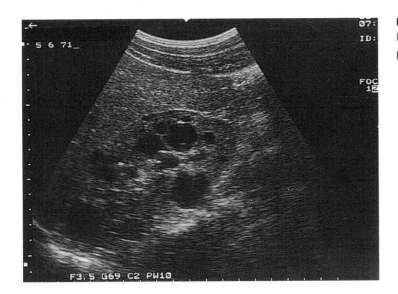

Figure 8.8
Ultrasound showing polycystic kidney.

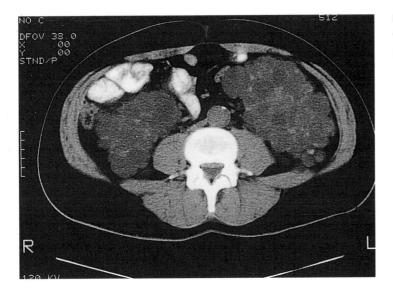

Figure 8.9
CT scan showing bilateral polycystic kidneys.

Diabetic kidney disease

The topic of diabetic hypertension is discussed in Chapter 14. High blood pressure is common in diabetics and is one of the best predictors of nephropathy and retinopathy.

Connective tissue disorders

Most of the connective tissue disorders can cause renal damage and are often associated with high blood pressure.

Scleroderma

Patients with scleroderma may suddenly develop accelerated or malignant hypertension and acute renal failure (Fig. 8.8). It is important, therefore, in these patients that blood pressure is measured and treated even when only mildly elevated. Some claims have been made that converting enzyme inhibitors may specifically prevent the development of accelerated malignant hypertension but whether this is correct or not is not clear at the present time. There are no diagnostic blood tests for scleroderma, so the diagnosis must rely on clinical examination.

Systemic lupus erythematosus

Systemic lupus erythematosus often involves the kidney, and hypertension and renal failure are common sequelae. Corticosteroids and cytotoxic therapy may delay the progression of the renal disease. Control of blood pressure is important in that a raised blood pressure may hasten the onset of renal disease. A reversible lupus-like syndrome can be caused by hydralazine therapy. Antinuclear antibodies (ANA) and extractable nuclear antigen (ENA) may be positive.

Polyarteritis nodosa

This connective tissue disorder, when it involves the kidney, can often cause severe hypertension resistant to treatment. The diagnosis is made usually on other features of polyarteritis and characteristic lesions will be seen on renal biopsy as well as aneurysms on renal arteriograms. ANA or anti-neutrophil cytoplasmic antibodies (ANCA) may be positive.

Retroperitoneal fibrosis

Fibrosis of the retroperitoneal tissues may occur after treatment with methysergide, or may be associated with retroperitoneal tumours. Most often, however, no cause is found. The ureters are pulled medially and may become obstructed, causing bilateral hydronephrosis.

Obstructive uropathy

Obstructive uropathy may be associated with high blood pressure, particularly if there is renal failure. In older patients with prostatic enlargement and chronic urinary retention, high blood pressure would be expected to be common, but it appears to be no more so than in the general population of that age.

FURTHER READING

Derkx FHM, Schalekamp MADH. Renal artery stenosis and hypertension. *Lancet* 1994; **344**:237–9.

Gonzalo A, Rivera M, Quereda C, Ortuno J. Clinical features and prognosis of adult polycystic kidney disease. *Am J Nephrol* 1990; **10**:470–4.

Gordon RD. Mineralocorticoid hypertension. *Lancet* 1994; **344**:240–3.

Ross EJ, Griffith DNW. The clinical presentation of phaeochromocytoma. *Q J Med* 1989; **71**:485–96.

3

Section Three

9 THE BENEFITS OF ANTIHYPERTENSIVE TREATMENT

BACKGROUND

Whilst the aetiology and pathogenesis of hypertension remain uncertain and the optimum method of reducing blood pressure is still controversial, there is no doubt that the value of reducing blood pressure is proven. Antihypertensive drugs can be regarded as having a major beneficial impact which ranks alongside that of antibiotic therapy in preventing premature death. Up until the early 1960s clinicians could only stand back and watch helplessly as their hypertensive patients inexorably deteriorated with strokes, heart failure, renal failure and coronary heart disease.

The dramatic reduction in stroke and coronary heart disease incidence over the last ten years can, in large part, be attributed to the advent of tolerable antihypertensive drugs. Furthermore the 'whole patient' approach to the management of hypertensive patients has further contributed to the fall in heart attacks and stroke rates observed in most developed nations.

The purpose of this chapter is to review the results of the randomized trials of antihypertensive therapy with particular reference to the large-scale and more reliable studies.

THE IMPORTANCE OF CLINICAL TRIALS

No pharmacological preparation should be administered unless there is firm evidence from well conducted, randomized, controlled trials that their use is beneficial. This is particularly important in hypertensive patients because the condition is usually symptomless; the decision to prescribe drugs on a long-term basis to otherwise fit people must be based on absolute proof that this is worthwhile. In addition, the fact that hypertension is so common means that the recommendation to give drugs to millions of people, with its cost implications, must be based on a large body of reliable data. The topic of hypertension has been particularly well served in this respect as a great many excellent clinical trials have been conducted. These initially concentrated on very severe hypertension but, as the years have gone by, trialists have turned their attention to milder cases where the immediate clinical risk is lower.

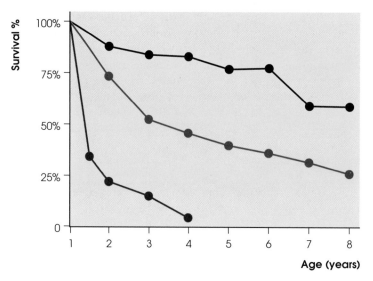

Figure 9.1
Survival rates for untreated and treated malignant hypertension.

—●— Diastolic blood pressure reduced to below 100mmHg

—●— Diastolic blood pressure remained above 100mmHg.

—●— Untreated malignant hypertension (*from Pickering 1968*)

TRIALS OF SEVERE HYPERTENSION

The introduction of the thiazide diuretics, methyldopa and the adrenergic neurone blockers (e.g. guanethidine) prompted the first wave of clinical trials in severely hypertensive patients where the risk of death was high.

Malignant hypertension

In this rare but rapidly fatal condition, no formal trials were conducted because it was rightly felt to be ethically unjustifiable to withhold drugs which lowered blood pressure as soon as they became available. The clinical observation that with treatment these sick patients survived at all meant that drug therapy was mandatory. An 80% 2-year death rate was transformed to a 70–80% 5-year survival rate (Fig. 9.1).

Hamilton, Thompson and Wisniewski (1964)

This was the first randomized controlled trial of drug therapy in relatively fit symptomless but severe hypertensives. Diastolic blood pressures exceeded 110 mmHg and, in more than half of the patients, the diastolic pressures were 130 mmHg or more. Ten men and 20 women received active drug therapy and 12 men and 19 women were treated with observation only. Amongst the men, eight vascular events (strokes and heart failure) developed in the untreated cases, whilst no events occurred in treated patients. In women there were eight events in those receiving no treatment and five in the treated group, a difference which was not statistically significant. However, in many of the treated women, blood pressures were not successfully reduced with the drugs available at the time. Hamilton and co-workers, therefore, re-analysed their data for women on the basis of whether or not diastolic blood pressure was reduced to below 110 mmHg. In 16 women, the blood pressure was successfully reduced and only one suffered a vascular event. In the 23 women whose blood pressures remained above 110 mmHg at follow-up, there were 12 vascular events. This was the only trial to provide information on the use of antihypertensive drug therapy in women until 1979.

Veterans Administration 1967

This was a placebo-controlled trial amongst similar patients to those studied by Hamilton and co-workers, but women were not included in the trial, 70 men received active treatment whilst 73 received placebo, and entry diastolic pressures were between 115 and 129 mmHg. At follow-up, four deaths and 27 morbid events developed in the placebo patients compared with no deaths and two morbid events in the patients receiving active therapy.

Other trials of severe hypertension

Several other small-scale randomized trials were also conducted in the 1960s but they provide little extra information when seen in isolation. In addition, there were some severe hypertensive patients included in the large-scale randomized trials discussed below which had mainly concentrated on the milder grades of hypertension. If the results of all of the trials of patients with diastolic pressures of 115 mmHg or more are pooled, then data are available on 1589 patients randomized to active therapy and 1629 control patients receiving no active treatment. Fatal or non-fatal strokes developed in 83 (5.2%) actively treated patients and 146 (9%) controls. Heart attacks developed in 109 (6.9%) actively treated patients and 147 (9%) controls.

TRIALS OF MILD TO MODERATE HYPERTENSION

By 1970, it was clearly established that it was no longer ethically justifiable to withhold drug therapy from patients with diastolic pressures of 110 mmHg or more. The trialists, therefore, turned their attention to the milder grades of hypertension where the individual risk of death was less but the number of eligible people was greater and the number of vascular complications was correspondingly greater.

Veterans Administration 1970

This trial was conducted in men with diastolic pressures between 90 and 114 mmHg. One hundred and ninety-four men received placebo tablets and 186 received active drugs. The results of this trial were impressive, with 35 morbid events and 16 deaths in the placebo group and nine morbid events and eight deaths in the active group. However, sub-group analysis of this study showed that the benefits were largely confined to patients with diastolic blood pressures between 105 and 114 mmHg. In the 170 men with entry diastolic pressures between 90 and 104 mmHg, 25% of placebo and 16% of actively treated patients suffered cardiovascular events, a trend which was not statistically significant. At this stage, it was generally considered that the reduction of coronary events with antihypertensive therapy was unimpressive, the benefits of antihypertensive therapy being largely related to prevention of strokes and heart failure.

The Hypertensive Detection and Follow Up Programme (HDFP) 1979

This is a much criticized study, but its size means that reliable information can be obtained. Hypertensive patients were randomized either to 'stepped care' in specially established clinics or to 'referral care' with their usual health care facilities; 10 940 men and women were randomized and, at follow-up, more of the 'stepped care' patients received active treatment than the 'referred care' patients and average blood pressures were thus lower. In the strata of the HDFP study which included mild hypertensive patients alone, there was an impressive reduction of both heart attacks and strokes but it is difficult to be certain whether this effect was due to differences in blood pressure or to differences in quality of health care. One cynic commented that the HDFP was a randomized trial of socialized medicine with efficient delivery of health care rather than a trial of antihypertensive drug therapy.

Australian National Blood Pressure Study (ANBPS 1980)

This was a well conducted placebo-controlled trial of the use of chlorothiazide or placebo in 3427 men and women with diastolic blood pressures between 95 and 109 mmHg. At follow-up, 17 cerebrovascular events developed in the actively treated group and 31 events in the placebo group. These differences were statistically significant. The results for coronary heart disease were less impressive, with 98 cardiac events with active treatment and 109 events with placebo. There were 30 less deaths from all causes in patients who received diuretic treatment.

The MRC trial of mild to moderate hypertension (1985)

The British MRC trial was also the source of much controversy. The entry diastolic pressures were between 90 and 109 mmHg and 17 354 men and women aged 35–64 years were randomized to placebo or active antihypertensive drugs. The actively treated group were further subdivided into half who received propranolol and half who received bendrofluazide in the astonishing dose of 5 mg twice daily. By the end of the study, 60 strokes occurred in the treated group and 109 in the placebo group, an effect which was statistically significant. No significant differences were found in overall rates of coronary events: 222 events occurred on active treatment and 234 in the placebo group. The main problem with the MRC trial was that there were considerably fewer cardiovascular complications in the placebo group than was expected. This was due to the fact that the average diastolic pressure in these untreated patients fell to 90 mmHg soon after the trial started and remained at this level for 5 years. This is a problem with trials where the run-in period is inadequate. Blood pressures fall on rechecking and seem only to 'bottom-out' at the fourth visit.

Several sub-group analyses were conducted *post hoc* from the results of the MRC trial. All-cause mortality was reduced in men and appeared to be increased in women. This finding needs to be considered with great caution. If a therapeutic intervention is shown to be of benefit for men and women considered together, and if one gender is shown to obtain particular benefit (i.e. the men), then, by the laws of mathematics, the drugs will appear to be harmful to the other gender (i.e. the women). As no other trial has suggested that antihypertensive therapy is harmful to women, this gender difference should be ignored. Another sub-group analysis suggested that beta-blocker therapy was associated with a reduction of coronary events in the men but not the women and furthermore that this benefit was confined to non-smoking men. Again this finding needs to be treated with caution. A similar finding was reported in a study of the treatment of hypertension with oxprenolol whereas in two other studies there was no evidence of coronary prevention in smokers or non-smokers treated with atenolol. By contrast, treatment with metoprolol was found in one sub-group analysis of a further trial to be beneficial in smokers only. Our view is that the cigarette smoking/beta-blocker interaction is probably not genuine and hypertensive patients should not smoke anyway.

The European Working Party on Hypertension in the Elderly (EWPHE)

This well conducted randomized placebo-controlled trial was conducted in 840 men and women aged 60 to 99 years. Many of the findings are relevant to non-elderly patients and the implications for the elderly are discussed in more detail in Chapter 15. By the end of the study, the 416 patients who received the diuretic-based regime suffered 48 heart attacks and 32 strokes. By contrast, in the placebo group, there were 59 heart attacks and 48 strokes. This trial was, therefore, the first to convincingly demonstrate coronary prevention as well as stroke prevention, and contrary to what some observers had expected, this was achieved with diuretic therapy. In this trial there was a significant reduction in cardio-vascular deaths, a benefit which had eluded the previous trials.

The Coope and Warrender trial

In this general practice-based study from England and Wales, 419 men and women were randomizdd to receive the beta-blocker atenolol whilst 465 were given no active therapy. The age range was 60–79 years. Atenolol alone proved ineffective in a great many patients, so a thiazide diuretic had to be added. As with other trials, there was a significant reduction in strokes but, in this study, there was no impact on coronary heart disease.

The Systolic Hypertension in the Elderly Programme (SHEP 1991)

This was a multi-centre trial in which 4736 patients aged 60 or more years were randomized to receive either chlorthalidone or placebo tablets. Of the participants, 42% were aged less than 70 years, so many of them were not particularly elderly. This trial

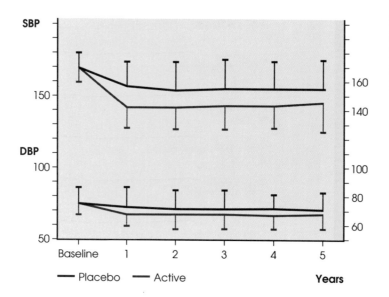

Figure 9.2
Baseline and follow–up blood pressure in the Systolic Hypertension in the Elderly Program (SHEP).

broke new ground because it was conducted amongst patients with a systolic pressure of more than 160 mmHg but diastolic pressures below 90 mmHg. Epidemiologists had long known that systolic blood pressure was a better predictor of cardiovascular risk than the diastolic pressure but this was the first trial to investigate the value of reducing systolic pressures. At follow-up, there were only minor differences in diastolic pressures between treated and placebo patients, but the reduction in systolic pressures was significant (Fig. 9.2).

The results after 5 years were spectacular, with statistically significant reductions of both heart attacks and strokes and reduction in heart failure, TIA and the need for coronary revascularization (Fig. 9.3). The trial included a highly selected group of patients and has its critics. However, in the light of this and other studies, particularly in older patients, it can now be said that the

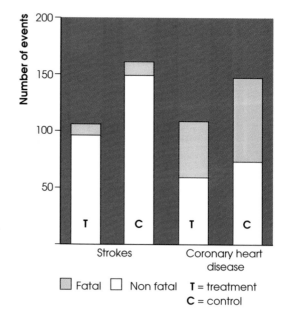

Figure 9.3
Results of treatment in the SHEP study.

treatment of isolated systolic hypertension has been validated, although the level of systolic pressure at which treatment should be given remains uncertain.

The Swedish Trial of Old People with Hypertension (STOP-H)

This multi-centre trial largely confirmed the findings of all other studies, with a significant reduction in strokes and some coronary prevention. It is not possible to be certain whether one drug group was better than another in coronary prevention.

The MRC trial of hypertension in the elderly

This second MRC trial was conducted in 4396 men and women who were randomized to receive either atenolol, a diuretic or placebo therapy. Patients were aged 65–74 years, so again the findings in this study are relevant to non-elderly patients. By the end of the study, there was a 25% reduction in strokes and a 19% reduction in coronary events in actively treated patients when compared to those receiving placebo tablets. Again, coronary prevention was achieved in the diuretic-treated patients but there was no prevention in patients randomized to the beta-blocker.

Some of the patients included for this trial were recruited on the basis of raised systolic blood pressures with diastolic pressures below 90 mmHg. A sub-group analysis of this group revealed that the treatment of isolated systolic hypertension lead to a reduction in both heart attacks and strokes, a finding similar to that of the SHEP study.

THE BENEFITS OF TREATING MILD HYPERTENSION

A major overview or meta-analysis of all of the above studies, along with sundry other smaller studies which individually lacked the power to prove anything, or showed only non-significant trends, was conducted in Oxford in 1994.

On the basis of epidemiological follow-up data from several large population surveys, the authors calculated that antihypertensive treatment for mild hypertension would be expected to bring about a 35–40% reduction in strokes and a 20–25% reduction in coronary heart disease events. Taking the results of all the outcome trials together, it was noted that the reduction in strokes was 38% (plus or minus 4%) while the reduction in CHD events was 16% (plus or minus 4%) (Fig. 9.4).

Thus the prevention of strokes was shown to be exactly on target and the prevention of coronary heart disease to be not significantly less than what would be expected. In general, the coronary prevention was less impressive in the younger patients and it was this finding that had lead some earlier commentators to take the erroneous view that antihypertensive treatment was ineffective in coronary prevention. There has been some speculation that the unimpressive effects on coronary prevention in the MRC trial of 35–64-year-olds was due to the high dose of bendrofluazide used, with its adverse effects on plasma lipid levels. Later trials used lower doses of thiazides which are equally effective at reducing blood pressure but have less effects on lipids. Another factor is that, over the age of about 65, epidemiological studies have demonstrated that plasma lipid levels may be less predictive of heart disease, so that the small rise in plasma cholesterol in older patients may be less important.

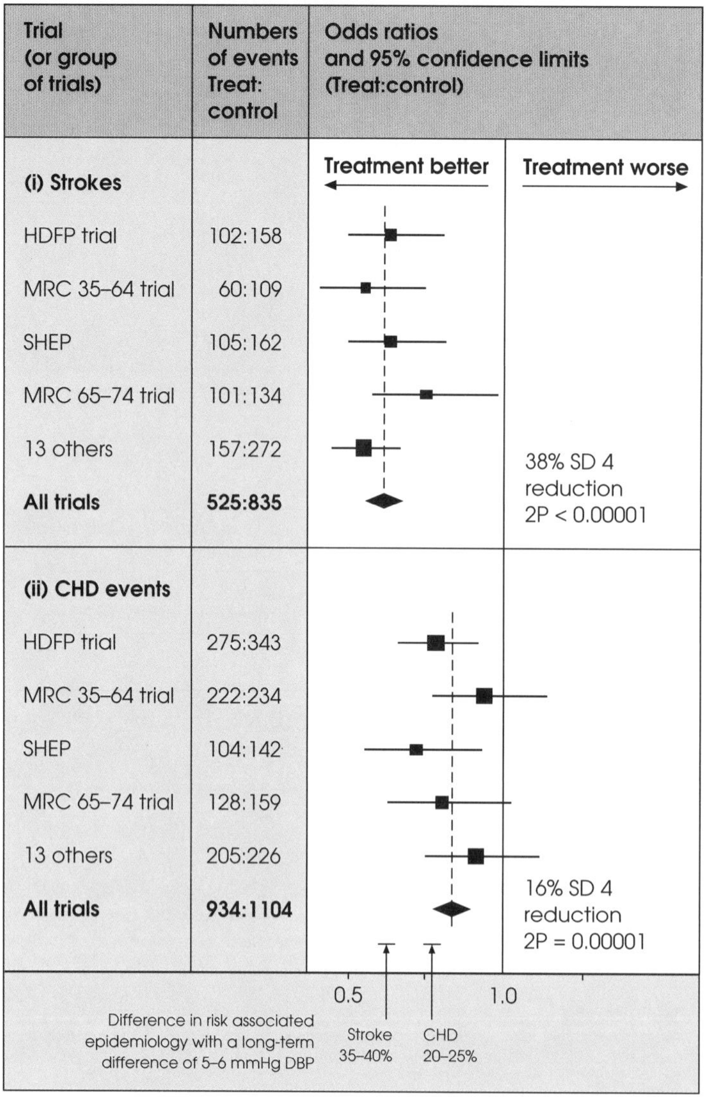

Trial (or group of trials)	Numbers of events Treat: control	Odds ratios and 95% confidence limits (Treat:control)
(i) Strokes		Treatment better / Treatment worse
HDFP trial	102:158	
MRC 35–64 trial	60:109	
SHEP	105:162	
MRC 65–74 trial	101:134	
13 others	157:272	
All trials	**525:835**	38% SD 4 reduction 2P < 0.00001
(ii) CHD events		
HDFP trial	275:343	
MRC 35–64 trial	222:234	
SHEP	104:142	
MRC 65–74 trial	128:159	
13 others	205:226	
All trials	**934:1104**	16% SD 4 reduction 2P = 0.00001
Difference in risk associated epidemiology with a long-term difference of 5–6 mmHg DBP		0.5 1.0 Stroke CHD 35–40% 20–25%

Figure 9.4
Meta–analysis of pooled results from the randomized trials of blood pressure reduction.

This overview meta-analysis also demonstrated that there was no significant difference in the coronary heart disease rates in those studies employing beta-blocker as first line therapy compared with those using thiazide diuretics.

Antihypertensive therapy and death

The Oxford meta-analysis has the statistical power to demonstrate that antihypertensive treatment is capable of preventing both fatal and non-fatal strokes and heart attacks, with

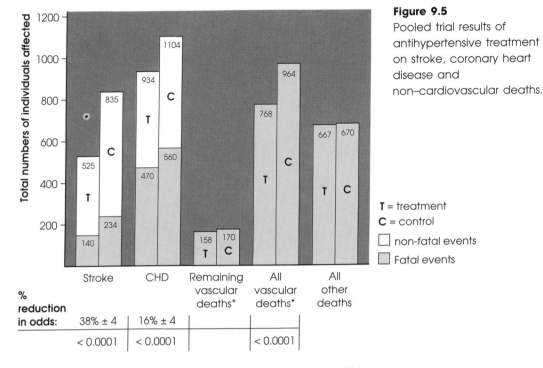

Figure 9.5
Pooled trial results of antihypertensive treatment on stroke, coronary heart disease and non–cardiovascular deaths.

T = treatment
C = control
☐ non-fatal events
▨ Fatal events

% reduction in odds:	Stroke	CHD	Remaining vascular deaths*	All vascular deaths*	All other deaths
	38% ± 4	16% ± 4			
	< 0.0001	< 0.0001		< 0.0001	

All available evidednce from randomised antihypertensive drug trials (mean DBP difference 5 – 6 mmHg for 5 years)

* Includes any deaths from unknown causes

a statistically significant reduction of deaths from all vascular diseases, and no adverse impact on deaths from all other causes. Antihypertensive treatment saves lives and has no adverse effects on cancer or other illnesses (Fig. 9.5).

The clinician can now be confident that his treatment is worthwhile in preventing strokes as well as heart attacks and prevents premature deaths, with no adverse effects on other diseases.

TRIALS STILL IN PROGRESS

There is still a need for more information on selected patient groups as well as clarification of the best choice of antihypertensive drugs and the optimum target pressures that should be achieved with drug therapy. These last few trials are now underway and should provide answers to those questions by the late 1990s.

Syst-Eur and Syst-China

These two trials, like the SHEP study, are investigating the value of the drug treatment of isolated systolic hypertension. The Syst-Eur trial is addressing subsidiary issues, including the effects of drug treatment on mental performance, and the value of 24-hour ambulatory blood pressure measurement in isolated systolic hypertension.

Hypertension Optimal Treatment (HOT) study

This trial is investigating the possibility of there being a J curve in relation to the complications of hypertension (particularly coronary heart disease) and the achieved diastolic blood pressure. Several open studies have suggested that if diastolic pressures are reduced to below 80 mmHg, the risk of heart attacks rises (Fig. 9.6). It is important to note however that there appears to have been no J curve effect with the SHEP study even though average diastolic pressures were reduced to 68 mmHg.

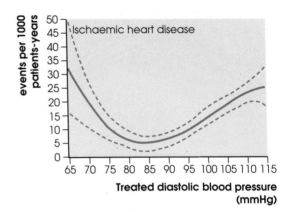

Figure 9.6
Combined results of several studies of blood pressure reduction which reported a J–curve.

Swedish Trial of Old People with Hypertension (STOP-H2)

This trial has been established to compare the efficacy of the newer and the older hypertensive drugs in the prevention of the vascular complications of hypertension. To date, only the beta-blockers and the thiazide diuretics have been shown to prevent strokes and, to a lesser extent, heart attacks. The newer agents (the ACE inhibitors, the angiotensin receptor antagonists the calcium channel blockers and the long-acting alpha-blockers) are equally effective in lowering blood pressure, and tend to have fewer side-effects, but they have not as yet been demonstrated to be able to prevent cardio-vascular events in mild to moderate hypertension. The ACE inhibitor and verapamil have, however, been shown to prevent reinfarction in heart-attack patients, and the ACE inhibitors also reduce proteinuria and preserve renal function in diabetic and non-diabetic hypertensives. The STOP-H2 and other studies should establish whether these beneficial effects of the newer agents are also seen in more routine cases of uncomplicated hypertension.

Hypertension in the Very Elderly Trial (HYVET)

This trial will investigate the possible value of treating hypertension in patients aged over 80 years. Epidemiological studies of the very old suggest that the height of the blood pressure becomes a very poor predictor of strokes or heart disease over the age of around 80 years. However, the value of reducing high blood pressures over this age does need to be investigated.

WHO BENEFITS FROM ANTIHYPERTENSIVE THERAPY?

With all the new information available since 1990, several expert committees have now published guidelines on the management of hypertension (British Hypertension Society, Canadian Hypertension Society, Joint National Committee on Detection, Evaluation and Treatment of High Blood Pressure (USA), New Zealand Guidelines and WHO/International Society of Hypertension). The findings of these committees demonstrate near unanimity and are summarized briefly below.

Diastolic blood pressure

If the diastolic blood pressure persistently exceeds 95 mmHg, then, up until the age of 80 years, antihypertensive medication should be prescribed.

Systolic blood pressure

If the systolic blood pressure persistently exceeds 160 mmHg in patients aged 60–80 years, then antihypertensive drugs should be prescribed, no matter what the diastolic pressure is.

The value of treating isolated systolic hypertension below the age of 60 years is uncertain, but the committees felt that it would be prudent to prescribe drug therapy.

Complicated hypertension

The topic of hypertension in the presence of pre-existing vascular complications is covered in Chapter 14. In general, the committees felt that in these high risk patients the threshold for instituting antihypertensive medication should be reduced to 90 mmHg.

HOW REPRESENTATIVE ARE PATIENTS IN LONG-TERM CLINICAL TRIALS?

There is a tendency amongst some clinicians to extrapolate directly from the results of the trials discussed here and to draw attention to the fact that a great many patients (often thousands) have to receive antihypertensive drugs in order to prevent one heart attack or one stroke. We believe that this can be a very misleading statistic as it only takes into account the absolute benefits of treatment in the participants of these particular trials. Patients who agree to co-operate in these long-term studies are not, in fact, at all representative of hypertensive patients in general. They tend to be rather well-to-do and have low overall cardiovascular risk (with a low prevalence of cigarette smoking). Afro-Caribbean patients tend to be under-represented. Most participants have no evidence of end-organ damage, and few have left ventricular hypertrophy (a powerful risk factor).

As the absolute number of cardiovascular events is often low, many thousands of participants are required if significant results are to be obtained and the trials take many years. It is not, therefore, correct to extrapolate directly from these trial results to patients in more normal clinical practice, where LVH, proteinuria and other risk factors are likely to be more common. In this respect, the results of the much criticized HDFP study more readily reflect clinical practice as there were many high risk patients and African Americans were included. It is better, therefore, to concentrate on the relative benefits of treatment in the trials (i.e. a 38% reduction of strokes and a 16% reduction in heart attacks) rather than the absolute benefits in the low risk trial participants. These relative benefits appear to be roughly similar at all grades of blood pressure elevation, including very high risk, severe hypertensive patients.

CONCLUSIONS

Antihypertensive therapy is successful in preventing both heart attacks and strokes. It is possible that the newer drug groups may be even more effective than the beta-blockers and the thiazides. Further studies are becoming necessary but they are difficult to achieve and take a long time to produce results. What is clear, however, is that the outcome for a hypertensive patient is closely related to the accuracy of blood pressure control with therapy, rather than the height of the blood pressure at first presentation. Severe hypertensives with good blood pressure control do well, whereas milder cases with poor control do badly. The prime concern for clinicians and public health staff is to ensure that this well validated treatment is effectively provided for all who need it.

FURTHER READING

Alderman MH, Cushman WC, Hill MN, Krakof LR. International round table discussion of national guidelines for the detection, evaluation and treatment of hypertension *Am J Hypertens* 1993; **6**:974–81.

Collins R, MacMahon S. Blood pressure, antihypertensive blood treatment and the risks of stroke and of coronary heart disease. *Br Med Bull* 1994; **50**:272–98.

Collins R, Peto R, MacMahon S et al. Blood pressure, stroke and coronary heart disease. Part 2 – short term reductions in blood pressure: overview of randomised drug trials in their epidemiological context. *Lancet* 1990; **335**:827–38.

Farnett L, Mulrow CD, Linn WD, et al. The J-curve phenomenon and the treatment of hypertension: is there a point beyond which blood pressure reduction is dangerous? *JAMA* 1991; **265**:489–95.

National High Blood Pressure Education Programme. The 1992 report of the joint national committee on detection, evaluation and treatment of high blood pressure. *Arch Intern Med* 1993; **153**: 154–83.

Sever P, Beevers DG, Bulpitt C et al. Management guidelines in essential hypertension: report of the Second Working Party of the British Hypertension Society. *Br Med J* 1993; **306**: 983–7.

10 NON-DRUG CONTROL OF BLOOD PRESSURE

BACKGROUND

Studies in the general population in Western countries have shown that approximately 20% of adults have a raised blood pressure, with either a diastolic pressure greater than 90 mmHg or a systolic pressure greater than 160 mmHg on first measurement (see Chapter 1). In this group there is an increased risk of cardiovascular disease which is related to the level of blood pressure. Also at risk are those in the upper half of the normal distribution, i.e. around 50% of the population.

While many of those who are found on screening surveys to have blood pressure above the so-called upper limits of normal are found on subsequent measurement to come within the normal range. The prospect of so many people taking blood pressure-lowering drugs must be viewed with alarm. Clearly, every effort needs to be focussed on whether we can prevent high blood pressure developing and lower blood pressure when it is in the upper range or above the the upper range of normal by lifestyle alterations rather than by the use of drugs.

Increasing evidence does suggest that various changes, particularly in the diet, may lower blood pressure and, furthermore, that these changes in lifestyle are often additive to drug therapy should this be necessary.

These changes in lifestyle should also be designed to reduce other cardiovascular risk factors for premature vascular disease.

EFFECT OF OBSERVATION

Repeated measurement of blood pressure during follow-up causes a fall in blood pressure. This was best seen in the MRC trial of mild hypertension where a group of patients were treated either with propranolol, bendrofluazide or a placebo and another group were observed without any treatment but had the same measurements of blood pressure. All patients were seen at regular intervals during the trial and there was a fall in blood pressure in all four groups. In the group receiving either the beta-blocker or diuretic it was only just significantly greater than in the other two. But perhaps most interestingly, placebo tablets had no further additional effect in lowering blood pressure compared with the follow-up alone with similar measurements of blood pressure. This fall in blood pressure seemed to reach a maximum at 3 months and there was no further fall with observation alone after this. This study allows us to draw three important conclusions:

1. Patients with mild hypertension who have their blood pressure measured regularly will as a group have a fall in blood pressure, and it is important, therefore, not to rush into any treatment, whether non-drug or drug therapy, in this group of patients.
2. If non-pharmacological therapy is started within the 3-month period the blood pressure fall may falsely be ascribed to the intervention when in fact it may be due to the measurement of blood pressure alone.
3. These findings clearly indicate that it is essential in any blood pressure-lowering clinical trial, with non-drug or drug therapy, to have proper controls to allow for the effect of the observation alone.

This chapter will consider the evidence that lifestyle alterations do lower blood pressure and the increasing evidence that these changes in lifestyle may be additive so that it is better when treating patients to give them a package of non-pharmacological advice. This will vary with the ability and enthusiasm of the patient to carry them out.

DIETARY ALTERATION

Increasing evidence suggests that the very high prevalence of cardiovascular disease in some Western countries compared to others is largely related to differences in diet, particularly sodium, potassium and saturated fat intake and a relative lack of fruit and vegetables. There is now accumulating evidence that alteration of sodium and potassium intake, even in those who already have raised blood pressure, may cause quite substantial falls in blood pressure.

Alteration of salt intake

Historical perspective

Salt plays a vital role in regulating the amount of extracellular fluid. During evolution, as animals moved away from the sea, salt was in short supply, particularly for those animals that were vegetarian and they relied entirely on the very small amounts of salt present in plants. Animals adapted by developing very powerful mechanisms to conserve salt or sodium within the body. Humans need a salt intake estimated to be between 1 and 5 mmol/day.

About four thousand years ago, the Chinese discovered that salt had the property of preserving food. The ability to preserve food, particularly during the winter, was essential to the development of the economies of these developing settlements. Salt became a very valuable commodity in view of its magical ability to preserve food. Salt became the main source of trade throughout the world. However, Huang Ti (The Yellow Emperor) observed that if too much salt is eaten, the pulse hardens (2000 BC). Most of the wealth of Venice was founded on the salt trade. Once food is consumed that has been preserved in salt, the taste receptors get accustomed to the high salt concentration and natural foods taste bland. When salt became readily available it was added to fresh food to bring it up to the same or near to the same concentration as in the preserved food.

With the invention of the deepfreeze and the refrigerator, food can be preserved without the addition of salt. Nevertheless we continue to add large amounts of salt unnecessarily to our food. Salt intake in most Western countries is, on average, between 150 and 250 mmol/day (equivalent to 8–14 grams of salt per day). There is now very strong evidence in animals, and accumulating evidence in man, that this unnecessarily high salt intake is an important precipitating or underlying cause for the development of high blood pressure. Growing evidence now suggests that we should all reduce our salt intake in order to reduce the number of people developing high blood pressure and to lower the whole population's blood pressure. Indeed, in most countries expert committees have advised that this should be done and, in the UK for instance, the Expert Committee on Dietary Reference Values has recommended a reduction in salt intake from the current average of around 160 mmol/day to around 70–80 mmol/day.

Two French nephrologists, Ambard and Beaujard, in the early 1900s were the first to show that severe restriction of salt intake did lower blood pressure in patients with renal failure and hypertension. This early work was largely ignored until Kempner in the mid-1940s found that a rice and fruit diet that was low in protein and sodium and rich in potassium was effective in patients with very severe hypertension. This diet was widely used at the time; it consisted of plain boiled rice and fruit and, it was incredibly monotonous. Patients found it difficult to tolerate. When the thiazide diuretics were introduced in the 1950s this severe form of salt restriction was abandoned and it was not until the early 1970s that more moderate forms of sodium restriction were first suggested to lower blood pressure. Studies from all over the world have now demonstrated that quite moderate restriction of salt intake from 10 to 5 grams per day does cause a fall in blood pressure which is equivalent to the effect of a single drug alone, e.g. a beta-blocker or diuretic. Studies have also shown that the greater the degree of salt restriction, the greater the fall in blood pressure (Fig. 10.1), and that patients with more severe hypertension (Fig. 10.2), older patients and black patients respond better to salt restriction. The reason for this is that these patients have a less responsive renin–angiotensin system to salt restriction and have less rise in renin release and less rise in circulating angiotensin II. This inhibition of the normal compensatory response allows a larger fall in blood pressure. This also explains why the addition of drugs that block the renin system, e.g. angiotensin converting enzyme (ACE) inhibitors, are particularly effective when combined with salt restriction.

Our recommendation therefore is that all patients with high blood pressure should reduce their salt intake. Some patients will find it much more easy to change their dietary habits, particularly those who eat at home and are able to avoid processed or convenience foods, which often have large amounts of added salt. One advantage of salt restriction is that after the initial 3–4 weeks when food tastes bland, particularly if large amounts of salt had been used, the taste receptors in the mouth become more sensitive to lower concentrations of salty food and patients find the same salt taste for much lower concentrations. When they try the very high salt foods that they used to enjoy, these taste unpleasant.

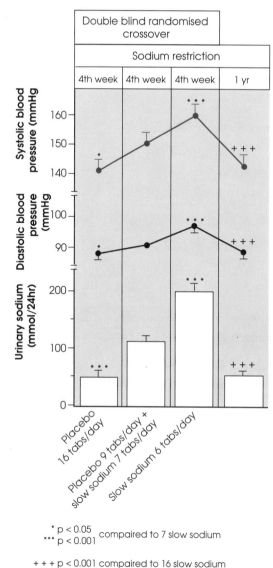

When giving advice about reduction of salt intake, it is important to assess the salt intake of the patient.

Assessment of salt intake

A dietary history is extremely inaccurate in reflecting salt intake. This is, in part, because it is extremely difficult to judge how much salt is in food and how much of that added is actually eaten, and the amount added in cooking is difficult to quantify. By far the best way of judging salt intake is to measure the 24-hour urinary sodium, as more than 90% of sodium intake is excreted in the urine. However, sodium consumption varies widely from day to day depending on the sort of food consumed, and urinary sodium excretion will follow these changes with an approximate 24-hour delay. One collection or, ideally, two consecutive 24-hour urine samples will give a reasonable estimation of whether a patient has a high sodium intake, i.e. more than 200 mmol of sodium per day (equivalent to around 11 grams of salt/day), an average sodium intake around 150 mmol a day (approximately 9 grams of salt/day) or a reduced sodium intake of less than 80 mmol a day (approximately 5 grams of salt/day). Contrary to the usual claims of difficulty in measuring 24-hour urine, this is relatively simple if the patient is properly instructed. Many patients are surprised by the amount of salt they consume when confronted with their 24-hour urinary sodium results. This is often because salt is hidden in food and very high amounts are present in many processed foods, particularly processed meat products, soup and ready-prepared meals. Indeed, in people who live exclusively on processed food, 80–90% of the sodium intake may be in the food rather than added in the cooking or at the table.

Figure 10.1

Effect of three salt intakes (10, 5 and 3 grams) on blood pressure showing a clear dose response and one-year follow-up where blood pressure remains controlled on the intake of 3 grams.

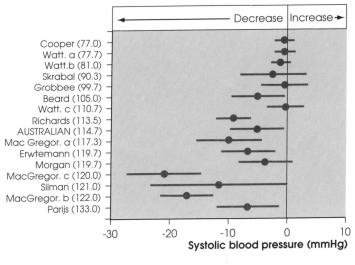

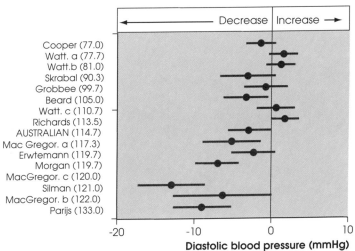

Figure 10.2
Effects of sodium restriction in different studies in order of severity of initial blood pressure.

How to reduce sodium intake

Any dietary change must be presented in an enthusiastic way and must fit in with the patient's lifestyle as well as the person who does the cooking in the household. In our view changes in diet should be presented as a package, that is a reduction in salt intake, an increase in potassium intake and a reduction in saturated fat and a lowering of cholesterol intake if high; specifically in relation to salt, patients and, more importantly, whoever cooks in the household should be instructed:

1. Not to add salt to the food at the table.
2. Not to add salt in the preparation of food and in the cooking.
3. To avoid processed foods that have a high sodium content. This particularly applies to processed meat products, dried soups, ready prepared meals, take-away food and many restaurant meals.

These simple steps can halve salt intake in most patients, that is to around 80 mmol or 5 grams a day. To reduce it further in most Western countries means finding a source of salt-free bread, as every slice of bread contains approximately 0.5 gram of salt. Where salt-free bread is available, it is then possible to reduce salt intake to around 50 mmol or 3 grams of salt a day.

Most countries are now introducing legislation which requires the salt content to be printed on the packaging of processed foods. However, many patients are confused by this labelling and may think that some foods which contain trivial amounts of sodium may be high in salt. Advice from the practice nurse or a dietitian can be very helpful.

The so-called 'salt controversy'

Until a few years ago there was controversy about the role of salt restriction in the treatment of high blood pressure, particularly because of the poor quality of the trials that had been done. However, there is now no dispute that moderate salt restriction is an effective way of lowering high blood pressure although the pro-salt lobby, financed by the food industry in the USA, UK and Europe, have continued to spend large amounts of money trying to confuse the issue. This is similar to the well-worn argument that was seen with cigarette smoking in the 1960s where it was claimed that the evidence was not absolutely clear cut and that more studies were needed before any action should be taken. This attitude is unhelpful, particularly to patients. More co-operation between the food industry and the medical profession could resolve this problem as it is quite unnecessary to add so much salt to processed food.

Increasing dietary potassium

Much evidence suggests that potassium has the opposite effect on blood pressure to sodium and that a high potassium intake may slow down or prevent the development of high blood pressure both in animals and in man. Indeed, it is often difficult to separate the two as, in general, high salt intakes are associated with low potassium intake and a low salt intake is often associated with a high potassium intake in fruit and vegetables. However, studies have shown that increasing potassium intake alone does have a blood pressure-lowering effect (Fig. 10.3). These studies were mainly done using potassium chloride, usually in the form of slow potassium (Slow K), as this made the studies more controlled and slow potassium placebos could be used in double-blind studies. A meta-analysis of all these studies clearly demonstrated that increasing potassium chloride intake does cause a fall in blood pressure approximately similar to that found with a beta-blocker or diuretic alone (Fig. 10.4). An important study from Italy has demonstrated that dietary alteration of potassium, predominantly by eating more fruit and vegetables, has a similar effect on blood pressure. This is important as some authorities have misinterpreted the trials of Slow K Tablets and claimed that potassium chloride tablets had been advocated in the non-pharmacological treatment of blood pressure. Potassium chloride tablets have no place in the non-pharmacological control of hypertension.

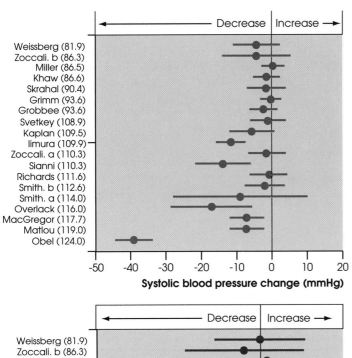

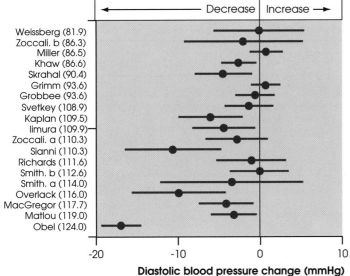

Figure 10.3
Effects of potassium restriction in different studies in order of severity of initial blood pressure.

Interestingly, evidence in some animals prone to high blood pressure and strokes shows that increasing potassium intake or decreasing salt intake prevents strokes independent of blood pressure. Some preliminary studies in man also suggest that a high potassium intake may protect from stroke, and a high salt diet may increase the

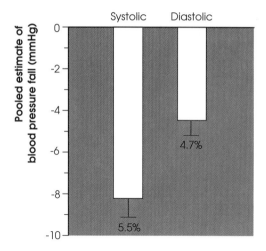

Figure 10.4
Pooled estimates of the treatment effect (and 95% CI) of potassium supplementation on blood pressure in untreated patients.

help with compliance with salt restriction, particularly for those who feel they must add some mineral to their food, and at the same time to increase potassium intake. The major problem with the pure potassium salt substitutes is that they taste unpleasant.

In view of this there are now several combinations of sodium and potassium chloride so-called 'salt alternatives' on the market. In general, these contain a smaller amount of salt (30–40%) and approximately 60–70% potassium chloride. In patients who feel that they must add some mineral to their food and are unable to stop the addition of salt to their food, they may be useful. It is important to tell patients that other forms of salt (e.g. sea salt and garlic salt) are almost identical to pure salt and should not be consumed.

likelihood of stroke independent of its effects on blood pressure.

How to increase potassium intake

Increasing potassium intake fits in with the 'healthy diet'. Potassium is mainly present in fresh fruit and lightly cooked vegetables. It is also present, in high concentrations, in most fish, so that increasing potassium intake fits in with reducing salt intake and reducing fat intake.

Salt substitutes

Salt substitutes containing potassium rather than sodium chloride have been used to

Calcium

There remains considerable controversy about the role of calcium intake as a precipitating factor for high blood pressure but in spite of much publicity, some years ago, that increasing calcium intake might possibly lower blood pressure, there is now overwhelming evidence that increasing calcium intake in the diet has no blood pressure-lowering effect.

Magnesium

Magnesium, like potassium, is an important regulator of the excitability of cell membranes and is present in many foods. Magnesium sulphate used to be given intravenously in pre-eclamptic toxaemia and, whilst it relieved the fits, there was no very good evidence that it lowered blood pressure. In carefully controlled double-blind studies in patients with essential hypertension, disappointingly, magnesium supplements had no effect on blood pressure when compared with placebo and therefore no specific recommendations for magnesium can be given to patients with high blood pressure at the present time.

Saturated fat and polyunsaturated fat

One study from Scandinavia reported that substituting saturated fat with polyunsaturated fat lowered blood pressure but more recent trials have not really substantiated this effect. Fish oil supplements have also been claimed to lower blood pressure but further studies have not been so clear cut. There is very strong evidence that high blood cholesterol levels and high low density lipoprotein (LDL) levels are important independent risk factors for arterial disease. Whilst cholesterol levels are in part due to the inherited differences in metabolism, they are also closely correlated with dietary saturated fat intake.

An increase in plasma cholesterol greatly increases the risk of cardiovascular disease for a given level of blood pressure. A meta-analysis of the published trials of cholesterol lowering strongly suggests that lowering saturated fat intake and thereby reducing cholesterol does reduce the risk of cardiovascular disease. All hypertensive patients should therefore have serum cholesterol levels measured and, whatever the level, they should be instructed to reduce their saturated fat intake. The degree of reduction of fat intake will obviously depend on the level of cholesterol and the ability of the patient to stick to the diet. Patients should be instructed to

reduce or stop consumption of all dairy products apart from fully skimmed milk, to avoid red meat and red meat products and to consume more fresh fruit and vegetables, fish, particularly oily fish, and chicken. Where oil is essential, it is better to substitute a monosaturated fat such as olive oil or rape seed oil, but if this is not available the second best is a polyunsaturated fat such as sunflower, corn oil etc (Table 10.1).

Dietary fibre

Dietary fibre consists of complicated carbohydrate substances that are not absorbed but decrease intestinal transit times and are useful in the prevention of constipation. One study suggested that increasing dietary fibre content might lower blood pressure. However, from this study it was not clear whether this was a direct effect of the increase of fibre in the diet or due to concomitant alterations in sodium intake or absorption. Increasing fibre content in the diet may have other advantages. It has been claimed to be important in preventing various intestinal diseases, particularly cancer of the colon, and may also have a cholesterol-lowering effect. Increasing fibre in the diet with greater consumption of fruit and vegetables has this advantage. However, many cereal products, which claim to have the above advantages, also have a high salt content.

Obesity and weight reduction

Many patients with high blood pressure are overweight and there is no doubt from population studies that there is a close relationship between blood pressure levels and body mass index, even when allowance

Table 10.1
Simple dietary guide for patients with high blood pressure.

Reduced salt intake	do not add salt at table do not add salt to cooking avoid processed foods with high salt content (e.g. bacon, cheese, dried soups, etc – look at label)
Reduced saturated fat intake	reduce red meat and products (e.g. paté, sausages, etc.) reduce milk products (fully skimmed milk allowed) reduce baked products with fat (e.g. pastries, biscuits)
Eat more	fish chicken and turkey fresh fruit and vegetables
Use	olive oil rape seed oil

has been made for the tendency to overestimate blood pressure in obese people. Well controlled studies in patients with high blood pressure and obesity have shown that when they reduce their weight there is a fall in blood pressure; these studies suggest that a 5 kg (11 lb) reduction in weight is associated with a 5 mmHg reduction in systolic pressure (Fig. 10.5). Some studies have reported that if the weight reduction is not associated with a reduction in salt intake the fall in blood pressure is much less.

Therefore, all patients who are overweight and have high blood pressure should be encouraged to lose weight. In many patients with mild hypertension, weight reduction combined with salt restriction may bring blood pressure to a level where drug treatment is no longer indicated.

Alcohol

Epidemiological evidence now strongly suggests that a high alcohol intake is associated with elevation of blood pressure and a fourfold increase in the risk of stroke. There is, however, some evidence that a moderate intake of alcohol, particularly in the form of red wine, may exert a modest protective effect against coronary heart disease.

The mechanisms of the alcohol–blood pressure link are uncertain and are almost certainly multifactorial. Acute alcohol consumption causes a rapid rise in blood pressure, presumably by a direct vasoconstrictor effect on some, but not all, vascular beds. Alcohol and its metabolites are sodium transport inhibitors and this may provide some explanation of why vasoconstriction occurs.

Very heavy alcohol intakes can cause severe hypertension by at least two mechanisms. Firstly, some alcoholic patients develop the alcoholic pseudo-Cushing's syndrome and the blood pressure may be related to mineralocorticoid or glucocorticoid excess.

Secondly, in heavy drinkers, the rise in blood pressure may be related to the stress of alcohol withdrawal rather than the effects

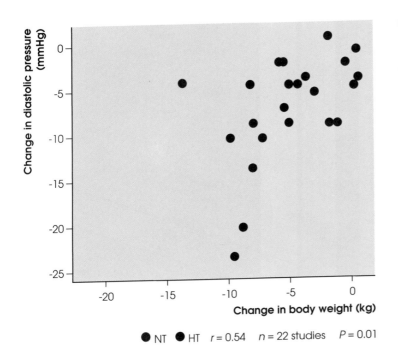

Figure 10.5

Fall in blood pressure related to reduction in weight. An overview of 22 studies.

● NT ● HT $r = 0.54$ $n = 22$ studies $P = 0.01$

of alcohol itself. In such patients, very high levels of plasma adrenaline and noradrenaline are found and a phaeochromocytoma-like crisis has been reported. Heavy drinkers, examined by the clinician the day after an evening with a high alcohol intake, may be in a state of subclinical alcohol withdrawal with resultant elevation of blood pressure. This state may not be immediately obvious to the clinician, who may mistakenly diagnose severe and pharmacologically resistant hypertension.

It is prudent to advise all people to avoid consuming more than the recommended maximum from the Expert Committees on Alcohol and Disease. The maximum weekly intake is 21 units (equivalent to 10.5 pints of beer or 4 bottles of wine) in men and 14 units in women (Table 10.2). It is also emphasized that binge drinking (which also causes strokes) should be avoided and there should be one alcohol-free day in each week.

Many hypertensive patients consume more than the amounts suggested above, and with counselling are happy to moderate their intake whilst not going without the pleasures of social drinking. As described in Chapter 7, there are clinical and laboratory features which suggest that alcohol intake is too high. These are a plethoric appearance with central obesity, hyperuricaemia not due to diuretics or renal disease, a raised mean corpuscular volume (MCV) and elevated levels of serum gamma glutamyl transferase. Otherwise, unexplained atrial fibrillation and

Table 10.2

Maximum recommended alcohol intake.

	Men	Women
Units/Week*	21	14
Beer (pints)	10½	7
Wine (glass)	21	14
Spirits (measures)	21	14
Sherry, etc (glass)	21	14

*1 unit of alcohol is equivalent to approximately 10 g.

inappropriate cardiomegaly suggest the diagnosis of alcoholic cardiomyopathy.

There are now many excellent randomized controlled trials which show that moderation of alcohol intake has a blood pressure-lowering effect which is independent of any effect on caloric intake, or sodium and potassium (Fig. 10.6). This reduction can be achieved with sympathetic non-confrontational counselling, particularly by appropriately trained nurses in a primary health care setting.

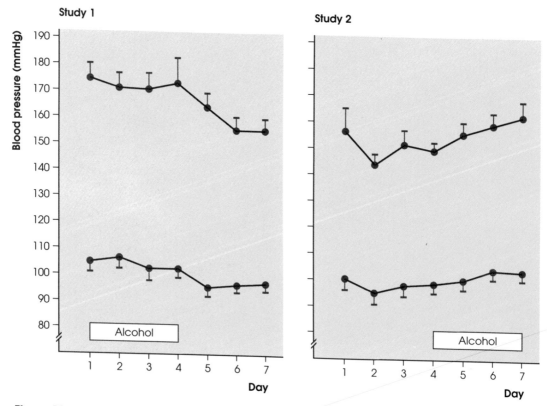

Figure 10.6

Change in blood pressure with cessation and restarting alcohol intake.

SMOKING

Smoking is an independent risk factor for the premature development of arterial disease. Overwhelming evidence has demonstrated that stopping smoking is of immense benefit for the prevention of further manifestations of cardiovascular disease, that is stroke, heart attack and peripheral vascular disease.

The mechanism whereby smoking may cause increased risk of arterial disease is still not clear and may in part be related to a direct effect of nicotine or more likely due to the high levels of carbon monoxide in the blood which make the development of vascular disease more likely. Smoking is, after high blood pressure, the most preventable cause of death in the Western world. It is estimated that in the UK alone over 200 000 persons per year die from smoking. Risks from smoking compound with the risks of high blood pressure and fat intake and cholesterol.

However, whilst smoking a cigarette causes an acute rise in blood pressure, epidemiological evidence suggests that it has no effect on blood pressure in the long term. Indeed, blood pressure may be slightly lower in smokers compared to non-smokers, although malignant hypertension and renal artery stenosis due to atheroma are strongly associated with cigarette smoking. All patients who smoke, whatever their blood pressure, should be told to stop. In view of the compounding risks of high blood pressure and smoking on premature vascular disease, it is particularly important that patients with high blood pressure stop smoking. A careful explanation of the synergism between high blood pressure and smoking may produce a greater determination in the patient to give up smoking. In middle-aged men, premature vascular disease which, in part, will be brought on by cigarette smoking may cause impotence, and this also may be a powerful motivating factor, at least for men or their partners, in increasing their resolve to stop smoking.

CAFFEINE

Drinking a cup of coffee does cause an acute rise in blood pressure. However, epidemiological evidence does not show any relationship between caffeine consumption and blood pressure. Cutting back on coffee intake does not seem to cause a fall in blood pressure.

COMBINED NUTRITIONAL ADVICE

Several studies from the USA have demonstrated that when patients had their drug therapy withdrawn and were advised to restrict salt and alcohol intake and reduce weight, many did not need to go back onto blood pressure tablets, compared with a control group where almost all of them had to go back onto drug treatment (Fig. 10.7). These studies, as well as the preceding individual studies in this chapter, strongly suggest that changes in diet in patients with high blood pressure should be presented as a package rather than on an individual nutrient level.

- All patients should therefore be instructed to cut the amount of salt in their food by not adding it to the cooking or at the table and avoiding foods that already have large amounts of salt added.
- All patients should cut back on their saturated fat intake and, if necessary, substitute monosaturated fats for saturated fats.

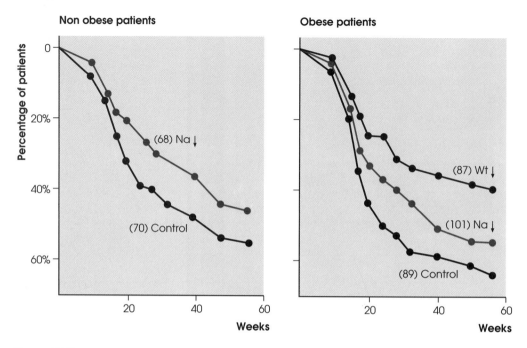

Figure 10.7
Proportion of patients needing to restart drug therapy with no dietary advice (controls), weight restriction advice and salt restriction advice.

- All patients should eat more fresh fruit and vegetables, fish, particularly oily fish, and chicken.
- Alcohol consumption should be moderate and not above the recommended levels.

OTHER WAYS OF LOWERING BLOOD PRESSURE

Relaxation

The most effective way of lowering blood pressure is to sleep. This fall in blood pressure during sleep is largely due to relaxation of voluntary muscles. The reflex can be clearly demonstrated by relaxation of all muscles followed by the measurement of blood pressure. The thumb is then opposed against the index finger in isometric contraction and this will cause a marked increase in diastolic pressure of approximately 10–20 mmHg.

All relaxation therapies, for example biofeedback, transcendental meditation, yoga, sleep therapy and psychotherapy, use this simple, but basic, physiological reflex. Only one well conducted randomized study did show a fall in blood pressure in both normotensive and hypertensive patients after relaxation therapy. However, more recent studies have demonstrated that this fall in blood pressure appears to be due to the ability of patients to learn to relax during the measurement of blood pressure, and whether the blood pressure is lower when they are going about their normal activities is not clear. It is sensible in all patients to review their lifestyle and ensure that they are not subjecting themselves to unnecessary stress but there is little point in forcing people to relax who do not want to.

Exercise

During dynamic exercise such as running, swimming or cycling, systolic pressure rises and diastolic pressure falls. In physically fit people the rises in systolic pressure and heart rate are less. During isometric exercise, there is contraction of muscles without movement, and very large rises in both systolic and diastolic pressure.

Several studies have now demonstrated that regular exercise does cause a fall in blood pressure (Fig. 10.8). There is some debate about the amount of exercise needed, with different studies showing falls in blood pressure with widely differing amounts of exercise. Currently, our view is that, where appropriate, regular exercise should be done three to four times a week and the exercise should be sufficient to cause sweating. Patients who become fit often feel better and this is sufficient reason in itself for encouraging patients to take plenty of exercise. However, sudden severe strenuous exercise may be harmful, particularly in patients who have marked coronary artery disease. Patients who are unfit should build up the exercise load slowly. Isometric exercise may be particularly harmful in patients with ischaemic heart disease.

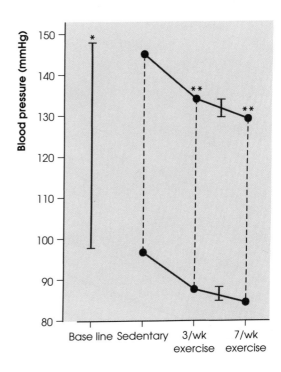

Figure 10.8
Effects on blood pressure of an exercise program, three or seven times a week.

Hospital admission

Putting patients into bed in hospital has a marked blood pressure-lowering effect, mainly due to the relaxation of voluntary muscles and also because there is a loss of sodium and water with decreased physical activity. There is no evidence that bedrest or admitting patients to hospital has any long-term effect on blood pressure. Increasingly, patients with severe or resistant hypertension who used to be admitted to hospital for investigation and treatment are now treated in daily outpatient clinics. Where patients are admitted to hospital, it must be remembered that control of blood pressure in the hospital does not necessarily mean that the blood pressure will be controlled when patients are leading their normal lives.

FURTHER REA DING

Cutler JA. Combinations of lifestyle modifications and drug treatment in management of mild-moderate hypertension: a review of randomized clinical trials. *Clin Exp Hypertens* 1993; **15**:1193–204.

MacGregor GA, Markandu ND, Sagnella GA, et al. Double-blind study of three sodium intakes and long-term effects of sodium restriction in essential hypertension. *Lancet* 1989; **ii**:1244–7.

Maheswaran R, Beevers DG. Effectiveness of advice to reduce alcohol consumption in hypertensive patients. *Hypertension* 1992; **19**:78–84.

MRC Working Party on Mild to Moderate Hypertension. Randomised controlled trial of treatment for mild hypertension: design and pilot trial. *Br Med J* 1977; **2**:1437–40.

Nelson L, Jennings GL, Esler MD, et al. Effects of changing levels of physical activity on blood-pressure and haemodynamics in essential hypertension. *Lancet* 1986; **2**:473–6.

Stamler R, Stamler J, Grimm R, et al. Nutritional therapy for high blood pressure. Final report of a four-year randomizing controlled trial - the hypertension control program. *J Am Med Assoc* 1987; **257**:1484–91.

11 A REVIEW OF ANTIHYPERTENSIVE DRUGS

BACKGROUND

Drugs that lower blood pressure were first introduced in the 1950s but were reserved for use in patients with very severe or accelerated hypertension. Prior to their introduction attempts to reduce blood pressure were made using either sedatives or tranquillizers like phenobarbitone together with a very low salt diet. The first drugs that were most commonly used were the ganglion-blocking drugs, e.g. hexamethonium, mecamylamine, pempidine and pentolinium. It soon became apparent that in those patients with very severe hypertension, lives were being saved. However, the side-effects of these drugs were so unpleasant that their use was only justified in the most severe cases.

Therefore, the subsequent introduction of the thiazide diuretics, methyldopa and adrenergic neurone blockers such as guanethidine, bethanidine and debrisoquine in the late 1950s and early 1960s meant that more tolerable blood pressure-lowering agents could be used in less severe hypertensives. Early clinical trials in 1964 and in 1970, where diuretics, reserpine and hydralazine were used, confirmed that these agents were saving the lives of patients with severe hypertension. However, all of these agents, apart from diuretics, have severe side-effects and are now regarded as obsolete except for methyldopa in pregnancy.

In the mid-1960s the beta-blocker propranolol was introduced for angina and shortly afterwards it was found to lower blood pressure. The beta-blockers or a diuretic then became the mainstay of treatment for blood pressure in the 1970s and were employed in most of the randomized trials looking at the benefits of treatment of mild to moderate hypertension. These trials (for further details see Chapter 9) clearly demonstrated a major reduction in stroke and a reduction in coronary heart disease. Nevertheless, the beta-blockers and diuretics have their own side-effects and in any case do not always control blood pressure. In view of this, the search for other drugs that are effective in lowering blood pressure has continued.

In the early 1980s two new classes of compounds, the calcium entry antagonists and the converting enzyme inhibitors, were introduced. These newer classes of compounds have not been the subject of randomized controlled clinical trials, but because of the absence of any biochemical side-effects of these drugs it is possible that they will be more effective than the thiazides at coronary prevention. Trials to prove this point are necessary and are currently ongoing. The alpha-blocking drugs indoramin and prazosin were introduced in the early 1970s but were never popular because of their side-effects. More recently, longer-acting alpha receptor antagonists, doxazosin and terazosin, have been introduced. Their modest lipid-lowering effects may be beneficial.

WHICH DRUG FOR WHICH PATIENT?

With the four main classes of drug that are now used to lower blood pressure, the doctor and, more importantly, the patient has a wide choice of treatment options. Ideally each patient should undergo some sort of assessment to decide which drug is the best tolerated and most effective in their particular case. After all, the patient is likely to receive this treatment for the rest of their life. Many of the drugs, while not having the serious side-effects of the older agents, may have more subtle effects which may reduce the quality of life on a long-term basis. In general, experience has shown that a combination of a low dose of two different drugs with an additive effect may well have fewer side-effects than the higher doses of one agent.

If one particular drug is not sufficiently effective, it is usually better to change to a different class of drug or to add a second agent in. These strategies, in our view, are preferable to increasing the dose of the first agent. Schemes for reducing blood pressure are discussed in the next chapter. This chapter discusses the many drugs that are available, their mechanisms and their side-effects.

DIURETICS

Diuretics have been the backbone of blood pressure-lowering therapy since they were introduced in the 1960s. At this time they largely replaced rigorous salt restriction. More recently, there has been considerable concern about their potential harmful metabolic effects and the possibility that they may also cause arrhythmias in some patients. In men, impotence has emerged as a major problem with higher doses of the thiazide diuretics. In spite of these concerns, all of the trial evidence suggests that diuretics do reduce strokes and also, particularly in the elderly, reduce coronary heart disease. Some evidence would suggest that in this regard they may be more effective than the beta-blockers.

Diuretics are additive to nearly all of the blood pressure-lowering drugs, particularly the beta-blockers and angiotensin converting enzyme (ACE) inhibitors. Before the advent of the calcium entry antagonists and the ACE inhibitors, arteriolar vasodilators like hydralazine and minoxidil were often added in to the beta-blocker. However, these drugs caused sodium retention, which offsets the blood pressure-lowering effect of the drugs. In this situation diuretics must be used.

Thiazide diuretics

All the thiazide diuretics have a fairly flat dose–response curve, so that increasing the dose has little further effect on blood pressure but markedly increases the metabolic consequences of the diuretic, e.g. lowering potassium, increased blood sugar and/or glucose intolerance, increased cholesterol and uric acid. Therefore it is best to use the minimum dose necessary as nothing is gained by giving larger doses.

There are only slight differences in the duration of action but major differences in the dosage (Table 11.1). All of them are given once daily as their effect on blood pressure lasts for several days. Related sulphonamide compounds such as chlorthalidone and metolazone are longer-acting and more powerful.

Mode of action

The thiazide diuretics act on the renal tubules to block sodium and chloride reabsorption. After a certain amount of sodium and water loss has occurred, compensatory mechanisms block the effect of the diuretic on the kidney so that, within a few days, no additional loss of sodium occurs and total body sodium is maintained at a slightly lower level. This causes a fall in the extracellular fluid volume and a small decrease in plasma and blood volume. With the loss of sodium and water, the kidney responds by increasing renin release, leading to the formation of the powerful vasoconstrictor angiotensin II. Therefore, the fall in blood pressure with a diuretic is largely determined by the fall in extracellular volume compensated by a reactive rise in plasma angiotensin II. This explains why diuretics are more effective in black patients and in older white patients, both of whom

Table 11.1
Dosage for diuretics.

	Normal daily dose for hypertension
Thiazides	
*Bendrofluazide	1.25–2.5 mg o.d.
Cyclopenthiazide	0.25 mg o.d.
*Hydrochlorothiazide	12.5 to 25 mg o.d.
Thiazide related compounds	
Chlorthalidone	12.5–25 mg o.d.
Indapamide	2.5 mg o.d.
Loop diuretics	
Bumetanide	1 mg b.d.
Frusemide	40 mg b.d.
Potassium sparing diuretics	
Amiloride	5 mg o.d.
Spironolactone	25–100 mg o.d.
Triamterene	50 mg o.d.

*Recommended for routine treatment

tend to have lower plasma renin levels to start with, and less rise in renin and angiotensin II with the diuretic.

Beta-blockers partially inhibit the renin release caused by diuretics, and the ACE inhibitors almost totally abolish the compensatory rise in plasma angiotensin II levels. For this reason beta-blockers and ACE inhibitors are very effective when used in combination with a diuretic.

Side-effects

Thiazide diuretics at low doses are reasonably well tolerated. They have rare severe reactions, occasionally causing skin rash, thrombocytopenia and leucopenia. However, the MRC Mild Hypertension Trial

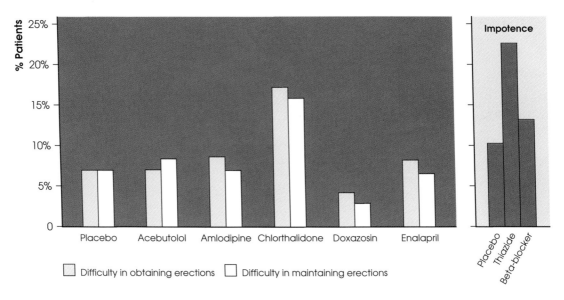

Figure 11.1
Thiazides and sexual function in men.

showed that larger doses of bendrofluazide caused impotence in a large proportion of men when compared with beta-blocker or placebo therapy (Fig. 11.1). It is important, therefore, that, when using a thiazide, men, at least, should be questioned about this as it is an important and under-recognized problem.

Metabolic problems of thiazide diuretics

Hypokalaemia

Almost all patients treated with thiazides sustain a small fall in plasma potassium. This fall varies with the dose of the thiazide given but averages anything from 0.3 to 1.0 mmol/l. Patients on a high salt intake will have a greater fall in plasma potassium with a diuretic, whereas in patients who are on a low salt intake the fall in potassium is much less. Whilst the dangers of hypokalaemia in patients with high blood pressure have not been clearly defined, much circumstantial evidence suggests that, potentially, it may be responsible for a greater number of arrhythmias and sudden deaths. For instance, in the MRC Mild Hypertension Trial there was a higher incidence of multifocal ventricular ectopic beats in the thiazide-treated patients compared with those receiving either a beta-blocker or a placebo. This effect may be increased by exercise. There is also evidence that patients who have suffered a heart attack have a worse prognosis if they have low plasma potassium.

The plasma potassium levels should be measured in all patients before starting diuretic therapy. If it is already low, further tests should be instituted, particularly to exclude primary or secondary aldosteronism. All patients who have started on diuretics should have a repeat plasma potassium check within a month or so of the start of treatment. In general, clinicians have neglected to watch plasma potassium levels, partly because hypokalaemia does not cause any obvious clinical effects.

How to avoid hypokalaemia on diuretics

Traditionally, potassium supplements were given. Nonetheless, these have their own side-effects, are not always effective and, in our view, are only rarely indicated. There are still some thiazide diuretics that are combined with potassium; however, as these contain trivial amounts of potassium they are of no benefit and should not be used. In fact, an effective way of ensuring that there is little fall in plasma potassium with a thiazide is to use a low dose, for instance 1.25 mg of bendrofluazide or 12.5 mg once a day of hydrochlorothiazide. In general these doses only cause very small falls in potassium and if they are combined with an ACE inhibitor or a beta-blocker, the fall may be entirely abolished. This is because these drugs on their own cause a slight rise in plasma potassium by virtue of their suppression of angiotensin II and aldosterone levels. Restricting salt intake will also reduce the fall in plasma potassium that occurs with the thiazide diuretics. It is also possible to combine the thiazide diuretics with a distally acting diuretic such as triamterene or amiloride (spironolactone should no longer be used for this purpose except in special situations). Whilst this may prevent the

hypokalaemia, our view is that in the majority of patients it is unnecessary as it brings in another drug which has its own side-effects and some of the fixed combination products contain too much thiazide diuretic.

If, in spite of these manoeuvres, plasma potassium does fall to low levels it is likely that the patient has some other cause and primary aldosteronism should be excluded.

Hyperuricaemia

All of the thiazide diuretics cause an increase in plasma uric acid levels and may occasionally precipitate gout. However, what is much more controversial is whether a symptomless rise in plasma uric acid level has any long-term consequences. Hyperuricaemia is common in hypertensive patients even without thiazides, but it is doubtful whether serum uric acid is an independent cardiovascular risk factor. Renal impairment and a high alcohol intake will also cause an increase in uric acid. Lower doses of a thiazide diuretic will have much less effect on uric acid.

Glucose intolerance

Many hypertensive patients have a degree of insulin resistance, and thiazide diuretics, when given long term, may cause a further deterioration in glucose tolerance. Some will develop elevated fasting blood glucose levels and, more rarely, frank diabetes may be precipitated. In patients who already have diabetes there may be a slight worsening of diabetic control but in patients who are on insulin this is not of great importance as the insulin dosage can be altered. However, patients who have maturity onset diabetes which is being controlled either by drugs or diet should not be given thiazide

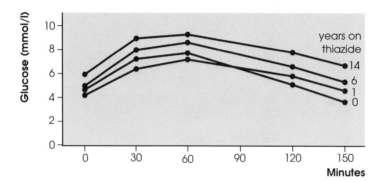

Figure 11.2
The long–term effect of thiazide diuretics on glucose tolerance.

diuretics unless absolutely necessary. Many of these patients who are followed in diabetic clinics can normalize their blood sugars by changing from a thiazide diuretic to another agent.

Blood lipids

A meta-analysis of all the studies of thiazides has clearly demonstrated that there is a small rise in plasma cholesterol and triglyceride levels with long-term treatment with thiazide diuretics. This is mainly due to a rise in LDL cholesterol and, in some studies, a fall in HDL cholesterol. Potentially this is likely to hasten the development of vascular disease and could partly offset the benefits of the reduction in blood pressure. However, the recent studies in the elderly have predominantly used a thiazide diuretic regime and have clearly demonstrated, not only a reduction in strokes, but also coronary heart disease.

Calcium

Thiazide diuretics can elevate plasma calcium levels to the range where a diagnosis of hyperparathyroidism should be consid-

ered. However, thiazide diuretics reduce urinary calcium excretion and cause a positive calcium balance. Several studies have now demonstrated that in the long term they cause an increase in bone mass, and in studies in both normotensives and hypertensives there have been reductions in the number of hip fractures in patients treated with thiazides compared to those given a placebo.

This aspect may be particularly important in postmenopausal women who have high blood pressure.

Other problems

In those patients who are sodium and water depleted, diuretics may cause further volume depletion. Patients with chronic renal disease may show a deterioration in renal function. Rarely, thiazides cause large falls in plasma sodium with frank hyponatraemia (e.g. serum sodium 110 to 125 mmol/l). Usually there is other intercurrent illness. Hyponatraemia may cause confusion, dehydration, vomiting and muscle weakness, particularly in the elderly.

A small rise in packed cell volume and haemoglobin level is common with diuretics.

Both are potential risk factors for strokes. Thiazides also increase platelet aggregation, which may cause an increased tendency to develop thrombotic disease. And, unless necessary, thiazides should not be used for hypertension in pregnancy as they may reduce placental blood flow (see Chapter 16).

Loop diuretics

The two most commonly used drugs in this class are frusemide and bumetanide. They act on the ascending limb of the loop of Henle and block sodium reabsorption. They are much faster acting diuretics than the thiazides, and have the disadvantage of a much shorter duration of action; they cause a loss of sodium and water within 2 to 3 hours of taking the diuretic but subsequently, during the rest of the day, there is sodium and water retention so that in patients with hypertension they cause little reduction in sodium balance. They are therefore not widely used in the treatment of hypertension. However, in patients with more resistant hypertension, when they are combined with other drugs and given twice a day, so that they have a sustained effect on sodium balance, they may be very effective, particularly in patients with renal impairment. In general, the loop diuretics have the same sort of problems as the thiazide diuretics but at lower doses they may possibly have fewer metabolic effects; however, this may relate more to their short length of action and therefore their ineffectiveness in hypertension.

Potassium-sparing diuretics

These drugs act on the distal renal tubule and reduce potassium excretion at the same time as increasing sodium and water loss. However, their effect on sodium and water loss is much less than that of the thiazides and diuretics. Currently there are three potassium-sparing diuretics available: spironolactone, triamterene and amiloride.

Spironolactone

Spironolactone is an aldosterone antagonist which may also have a direct effect on the distal renal tubule. Given alone, usually in large doses, it can control blood pressure in patients with primary aldosteronism prior to surgery or in cases where surgery is contraindicated or in patients with bilateral adrenal hyperplasia. It is as effective as a thiazide diuretic but has a slower onset of action. However, spironolactone has endocrine side-effects, including gynaecomastia, loss of libido in men and intermenstrual or premenopausal bleeding. It can also have gastrointestinal side-effects, particularly dyspepsia. In view of these side-effects, spironolactone is no longer recommended for the treatment of hypertension except for patients with primary aldosteronism, where it may be very useful, particularly in those with more resistant blood pressure.

Triamterene

This drug is less effective in lowering blood pressure than spironolactone but it does partially block the potassium-lowering effect of thiazide diuretics. It has therefore been combined with thiazide diuretics to prevent the fall in plasma potassium.

Amiloride

Although structurally different to triamterene, amiloride has a similar action on the distal tubule. It has been widely marketed in combination with a thiazide diuretic, but the most widely used form of it contains 50 mg of hydrochlorothiazide, and this is far too much diuretic for the treatment of hypertension. There is now a half-strength dose containing 25 mg of hydrochlorothiazide and 2.5 mg of amiloride. Even this is too high an amount of thiazide for many patients. If a lower dose of thiazide is given, e.g. 12.5 mg, it may well not be necessary to add in the amiloride. However, amiloride is relatively free of side-effects and is a reasonable alternative for the treatment of primary aldosteronism, where spironolactone cannot be used.

All of the distal-acting diuretics may cause dangerous hyperkalaemia in patients with renal failure and particular care must be used with these drugs in patients with renal disease and, in particular, where there has been or may be a rapid deterioration in renal function.

Indapamide

This diuretic has been claimed to be different from thiazides in that it may have additional blood pressure-lowering effects independent of the loss of sodium. This claim has often been made for the thiazide diuretics themselves but there is little evidence to support it. Indapamide appears to be very similar to a low dose of any other thiazide diuretic.

BETA-BLOCKERS

The beta-adrenergic receptor blockers were originally introduced in the early 1960s for the treatment of angina pectoris, and their blood pressure-lowering effects were not initially appreciated. During the 1970s and 1980s they were the mainstay of blood pressure-lowering treatment but, in view of their rather subtle side-effects, they have become less popular. They have been shown clearly to reduce the risk of reinfarction in patients who have already had a heart attack. However, whether they reduce coronary heart disease in patients with hypertension who have not had an infarct is not certain.

Mode of action

The beta-blockers compete with the endogenous catecholamines for adrenergic beta receptors. Beta receptors can be divided into two classes: β_1 and β_2 receptors. Blocking the β_1 receptors reduces the heart rate and the contractility of the heart, with a concomitant reduction in cardiac output. This may be part of the mechanisms of the blood pressure-lowering effect. Blockade of the β_2 receptors causes vasodilatation in voluntary muscle but may cause bronchoconstriction, particularly in asthmatic subjects. Beta-blockers also inhibit renin release, leading to falls in plasma angiotensin II levels which probably explains most of their blood pressure-lowering action. This also explains why beta-blockers are less effective in patients with low plasma renin levels such as blacks and older hypertensive patients.

Differences between beta-blockers

For all practical purposes all of the beta-blockers are as effective as each other in reducing blood pressure. However, some important other differences between them have emerged.

Cardioselectivity

Some beta-blockers are not cardioselective (for example, propranolol and oxprenolol) as they block both β_1 and β_2 receptors equally. The cardioselective beta-blockers such as acebutolol, atenolol and metoprolol have a greater effect on cardiac β_1 receptors. However, there does not appear to be any difference in the blood pressure-lowering effect between selective and nonselective beta-blockers.

Intrinsic sympathomimetic activity

Like many competitive inhibitors, some beta-blockers stimulate the beta receptors as well as block them, particularly when endogenous levels of catecholamines are low. This intrinsic sympathomimetic activity (ISA) or partial agonist activity is seen particularly with pindolol, oxprenolol and, to a lesser extent, acebutolol. These agents are therefore less prone to cause bradycardia, but may possibly be less effective in lowering blood pressure.

Lipophilicity

Some beta-blockers are more lipid-soluble than others. Lipid-soluble (lipophilic) drugs are more likely to enter the brain and cause central side-effects such as tiredness, sleep disturbance and vivid dreams. The less lipid-soluble, that is more hydrophilic, drugs such as atenolol, acebutolol, sotalol and nadolol should potentially cause less central side-effects. However, clear evidence for this has not been provided. Lipid-soluble drugs are mainly metabolized by the liver whereas the water-soluble ones are excreted by the kidney. This is important if there is either hepatic or renal impairment and may influence the choice of beta-blocker.

Duration of action

Most beta-blockers reduce blood pressure within 1–2 hours of a single oral dose and most of them can be given once a day. However, oxprenolol, propranolol and metoprolol are relatively shorter acting than other beta-blockers and are normally prescribed twice daily. By contrast atenolol, nadolol, sotalol and bisoprolol are longer acting. In many patients much lower doses of beta-blockers can be given, often with a reduction of the more subtle side-effects. However, at lower doses the drug may need to be given more often. For instance, atenolol 12.5 mg (half tablet) once a day probably does not work for 24 hours whereas the same dose twice a day may well do so (Table 11.2).

Table 11.2
Dosage for beta-adrenoceptor blockers.

Acebutolol	200 mg–800 mg
Atenolol	25–100 mg
Bisoprolol	5–10 mg
Metoprolol	50–400 mg
Non-selective beta-blockers	
Propranolol	80–360 mg
Sotalol	80–160 mg
Beta-blockers with partial agonist activity	
Celiprolol	200–400 mg
Oxprenolol	80–320 mg
Pindolol	5–15 mg

Table 11.3

Some side-effects of beta-blockers.

Sleep disturbance	Heart failure
Nightmares	Reduction of exercise tolerance
Lethargy	Raynaud's syndrome
Bronchospasm	Claudication
Bradycardia	Impotence

hands warm and wearing gloves may suffice. However, they also worsen symptoms of Raynaud's disease and intermittent claudication. In severe peripheral vascular disease, gangrene has been precipitated by the use of beta-blockers. It is possible that beta-blockers with partial agonist activity, for example pindolol, oxprenolol and celiprolol, may be less likely to do this but beta-blockers are best avoided and calcium entry antagonists or ACE inhibitors should be used instead.

Side-effects of beta-blockers (Table 11.3)

Heart failure

When beta-blockers were first introduced, there was some concern that they might precipitate heart failure, particularly in patients with angina, who may already have had damaged heart muscle. In patients with high blood pressure, where the left ventricle is performing well, beta-blockers are unlikely to precipitate heart failure. Nevertheless, patients with high blood pressure and heart failure should not be given beta-blockers except under very carefully supervised conditions (see Chapter 14). In view of the slowing of AV conduction that the beta-blockers can cause, they should not be given to patients with any form of heart block.

Reduction in peripheral blood flow

Because of the reduction in cardiac output and the reflex increase in peripheral resistance, all beta-blockers tend to reduce peripheral blood flow and cause cold hands and feet, particularly in colder climates. If symptoms are mild, advice about keeping

Bronchospasm

All beta-blockers may precipitate bronchospasm, especially if there is a preceding history of asthma. However, an upper respiratory tract infection may precipitate asthma *de novo* in patients on a beta-blocker. It is claimed that the more cardioselective beta-blockers, such as atenolol, metoprolol, acebutolol and celiprolol, are less likely to have this effect. However, in our view beta-blockers should not be given to anyone with asthma or who is likely to develop asthma. Other drugs which do not have this problem should be used.

Reduction in exercise tolerance

All beta-blockers cause a reduction in exercise tolerance and this can be a major problem for active young patients. Most patients feel tired when climbing stairs, particularly with a feeling of heaviness in the legs.

Central nervous problems

Beta-blockers may cause sleep disturbance, vivid dreams and nightmares. These possibly may be more common with the lipid-soluble beta-blockers such as propranolol and oxprenolol.

More subtle side-effects

Beta-blockers commonly cause a loss of drive and energy. These side-effects can be very subtle and are not always noticed by the patient but are usually fairly obvious to the spouse or people who live with the patient. In the past these more subtle effects of beta-blockers were ignored but they are now the most common reason for not using or discontinuing a beta-blocker.

Diabetes mellitus

Theoretically, beta-blockers can interfere with insulin secretion, but this a fairly minor effect. However, they can interfere in some patients with the symptoms and metabolic response to hypoglycaemia. This is particularly important in insulin-dependent diabetics, who may not show the usual symptoms when they have become hypoglycaemic. However, this problem has probably been exaggerated and, provided patients are aware of it, beta-blockers can be used in insulin-dependent diabetics.

CALCIUM CHANNEL BLOCKERS

These drugs were known to lower blood pressure many years ago, but it was only in the early 1980s that they really came into use as blood pressure-lowering agents. They are effective blood pressure-lowering agents, particularly as they become more effective with increasing blood pressure. Their exact

Table 11.4
Dosage for calcium channel blockers.

	Normal daily dose
Dihydropyridines	
Amlodipine	5–10 mg o.d.
Isradipine	1.25–5 mg b.d.
Lacidipine	2–6 mg o.d. or b.d.
Nicardipine	20–30 mg t.d.s.
Nifedipine tablets	10–20 mg b.d. or t.d.s.
Nifedipine LA	30–60 mg o.d.
Verapamil	80–160 mg b.d. or t.d.s.
	Slow release 120–240 mg b.d.
Diltiazem	
Diltiazem	60–240 mg daily
	Dosage and frequency will
	depend on formulation

mode of action in causing peripheral vasodilatation is not fully understood, but it is likely that they cause a reduction in calcium within arteriolar smooth muscle, causing arteriolar vasodilatation. The calcium channel blockers, particularly the dihydropyridines, have also been shown to be natriuretic, and chronically they have a mild 'diuretic' action which, at the very least, prevents tolerance to these drugs and may, in part, be responsible for the blood pressure fall. There are three major groups of calcium antagonists: (*a*) the dihydropyridines, the first of which was nifedipine – there are now a large number of similar drugs; (*b*) verapamil, which has a greater negative ionotropic and chronotropic effect on the heart. Although many derivatives of verapamil are being developed, none of them are currently widely used; (c) diltiazem appears to lie between the dihydropyridines and verapamil.

Dihydropyridines

These drugs are both peripheral and coronary vasodilators and can be used to treat angina as well as hypertension. However, unlike verapamil, they appear to have no effect on cardiac conduction. The dihydropyridines have different durations of action and speed of onset. When a dihydropyridine is rapidly absorbed, there is a rapid rise in plasma level and this causes the well-known vasodilating effects of the dihydropyridines: flushing, headache, which is often associated with dizziness as well. This was particularly so with the nifedipine capsules which are rapidly absorbed and should no longer be used. Naturally long-acting drugs, such as amlodipine, which have a longer half-life, cause less of these vasodilating effects because there is a slow rise in the plasma level with the initiation of treatment and a constant level after about 7 days of treatment. The duration of action is also important in that not only are the older dihydropyridines rapidly absorbed, but they are short-acting because of very fast metabolism in the liver. Therefore, they cause large peak/trough variations in the plasma levels of the drug and, thereby, large variations in blood pressure and increased vasodilating symptoms. In spite of this knowledge, many doctors seem unaware of this and persist with prescribing short-acting dihydropyridines which have very impressive but fairly transient effects on blood pressure every time a tablet is taken. Indeed, one of the most frequent hospital referrals for variable blood pressure from general practitioners has been, in our experience, the use of short-acting dihydropyridines.

Nifedipine

This was the first dihydropyridine to become available, initially in a capsule formulation. The capsule formulation has a rapid onset of action and a rapid offset and should no longer be used except in the very rare circumstance of an unconscious patient with hypertensive encephalopathy where, for some reason, intravenous drugs cannot be given. It should not be given to patients with severe hypertension who are otherwise well, as it causes a very rapid fall in blood pressure which may be dangerous. The most frequently prescribed form of nifedipine is now a tablet. These tablets are less rapidly absorbed, but again are relatively short-acting, needing at least twice a day therapy and, in many patients with more severe hypertension, three or four times a day therapy. In view of the rapid metabolism of nifedipine, various attempts have been made to slow down its absorption, and there are now several different slow-release formulations of nifedipine available, with different formulations in different countries. However, as far as we are aware, the most effective is the slow-release formulation that uses a gastro-intestinal transport system, the so-called nifedipine GITS. This formulation gives a fairly constant plasma level over the 24 hours, and is therefore the most preferable way of giving nifedipine for the long-term treatment of high blood pressure.

Amlodipine

Amlodipine is the only dihydropyridine currently available with a long half-life of at least 36 hours. Steady state plasma levels are reached after about 7–8 days and the drug does not accumulate and there is very little peak/trough change in plasma levels with once daily dosing. Because of these pharmacokinetics, amlodipine has a slow onset, taking several days to reach a maximum effect and when the drug is stopped, it takes several days for the blood pressure to rise back to the pretreatment levels. Several studies have suggested that it causes fewer vasodilating effects because of this slow onset, but is as effective in lowering blood pressure as the other dihydropyridines, yet with the major advantage of less peak/trough differences in blood pressure. There is also evidence, like with the other dihydropyridines, of a good dose response, that is the higher the dose, the greater the fall in blood pressure so that if 5 mg is not effective, the dose can be doubled to 10 mg.

Other dihydropyridines

There are several other dihydropyridines. Most of them are short-acting like nifedipine and need to be given at least twice a day. Most are now available in slow release formulations, but whether these formulations give constant plasma levels is a matter of controversy and, in particular, whether blood pressure is consistently controlled throughout the 24 hours, is also a matter of some debate at the present time.

Indications for dihydropyridines

These drugs are now widely used for the first-line treatment of hypertension. They are particularly effective in older patients, black patients and in patients with more severe hypertension (i.e. where their blood pressure-lowering effect becomes greater, the higher the initial blood pressure). Whilst they act as vasodilators, they do have a mild natriuretic effect (diuretic) and this may also be part of the mechanism whereby they lower blood pressure. Unlike the beta-blockers and diuretics, they have no metabolic effects on cholesterol, potas-

sium or blood sugar. Special indications for dihydropyridines are when beta-blockers and diuretics are contraindicated, and they are widely used in patients with renal failure where they are effective. Animal studies have also demonstrated a reduction in the rate of deterioration of renal impairment with these drugs. They have a marked additive effect on blood pressure when added to a converting enzyme inhibitor. This is now a very widely used combination in the treatment of more severe hypertension. They are also additive to betablockers. This is useful in treating patients with associated coronary artery disease and hypertension, particularly those with angina. Interestingly, when thiazide diuretics are added to a dihydropyridine, there is no further fall in blood pressure, but all the metabolic effects of the diuretic are seen. Therefore, in patients treated with dihydropyridines alone, there is no point in adding a diuretic. However, when the dihydropyridine is given to a patient who is on a diuretic, there is often a further fall in blood pressure and the diuretic can then be withdrawn.

Side-effects

There are two well recognized side-effects of the dihydropyridines; the first is a vasodilating effect which is mainly due to a rapid rise in the plasma level, particularly seen with the short-acting dihydropyridines. This causes headaches, flushing and dizziness. These effects can be minimised by using the long-acting dihydropyridine, amlodipine or a slow-release formulation of a shorter acting dihydropyridine that is not rapidly absorbed. Even using this approach some patients may have a slight headache with the start of therapy and they should be warned about this. This usually disappears with continuing

Table 11.5

Side-effects of dihydropyridines and verapamil.

Dihydropyridines	(a)	rapidly-absorbed drugs facial flushing headaches
	(b)	All – ankle oedema nocturia
Verapamil		Constipation

therapy. The second side-effect of the dihydropyridines that occurs is a shift of sodium and water into the legs owing to a change in capillary haemodynamics. This may cause ankle oedema in some patients, particularly those who have a tendency to develop swollen ankles. Interestingly, this oedema is not related to sodium and water retention. Indeed, this class of compounds causes a slight loss of sodium and water from the whole body, and the swelling in the legs is entirely due to greater filtration of fluid in the upright position and a difficulty with clearing the fluid in some patients. Not surprisingly, therefore, if oedema develops it is resistant to salt restriction and diuretic treatment but will clear with elevation of the leg. With the initiation of therapy, there may often be transient oedema or discomfort in the legs, though this improves after a few days. However, if the oedema persists, a reduction in dose should be tried, but if this does not help then it is better then to switch to a different form of therapy or a different type of calcium antagonist. An important but under-reported side effect of the dihydropyridines is nocturia, particularly in middle-aged men and this may be mistaken for prostatic symptoms. There are also rare reports of gingival hyperplasia which regresses on withdrawal of therapy.

DILTIAZEM

This is an effective blood pressure-lowering drug which can also be used for angina pectoris. However, it has less negative inotropic effects than verapamil, but slightly more than the dihydropyridines. Like nifedipine it is rapidly metabolized and, in conventional formulation, needs to be given at least twice if not three times a day. A variety of slow-release forms of diltiazem have become available. It is important, therefore, for the prescriber to reassure themselves that the particular slow-release formulation of diltiazem they use does, in fact, work. This can be judged by the plasma level at peak and trough, that is, the amount of drug present at peak compared to just before they take the next tablet. Several of the formulations that are claimed to be long-acting, when looked at in this way do not come out as well as the manufacturers might like them to do. This means that patients will have considerable fluctuations in blood pressure.

Side-effects

Diltiazem seems to cause less of the vasodilating symptoms of the dihydropyridines and probably slightly less oedema, and causes less constipation than verapamil. However, as with the other calcium antagonists, the side-effects of diltiazem are dose-related.

Indications for diltiazem

Diltiazem is widely used in some countries as first line therapy for hypertension. It is additive to ACE inhibitors. In view of its slightly negative ionotropic and chronotropic effect, there has been some concern about adding it to beta-blockers, but the addition of a diuretic to diltiazem may have a slightly greater blood pressure-lowering effect than adding a diuretic to the dihydropyridines, however, it is not a markedly additive combination.

VERAPAMIL

Verapamil was originally introduced in the late 1960s as a beta-blocker and was used intravenously as an antiarrhythmic agent. Subsequently, it became clear, that it was a calcium entry antagonist and was an effective blood pressure-lowering drug like the other calcium antagonists. However, there were particular concerns when patients who were receiving a beta-blocker were given intravenous verapamil. It precipitated sinus arrest in a few patients. In view of this there has been concern about combining oral verapamil with a beta-blocker.

Like many of the other calcium antagonists, verapamil is rapidly metabolized and in conventional formulation needs to be given at least twice or three times a day. A variety of slow-release preparations have been developed. These will vary from country to country, particularly as verapamil is now off patent. The doctor prescribing verapamil needs to be sure that the slow release formulation that they use does maintain plasma levels throughout the 24 hours and that there are minimum peak/trough effects of the drug.

Side-effects

The major side-effect of verapamil is constipation. This occurs particularly when higher doses are used. It can be largely overcome by patients consuming a high fibre diet, e.g. eating bran, fruit and vegetables. In some patients the constipation may be so severe that the verapamil has to be stopped. Verapamil should not be used in combination with a beta-blocker unless there is some very good reason to do so. However, it is additive to an ACE inhibitor and probably the addition of a diuretic does have a slight effect on blood pressure compared to the addition of a diuretic to a dihydropyridine. One advantage that verapamil has, compared to the dihydropyridines, is that it has been shown to be almost as effective as beta-blockers in secondary prevention following myocardial infarction.

ANGIOTENSIN CONVERTING ENZYME INHIBITORS (ACE INHIBITORS)

These drugs were specifically designed to block the enzyme that is responsible for converting the inactive peptide angiotensin I to the active and powerful vasoconstrictor angiotensin II. The first inhibitor was found in snake venom and, from this, an injectable peptide was developed. Subsequently, compounds that could be taken orally were synthesized. Captopril was the first of this entirely new class of compounds. Since then a large number of other ACE inhibitors have been developed and are available for treatment. In general, this class of drugs is remarkably well tolerated. At present there do not seem to be any major differences between the ACE inhibitors that are available, apart from two factors. One is that some ACE inhibitors are taken as 'pro-drugs', that is, they are metabolized to the active compound in the liver. This is

Table 11.6
Dosage for ACE inhibitors.

	Normal daily dose
Captopril	12.5–50 mg b.d. or t.d.s.
Cilazapril	5–20 mg o.d. or b.d.
Enalapril	2.5 g–20 mg o.d. or b.d.
Fosinopril	10–20 g o.d. or b.d.
Lisinopril	2.5–20 mg o.d. or b.d.
Perindopril	2–8 mg o.d. or b.d.
Quinapril	5–20 mg o.d. or b.d.
Ramipril	1.25–5 mg o.d. or b.d.
Trandolapril	1–4 mg o.d. or b.d.

because the pro-drug is better absorbed. However, the disadvantage is that the ACE inhibitors may not be converted when there is hepatic impairment. The other important difference is in the pharmacokinetics of the drugs. Some of the ACE inhibitors are rapidly metabolized and are short-acting.

Mode of action

It is now realized that the renin–angiotensin system is important in the control of blood pressure. Circulating angiotensin II has multiple actions, e.g. direct vasoconstriction of arterioles, sodium and water retention both directly and through aldosterone, as well as stimulation of the sympathetic nervous system. Unsurprisingly, therefore, when the formation of angiotensin II is blocked by an ACE inhibitor, blood pressure falls. There is controversy about the importance of the local renin-angiotensin system. What has become clear, however, is that when angiotensin II is generated in the tissues, the renin that is available is derived from the kidney. The ACE inhibitors may also prevent the breakdown of bradykinin,

a potential vasodilator. However, in spite of a large body of work, it still remains very unclear how important, if at all, this effect is. It is likely that the role of bradykinin has been exaggerated. Perhaps more importantly, ACE inhibitors through angiotensin II may influence prostaglandin metabolism and this may contribute to the blood pressure fall that occurs.

Side-effects

The commonest side-effect of ACE inhibitors is an irritating dry cough which may occur in up to 15% of patients. This occurs with all of the ACE inhibitors and there is, as yet, no evidence that one ACE inhibitor causes less cough than another. There are some suggestions that it is more common in middle-aged females, smokers and possibly in Chinese. The mechanism of the cough is unknown. In severe cases, a reduction in dose or a switch to another ACE inhibitor can be tried. Usually this has little effect and the drug has to be stopped. Many patients may not associate the cough with the treatment, so it is important to question them. However, on the other hand, a cough is a very common symptom and ACE inhibitors should not unnecessarily be withdrawn unless there clearly is an association. If in doubt, the ACE inhibitor can always be restarted to see if the cough recurs.

Of all the drugs, the ACE inhibitors seem to have the least adverse effects and most patients feel extremely well on these drugs. They do not have the subtle effects on mentation that the beta-blockers have. They do not impair exercise ability. However, ACE inhibitors can occasionally cause a deterioration in renal function. This is likely to occur in patients who have renal artery stenosis, particularly if there is bilateral narrowing of both arteries or a narrowing to

Table 11.7

Side-effects of ACE inhibitors.

Dry irritating cough
Deterioration of renal function in renal artery stenosis
Rare – angioneurotic oedema
Hypotension if prior volume depletion or severe
Heart failure

a single functioning kidney. ACE inhibitors should not be used in these patients unless there are exceptional circumstances. Renal artery stenosis is much more common than thought previously, and occurs in many older patients who are cigarette smokers, particularly if they already have peripheral vascular disease. In these patients, if an ACE inhibitor is being given then renal function must be checked before and after one or two weeks of starting the ACE inhibitor. If there is a deterioration in renal function this strongly suggests that these patients have renal artery stenosis. Care should also be taken in patients who already have renal impairment and who are volume-depleted, particularly after large doses of diuretics, as these patients may also have a deterioration in renal function.

ACE inhibitors, particularly captopril, may occasionally cause a skin rash which is characteristically morbilliform. Much more rarely, it may cause a loss of taste, and, when used in very high doses, captopril and enalapril did occasionally cause proteinuria and leucopenia. However, with the lower doses of ACE inhibitors that are now used, these effects are extremely rare. Due to the fall in angiotensin II and, thereby, the fall in aldosterone, there is a slight rise in plasma potassium levels with ACE inhibitors. This is of benefit in general, particularly when combined with a low dose of diuretic preventing the fall in potassium. However, in patients with severe renal failure, particularly if they are being given potassium-sparing diuretics, there may be an increase in plasma potassium.

How to use ACE inhibitors

The blood pressure-lowering effect of the ACE inhibitors will largely depend on the level of angiotensin II and renin in that particular patient. This will depend on salt intake. The effectiveness of these drugs is therefore markedly influenced by salt intake, and if patients are prepared to restrict salt, the drug becomes much more effective. Similarly, diuretics are additive to ACE inhibitors and several studies have shown that quite low doses of diuretics are very effective. All of the calcium antagonists are markedly additive to the ACE inhibitors. However, there is some controversy about the additional effect of beta-blockers with ACE inhibitors, and it appears that they are not very additive.

Heart failure

For many years it was recognized that ACE inhibitors alleviated the symptoms of heart failure when added to a diuretic. More recent studies have confirmed this effect and importantly have shown a reduction in mortality. This is a major advantage of the ACE inhibitors. Therefore, all patients with heart failure who require a diuretic should also be treated with an ACE inhibitor, unless there are specific contraindications.

More recently, studies in patients following a heart attack have shown that in those patients who have impairment of left ventricular contraction, ACE inhibitors may also reduce mortality.

DIFFERENT ACE INHIBITORS

Captopril was the first drug that was developed. It is rapidly absorbed and has a short duration of action. This may be useful where there is concern about a large fall in blood pressure, or in patients with severe heart failure. However, in the routine treatment of hypertension, captopril needs to be given at least twice daily, and in many patients, more frequently. The other ACE inhibitors are longer acting and claims have been made that they can be given once a day. In our experience, this is not always so. When given once a day there are quite large peak/trough effects with the ACE inhibitors. Blood pressure should be checked before patients take the next dose to make sure it remains controlled throughout the 24 hours. In many patients it may be better to give a lower dose of the longer-acting drugs twice a day rather than a high dose once a day. Most of the ACE inhibitors are excreted by the kidney. Depending on the exact mode of excretion and whether some of the metabolites are active, they may accumulate in patients with renal impairment. Claims have been made that some drugs that are excreted mainly by the liver may be better in these patients.

Enalapril worldwide is the most widely used ACE inhibitor. It is a pro-drug that is converted in the liver to its active form and it is longer-acting than captopril so that it can be given in some patients once daily, but many patients require twice daily dosing. Lisinopril is a lysine analogue of enalaprilat, the active metabolite of enalapril. It is therefore directly absorbed and acts directly. It is excreted by the kidney and may accumulate in renal disease. It appears to be slightly longer-acting than enalapril.

ANGIOTENSIN RECEPTOR ANTAGONISTS

This is a new class of drug that has recently become available which blocks angiotensin II receptors. Blocking the renin angiotensin in this major new way has proven effective in the treatment of hypertension as well as heart failure. Peptide receptor antagonists have been available since the mid-1970s, but these had the major disadvantage that they had to be given intravenously. They also had some capacity to stimulate receptors when the angiotensin II levels were low. However, over the last decade orally active drugs that are effective in blocking angiotensin II receptors have been developed. It has become clear that there are two classes of angiotensin II receptors: the AT1 receptor which appears to be responsible for nearly all of the physiological actions of angiotensin II; and AT2 receptors whose role at present remains ill-defined. There are now more than ten angiotensin II receptor antagonists being developed.

Losartan

The first of the angiotensin II receptor antagonists is Losartan. It, and its metabolite E3174, specifically blocks the AT1 receptors for angiotensin II. The metabolite is responsible for the long duration of action which allows once a day dosing. Clinical studies have shown that Losartan at 50 and 100 mg is effective in lowering blood pressure; furthermore, it was as effective in a double-blind comparison study as enalapril 10 mg once a day. Other studies have shown that it is as effective as a dihydropyridine or a beta-blocker. Losartan is additive to diuretics and calcium antagonists. In clinical trials, Losartan has been well-tolerated: patients who had developed a cough on Lisinopril and were rechallenged in a careful double-blind study to make sure that they developed a cough the second time on Lisinopril, were then entered into a double-blind study of Lisinopril against Losartan. The trial clearly demonstrated that Losartan is not associated with cough.

Losartan is as effective as an ACE inhibitor and is likely to be used particularly in those patients who are at risk of developing a cough on an ACE inhibitor, or have already developed a cough. Assuming that its side-effect profile is as good as the clinical trials show thus far, it is likely to become a major new class of drug for hypertension. A major advantage of Losartan over ACE inhibitors apart from the lack of cough is its longer duration of action.

mg twice daily, but much larger doses may need to be used until the blood pressure is controlled. Once the phenoxybenzamine is introduced, a beta-blocker can be given to control the heart rate if this is increased. Phenoxybenzamine invariably causes some postural hypotension and problems with ejaculation.

Phentolamine

Phentolamine is a much shorter-acting alpha-blocker that is available only by intravenous injection. It can be used in hypertensive crises, particularly where patients have a phaeochromocytoma, or where there is rebound hypertension following clonidine withdrawal, or reactions to monoamine-oxidase inhibitors. Outside these indications, it should not be used.

ALPHA RECEPTOR ANTAGONISTS

This class of drug has not been particularly popular because of the difficulty of dosage regimes and the high frequency of side-effects. However, recently, two longer-acting alpha blockers have been developed, doxazosin and terazosin. This has led to renewed interest in the alpha receptor antagonists.

Phenoxybenzamine

Phenoxybenzamine should only be used in patients with phaeochromocytoma, where it is extremely effective. The usual dose is 10

Table 11.8

Dosage for alpha-adrenoceptor blockers and alpha and beta-receptor antagonists.

Alpha-adrenoceptor blockers	Normal daily dose
Doxazosin	2–16 mg o.d.
Phenoxybenzamine	10–50 mg once or twice daily
Prazosin	0.5–5 mg three times daily
Terazosin	1–20 mg daily
Alpha and beta-receptor antagonists	
Labetalol	200–400 mg twice daily

Prazosin

Prazosin is a short-acting alpha-blocker. It often causes postural drops in blood pressure and is not frequently used for the treatment of hypertension. It may have the advantage of relieving some of the symptoms of enlarged prostate and has been used in some men pending prostatectomy. With the advent of the longer-acting alpha-blockers, in our view prazosin should no longer be used.

Doxazosin and terazosin

These are both longer-acting alpha-blockers that can be given once daily. They appear to have less of the side-effects of the shorter-acting alpha-blockers, such as prazosin, and are effective in lowering blood pressure. In view of the fact that they do cause slight falls in cholesterol, claims have been made that they may have major advantages in the long-term treatment of hypertension, but these have yet to be clearly demonstrated. They are claimed to be additive to diuretics, beta-blockers, calcium antagonists and ACE inhibitors. When combined with other drugs they can cause postural drops in blood pressure; this should be borne in mind and standing blood pressures should be measured.

COMBINED ALPHA AND BETA RECEPTOR ANTAGONISTS

Alpha receptor antagonists and beta-blockers have been used together to treat hypertension. Only one drug combines alpha and beta blockade.

Labetalol

Labetalol is both a beta-blocker and a weak alpha-blocker when taken orally. However, when given intravenously, it has much greater alpha-blocking properties and invariably causes postural hypotension. Intravenous labetalol is sometimes used in hypertensive emergencies. When given orally, its long-term effect on blood pressure is similar to that of beta-blockers, except when very high doses are given, and the alpha-blocking property is then apparent, particularly in causing postural. Labetalol also appears to have more side-effects than many of the beta-blockers, particularly causing itchiness of the scalp. Several studies have been done in pregnancy hypertension, and it has been shown to be useful in this situation. It is no longer widely used outside this indication.

CENTRAL ALPHA RECEPTOR AGONISTS

Central alpha receptor agonists were first introduced in the 1960s, and became, in many countries, the most commonly used blood pressure-lowering drugs after the diuretics. Exactly how methyldopa works is not clear. It was originally thought that it inhibited the enzyme converting dopa to dopamine. However, more recent research has shown that, probably, both methyldopa and clonidine lower blood pressure by central alpha receptor stimulation. Whilst they are effective in lowering blood pressure, and are additive to many of the other blood pressure-lowering regimes, their side-effects, in comparison to the more modern drugs, are such that most physicians no longer use this class of drugs.

Methyldopa

Methyldopa is an effective blood pressure-lowering drug but has a large number of side-effects. Nearly all patients notice they feel sleepy, particularly during the first few weeks of therapy, and many feel debilitated. This may only become apparent when patients stop long-term methyldopa and suddenly feel much better. It can cause severe depression, and it may also cause erectile impotence. Several severe drug reactions can occur with methyldopa. These include severe liver dysfunction, hepatitis, a positive direct Coomb's test and, more rarely, haemolytic anaemia and drug fever. Many patients who started on methyldopa in the 1960s and 1970s have continued with it and have learned to live with their side-effects. Our view is that all patients receiving long-term methyldopa should be offered a trial of alternative therapy, as it is our experience that, in general, patients feel very much better when they have stopped methyldopa, even though at the time they may not have realized how their life was being impaired.

The only indication for methyldopa is in pregnancy-related hypertension, where early studies show that it appears to be safe to the fetus. As it is only given for a short time, it remains useful in the treatment of high blood pressure associated with pregnancy, but is gradually being replaced by other drugs.

Clonidine

This is very similar to methyldopa. It is an effective drug in lowering blood pressure, but it causes much the same sort of side-effects of sedation and nasal stuffiness. However, unlike methyldopa it does not cause hepatic and haemotological problems.

More worrying is the rebound hypertension that occurs when clonidine is withdrawn. This is particularly dangerous if patients are also receiving a beta-blocker, when the omission of even one dose of clonidine may result in a hypertensive crisis. Because of this and its side-effect profile, clonidine should no longer be used. Where patients are stopping clonidine, it is very important to withdraw the beta-blocker first and to substitute a calcium antagonist. The dose of clonidine should gradually be reduced and blood pressure should be closely monitored.

DIRECT-ACTING VASODILATORS

The direct arteriolar vasodilators, such as hydralazine, cause a decrease in peripheral vascular tone but have the disadvantage of causing a reflex activation of the sympathetic nervous system and an increase in heart rate. This increase in sympathetic nervous activity and the rise in angiotensin II also account for the retention of sodium and water that occurs with these drugs. However, when they are given in combination with a beta-blocker and diuretic, these side-effects are minimized and this was a widely used combination in the 1970s.

Table 11.9
Dosage for peripheral vasodilators.

	Normal daily dose
Hydralazine	25–100 mg twice daily
Minoxidil	2.5–20 mg twice daily

Worldwide, hydralazine is still frequently used, usually in combination with reserpine and a thiazide.

Hydralazine

Hydralazine has a direct effect on smooth muscle cells in the peripheral arterioles and only a small effect on veins. It is largely metabolized by the liver. On its own, it is not that effective in lowering blood pressure because of reflex sympathetic stimulation. However, when added to a beta-blocker it is an effective drug, particularly if a diuretic is added to overcome the sodium retention that invariably occurs with hydralazine. With the advent of the calcium antagonists and the ACE inhibitors, hydralazine is not so widely used, mainly because of its side-effects.

Side-effects

Many patients develop symptoms of peripheral vasodilatation, including headaches, flushing and palpitations. This is alleviated to some extent by adding a beta-blocker. However, frequently patients develop a Lupus-like syndrome with arthritis, pyrexia and general malaise. This usually occurs at higher doses or in patients who metabolize the drug slowly (slow acetylators). It is likely that this syndrome is more common than has been recognized previously because the symptoms may be quite mild.

Minoxidil and diazoxide

Minoxidil is the most potent vasodilator known. It is thought to act in a similar way to hydralazine, and again causes reflex sympathetic stimulation, leading to tachycardia and to gross sodium and water retention with oedema. At the same time it also causes severe hair growth and, in view of this side-effect, it was largely reserved for men with very severe, uncontrolled hypertension. With the advent of the calcium antagonists and ACE inhibitors the need for minoxidil has diminished. Nevertheless, in patients who are resistant to all other therapy, it still has a role. The major problem with the drug is sodium and water retention, and this is prevented by the use of diuretics. Frusemide is almost always needed, often in very large doses. Like hydralazine, it is best used in combination with a beta-blocker. All patients will notice an increase in hair growth and this virtually precludes its use in women. Diazoxide is a similar vasodilator. Orally, it is hardly ever used. However, intravenous diazoxide still has a role in the control of severe hypertension, where parenteral treatment is thought to be necessary. It should not be given as a bolus dose, as this can cause severe hypotension. It should be used in small, graded amounts (a maximum of 50 mg at a time) or as an infusion (for further details see Parenteral treatment of high blood pressure).

OTHER ANTI-HYPERTENSIVE DRUGS

Rauwolfia alkaloids

These drugs were widely used in the late 1950s and 1960s and have both central and peripheral effects on noradrenaline release. Reserpine was the most widely used drug. However, it was found to cause sedation and depression and even suicide. Nevertheless, at lower doses, 0.1–0.2 mg given at night and combined with a diuretic, it is an effective drug in lowering blood pressure and because it is very cheap it remains the most widely used combination in many developing countries.

Postadrenergic blockers (guanethidine, bethanidine and debrisoquine)

All of these drugs have serious side-effects, including postural hypotension, exercise-induced hypotension, failure of ejaculation, impotence and, rarely, severe diarrhoea. These drugs should therefore no longer be used and patients already on them should be changed to more modern treatment.

FURTHER READING

Lyons D, Petrie JC, Reid JL. Drug treatment: present and future. *Br Med Bull* 1994; **50**:472–93.

Materson BJ, Reda DJ, Cushman WC, et al. Single-drug therapy for hypertension in men: a comparison of six antihypertensive agents with placebo. *N Engl J Med* 1993; **328**:914–21.

Neaton JD, Grimm RH, Prineas RJ, et al. Treatment of mild hypertension study: final results. *JAMA* 1993; **270**:713–24.

12 Schemes for Reducing Blood Pressure

Background

There are well over one hundred different drugs that lower blood pressure with approximately twenty different mechanisms of action. New types of drugs and/or new formulations or combinations of existing agents are continuously being developed. Often, by the time definitive evidence of the usefulness of one particular group of drugs has become available, new products have been developed that may have advantages and in particular fewer side-effects. It is not surprising, therefore, that there is some disagreement even between experts about which drugs or combinations of drugs are best for individual patients.

At the same time, some of the drugs may have additional benefit or fewer harmful effects which are independent of their blood pressure-lowering action. For example, while the thiazide diuretics have been shown to prevent strokes and heart attacks, particularly in the elderly, their metabolic effects on potassium, glucose and lipids continue to cause concern. On the other hand, the ACE inhibitors, which have not as yet been studied in terms of whether they reduce strokes or heart attacks, have very few metabolic effects and have been shown to reduce mortality in heart failure. In general, it is probably true that it does not really matter how blood pressure is reduced, but the patient must continue to feel well.

Up to recently, the treatment of most forms of high blood pressure was relatively simple. Patients were started either on a beta-blocker or a thiazide diuretic, and if one drug was insufficient, the two were used in combination and further drugs were added in sequentially. This so-called 'step-care' approach has now been abandoned, as it is clear that individual patients respond to different drugs in different ways, and many patients may develop subtle side-effects on some of the drugs which seriously impair their quality of life, particularly as most patients are completely well before treatment, and treatment is for the rest of their lives.

The guiding principles should be to control blood pressure, both diastolic and systolic, making sure that the right drug or combination of drugs that are used, and to leave the patient feeling completely well.

WHAT IS THE LEVEL OF BLOOD PRESSURE TO AIM FOR?

The clinician's objective in drug therapy should be to reduce the blood pressure to the normal range, that is a diastolic below 90 mmHg but not below 80 mmHg, and to control systolic, that is to keep the systolic below 160 mmHg. The better the control of blood pressure, the lower the risk of premature death or illness from cardiovascular, cerebrovascular and renal disease. At the same time, the more severe the hypertension before treatment, the greater is the risk of death, but greater too are the benefits of treatment. In general, the same drugs are used whatever the level of blood pressure, but in patients with more severe hypertension there is a greater urgency to reduce blood pressure so that there is less time to establish the best approach for the individual patient. However, the urgency of treatment is commonly overstressed and, apart from cases with hypertensive encephalopathy, gross hypertensive left ventricular failure or hypertension associated with aortic dissection, there is rarely a need to reduce blood pressure over minutes or hours. Even in patients with accelerated hypertension, blood pressure should be lowered only over 24–48 hours and, in that period, it should not be reduced to normal. Over-rapid blood pressure reduction in patients with severe hypertension can cause, and has caused, both strokes and heart attacks.

BLOOD PRESSURE-LOWERING REGIMES

Non-pharmacological blood pressure reduction

All patients should be instructed on non-pharmacological ways in which blood pressure may be lowered (see Chapter 10). Non-pharmacological treatment is most often stressed to patients with only mild hypertension, but it is also effective in combination with drug treatment. All patients with hypertension should be instructed on how they can lower their blood pressure by salt restriction, and where relevant by weight loss and moderation of alcohol intake. Several studies have now clearly demonstrated that salt restriction is additive to many of the blood pressure-lowering drugs or combinations.

First line antihypertensive drug therapy

There are now at least five classes of first line antihypertensive drugs. These are:

(*i*)   the thiazide diuretics
(*ii*) the beta-blockers
(*iii*) the calcium entry antagonists
(*iv*) the ACE inhibitors
(*v*)   the selective alpha-blockers

It is our view that any of these drugs can be used as first line therapy. However, some physicians adopt a more conservative approach, saying that as long-term outcome trials have only been conducted so far with diuretics and beta-blockers, these drugs should be used first. Only when they fail, or patients have side-effects, should the other classes of compounds be used. Each physician has to make up his own mind as to what he feels is best for a patient. Studies are being set up to look at all the different classes of compounds currently being used for treating high blood pressure, but a definitive answer will not be to hand for at least five to ten years. We feel, therefore, that the best approach is to make sure that

Table 12.1
A guide to blood pressure treatment.

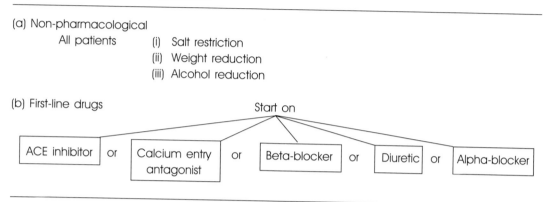

(a) Non-pharmacological

All patients   (i)   Salt restriction
                      (ii) Weight reduction
                      (iii) Alcohol reduction

(b) First-line drugs   Start on

| ACE inhibitor | or | Calcium entry antagonist | or | Beta-blocker | or | Diuretic | or | Alpha-blocker |

the blood pressure is well controlled, with whatever drugs are necessary, and that, just as importantly, the patient should not be made to feel in any way unwell. In other words, side-effects should be positively sought.

GUIDELINES

Various bodies in different countries have pontificated about advising doctors how to treat high blood pressure. This plethora of guidelines has been partly brought about by the financial pressures related to the cost of treatment and a genuine desire to improve patients' blood pressure control and their quality of life. All of the guidelines suffer from one major problem, that is, we still do not know from clinical trials whether the newer drugs (e.g. ACE inhibitors and calcium antagonists) prevent strokes and heart attacks. Nevertheless, these two classes of drugs are very widely used as they are effective, and lack or have a different range of side-effects compared to the beta-blockers and diuretics.

The guidelines published by the British Hypertension Society are probably the easiest to digest. They are very brief, particularly compared to the American guidelines and the Committee of the Society was honest enough to publically disagree as to whether all four classes of compounds should be given as first line therapy or whether beta-blockers and diuretics should be given initially and the other classes of compounds only given where there were side-effects or problems. The recent American guidelines now contradict their previous advice in stating that beta-blockers and diuretics should be reserved for first line treatment and other classes of compounds should only be used if there are other indications. Most of the other guidelines, from New Zealand and the World Health Organization fall between these two views. Perhaps the most rigorous approach is the New

Zealand approach of a complicated calculation of risk profile to decide whether treatment is justified or not. Clearly, in the circumstances, it is up to each doctor and, perhaps, the patient to decide what is the best treatment. Too often patients have not been involved in these decisions and yet it is they who will have to take the drugs for the rest of their lives. It is therefore vital that the doctor prescribing the drugs does understand the side-effects of those drugs, seeks them out and also understands the unpredictability of the response in individual patients.

Our view is essentially pragmatic and in our practice we have found that it is essential to use all classes of drugs to achieve the aims of good control of blood pressure without side-effects.

THE FIRST STEP

In this section we outline the five classes of compounds and the various indications for the drugs as first line therapy, as well as our preferred choices of treatment in each class of compound, and the starting and maximum doses that should be used in the average patient (Table 12.1).

Diuretics

There are no basic differences between the many thiazide diuretics. If this group of drugs is to be used then the best option is to prescribe the cheapest, at the lowest possible dose. Remember that thiazides have a flat dose response on blood pressure. Little is achieved by using bigger

doses in terms of blood pressure reduction, but the metabolic side-effects are much greater with the higher doses. It is our practice to either use bendrofluazide in a single daily dose of 1.25 or 2.5 mg or hydrochlorothiazide 12.5 mg to 25 mg daily as this minimizes the clinical and metabolic side-effects. Studies in elderly patients have clearly demonstrated that the thiazides reduce not only strokes, but also coronary heart disease.

Thiazide diuretics are most useful in:

- Black patients
- Elderly patients
- Patients with mild or incipient heart failure

In general, they are best avoided in:

- Patients with maturity onset diabetes
- Patients with hyperlipidaemia
- Pregnancy
- Patients with gout

One of the major side-effects of thiazide diuretics is impotence, and they should be discontinued in men complaining of impotence, and in patients who develop hyperglycaemia or hyperlipidaemia.

Patients receiving diuretics of any type should have their serum electrolytes checked after about two months and, thereafter, at least annually. It is not our practice to prescribe potassium supplements; nonetheless, an increase in dietary potassium is advised. Combined diuretic and potassium tablets should not be used as they only contain small amounts of potassium.

If the serum potassium falls then the potassium-sparing diuretics (amiloride or triamterene) may be added. The addition of a beta-blocker or an ACE inhibitor to a low dose of a thiazide diuretic also blunts the fall in serum potassium. Patients on long-term thiazide therapy should have occasional checks of their urine or blood for glucose, and their serum lipid levels should be checked. If marked hypokalaemia develops with the use of thiazide diuretics, a diagnosis of primary hyperaldosteronism should be considered.

Beta-blockers

The differences between the many beta-blockers are not great. Nearly all of them can be given in once a day dosage regimes, and the contraindications are well recognized. As with the thiazide diuretics, it is generally advisable to use the lowest dose, although this may have to be given twice a day.

Beta-blockers are most useful in:

- Younger patients
- Anxious patients
- Non-smokers
- Angina pectoris
- Patients who have had a myocardial infarction

Beta-blockers should be avoided in:

- Patients with asthma or a history of asthma
- 'Brittle' insulin-requiring diabetics
- Any patients with peripheral vascular disease
- Patients with intermittent claudication
- Raynaud's syndrome
- Second and third degree heart block
- Patients with heart failure

Beta-blockers should be discontinued in:

- Patients who develop heart failure
- Patients who develop asthma

Unlike with the thiazide diuretics, there are some small differences between some of the beta-blockers.

Hydrophilic beta-blockers (atenolol, nadolol and sotalol)

These may cause less tiredness and loss of exercise tolerance.

Cardioselective beta-blockers (atenolol, acebutolol, metoprolol, celiprolol, bisoprolol)

These drugs may possibly have fewer effects on airways resistance but should not, in any case, be given to asthmatics; and may cause less interference with autonomic and metabolic responses to hypoglycaemia.

Intrinsic sympathomimetic activity beta-blockers (oxprenolol, pindolol, acebutolol)

These may cause less reduction of peripheral blood-flow.

While the beta-blockers are effective drugs, the major problem that has emerged is their more subtle side-effects. In particular, they cause a reduction in exercise tolerance with a feeling of heaviness in the legs on climbing stairs or running. The other major side-effect is a subtle change in mentation with a lack of drive and vigour, often noticed by the spouse or work colleagues but only apparent to the patient when the beta-blocker is stopped.

Calcium entry antagonists

There are two major distinct types of calcium entry antagonists: the dihydropyridines, such as amlodipine and nifedipine, which do not affect heart rate, and verapamil, which is not only a vasodilator, but also slows the heart rate. Diltiazem lies between the two of these.

Calcium antagonists are most useful in:

- Older patients
- Black patients
- Patients with peripheral vascular disease
- Patients with cerebrovascular disease
- Patients with angina pectoris

However, verapamil should be avoided in:

- Patients with cardiac failure
- Patients with heart block
- Patients already on a beta-blocker

One major disadvantage in the past was that the calcium antagonists had a short half-life and this necessitated at least twice a day or, in many, three times a day therapy. Amlodopine is the only long-acting calcium antagonist, and the others are now in slow-release formulations which means they do not have to be given so often. Care, however, needs to be taken with each of these formulations as not all of them are as effective as their manufacturers may claim. The calcium antagonists have the advantage of, on the whole, not causing any subtle side-effects, particularly on mentation. However, they do have obvious side-effects; the shorter-acting dihydropyridines causing flushing and headaches, the short-acting and longer-acting ones both causing some gravity-dependent oedema. Verapamil may cause constipation.

Angiotensin converting enzyme (ACE) inhibitors

Except for cough, this group of drugs has the fewest side-effects of all the blood pressure-lowering drugs. Apart from their length of action and frequency of dosage, it is doubtful whether there are any major differences between the ACE inhibitors when used in the correct dosage.

ACE inhibitors are particularly useful in:

- Younger patients
- Patients with incipient or mild heart failure
- Patients who develop side-effects with other drugs
- Diabetic hypertensives

ACE inhibitors should be used with great care in:

- Renal artery stenosis
- Severely fluid-depleted patients, especially those already receiving a loop diuretic such as frusemide

and should be avoided in:

- Pregnancy
- Premenopausal women

Captopril, the first of the ACE inhibitors, necessitates in hypertension a three or four times a day dosage regime to avoid large peak/trough differences. It is better, therefore, to use a longer-acting ACE inhibitor such as enalapril or lisinopril. However, even with these, in many patients it may be better to give a low dose twice a day rather than a higher dose once a day, as most of the ACE inhibitors currently available wear off at the end of 24 hours after the last dose.

Alpha-blockers

Alpha-blockers are drugs that up to recently had quite severe side-effects, particularly causing severe postural hypotension. However, the long-acting selective alpha-blockers such as doxazosin and terazosin are effective in lowering blood pressure and lack the side-effects of their predecessors. They also have the advantage of causing a small reduction in cholesterol.

Other blood pressure-lowering drugs

The centrally acting antihypertensive drugs such as clonidine, methyldopa and reserpine should not be used as first line therapy in any patient. Their major side-effects of sedation and depression mean that they should no longer be used. The adrenergic blockers, guanethidine, bethanidine and debrisoquine, should no longer be used, and the directly acting vasodilators such as hydralazine, minoxidil and diazoxide should not be used as first line therapy. It is our view that when patients are encountered taking such drugs, even if blood pressure is well controlled, it may be well worth switching them to more modern drugs as they may feel considerably better.

Table 12.2

Suggested therapeutic combinations to reduce blood pressure.

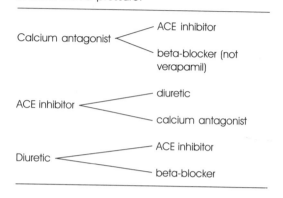

then a second drug should be tried. There is considerable argument about whether all of the drugs should be tried as initial therapy before going on to adding in a second drug. Clearly, a balance has to be struck between what is practical for the individual doctor and patient, and what results in the best control of the blood pressure with the patient feeling completely well. Another argument which, perhaps, has not received enough attention is that when two additive drugs are combined, much lower doses of the two drugs can be used. This may lessen side-effects associated with the drugs.

FAILURE OF FIRST LINE THERAPY

If the first drug does not lower blood pressure or does not lower it sufficiently, there are two options. One is to change to another first line drug or to add in a second drug. If the first line drug causes side-effects,

THE SECOND STEP

If optimum blood pressure control is not achieved with the first line drugs when used appropriately and in the correct dose, then another type of blood pressure drug can be added in. Some combinations are much

Table 12.3
Therapeutic combinations not usually recommended.

verapamil + beta-blocker
dihydropyridine + diuretic
ACE inhibitor + beta-blocker

Table 12.4
A guide to resistant blood pressure control (i.e. not controlled by two drugs).

(a) Check compliance with lifestyle changes
    (i)   salt restriction
    (ii) weight reduction
    (iii) alcohol restraint

(b) Check therapeutic compliance
    (i)   tablet counts
    (ii) monitor drug levels in blood if possible
    (iii) simplify therapeutic regime

(c) Investigate further for underlying cause of hypertension
    (i)   Renal arteriogram
    (ii) Urinary catecholamines
    (iii) Renin/aldosterone

more additive than others (Table 12.2), and some may have little additive effect, or may be potentially harmful (Table 12.3).

RESISTANT HYPERTENSION

If patients have been tried on two additive drugs and blood pressure is not controlled, it is important to think why their blood pressure is not being lowered by the combination (Table 12.4).

Check compliance

Enquire whether the patient is taking the prescribed drugs and whether they find the tablet regime difficult to remember. There are certain clues to non-compliance such as no fall in heart rate with beta-blocker, or no fall in serum potassium with thiazide diuretic. Tablet counts or discussion with relatives may produce surprises in patients who are apparently compliant.

Simplify the regime

Complex regimes can lead to poor compliance. It is reasonable to try to convert patients to a once-daily regime. However, this should not be done at the expense of losing control of the blood pressure towards the end of the 24 hours.

Salt restriction

Many patients may be eating large amounts of salt and this is a major reason for lack of response to the drugs. This can easily be checked by collecting a 24-hour urine and measuring sodium excretion, which will give a good guide to the patient's usual salt intake.

Surreptitious alcoholics

Withdrawal from alcohol can cause large rises in blood pressure and these patients may stop drinking 24 hours before seeing the doctor with a large rise in pressure.

Check for underlying causes of hypertension (see Chapter 8)

Most patients with secondary causes do have severe hypertension which is often resistant to therapy, e.g. renal artery stenosis, primary aldosteronism. It is vital that these patients are investigated to exclude an underlying cause

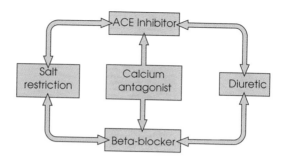

Figure 12.1

Additive combinations for blood pressure reduction.

THE THIRD STEP

Patients whose blood pressure is resistant to double therapy in the combinations suggested above have a high risk of cardiovascular complications of hypertension. It is advisable for such patients to be referred to specialized blood pressure clinics. Particularly, it is important to exclude an underlying cause for hypertension. Combinations that can be used in more resistant hypertension are as follows (Fig. 12.1).

A long-acting ACE inhibitor can be used combined with a long-acting calcium antagonist with either the addition of a diuretic or beta-blocker or both. In our experience it is unusual for patients not to be controlled on this regime. However, in some patients it may be necessary to add in frusemide twice a day, or a long-acting alpha-blocker such as doxazosin. It has also been our experience that adding different calcium antagonists to each other may have additive effects with less side-effects. For instance, adding verapamil to a dihydropyridine can be very effective in these patients. Also, the addition of hydralazine or minoxidil may be effective in very resistant patients, but its side-effects, particularly hair growth, have necessitated limiting its use.

Occasionally a patient is encountered whose blood pressure, while never dangerously high, appears to be resistant to all treatment. It is worth checking whether the patient has only transient elevations of pressure in response to attending the clinic. If he or she rests in a quiet room for half an hour, and the blood pressure is checked by a reliably trained nurse, lower readings may be achieved. Twenty-four-hour ambulatory monitoring can be performed to see what level blood pressure falls to when the patient is outside the clinic environment. If such patients have normal blood pressure, and have absolutely no evidence of cardiac, renal or cerebral damage, and, particularly, if ECG shows no evidence of left ventricular hypertrophy, then it may be reasonable to accept less than optimal control of clinic blood pressure. It may be, in such patients, that home blood pressure monitoring may be a better way of controlling the blood pressure.

MALIGNANT HYPERTENSION

All patients with the malignant phase of hypertension (i.e. those with retinal haemorrhages, exudates with or without papilloedema) should, as soon as the diagnosis has been made, be treated as a medical emergency and be admitted to hospital for controlled blood pressure reduction, as well as detailed investigation to find whether there is an underlying cause for their hypertension, and to try to prevent the development of renal failure. Indeed, if the blood pressure is not adequately reduced, the disease progresses rapidly to end-stage chronic renal failure requiring dialysis, or to death from cardiac failure or stroke. However, too rapid control of blood pressure may be dangerous, and has been shown to cause both stroke and myocardial infarction as well as marked deterioration in renal function or acute renal failure. The aim, therefore, should be to lower the diastolic pressure, with the use of oral therapy, only to around 110 mmHg over a period of 24–48 hours, and to lower it to around 90–100 mmHg only after a week or two, often after the patient has been discharged from hospital. Intravenous therapy is only justified if there is hypertensive encephalopathy, hypertensive heart failure or aortic dissection.

Regimes for malignant hypertension

The beta-blockers, ACE inhibitors and calcium antagonists will all lower blood pressure in most patients with malignant hypertension. Whilst theoretically the ACE inhibitors have some attractions, as they directly oppose the immediate cause of the high blood pressure, i.e. the rise in angiotensin II, they can cause progressive deterioration in renal function if there is underlying renal artery stenosis, or if the patient is severely volume-depleted. If ACE inhibitors are used, intravenous saline should be ready in case the blood pressure falls precipitously. Calcium antagonists are

very effective in these patients but if used in a rapidly absorbed formulation will lower blood pressure too quickly. Probably the best regime is an initial trial of treatment with nifedipine 10–20 mg in a tablet formulation that has a peak effect at 1–2 hours with an aim to reduce the diastolic pressure to around 110 mmHg. Many of these patients, once blood pressure has been lowered to about 110 mmHg, will thereafter require several drugs to keep it at this level. Many patients are volume-depleted and it is a good idea, if this is so, to increase their salt intake temporarily to bring their body weight up to increase perfusion of the kidneys. All these patients should be referred to a specialist unit for further investigation. Around 50% of patients with malignant hypertension have an underlying cause such as a phaeochromocytoma, renal artery stenosis etc.

HYPERTENSIVE EMERGENCIES

Many blood pressure-lowering drugs can be given intravenously or intramuscularly and lower blood pressure very rapidly. They were, and in some cases continue to be, used far too widely in hospital practice. The danger of precipitating a stroke or heart attack outweighs any benefit there might be from rapid reduction of blood pressure. However, in patients who have hypertensive encephalopathy, gross ventricular failure directly due to the severe hypertension or dissecting aortic aneurysm, intravenous treatment is mandatory. There are a range of different drugs that can be used, but some can only be used in an intensive care unit setting and should be reserved for that.

Diazoxide

This drug has been widely used as a parenteral agent and, some years ago, it was recommended to be given rapidly as an intravenous bolus of 300 mg. This produced an immediate and precipitous fall in blood pressure of 30–40% within 2–3 minutes and serious complications have been described. A much better way of giving diazoxide is either by infusion or in 50 mg intravenous injections given slowly and not repeated for at least 10 minutes. This will give a gradual reduction in blood pressure and the blood pressure may be reduced over 30 minutes to 2 hours to the desired level, thereby avoiding any precipitous falls.

Labetalol

Labetalol is a combined alpha–beta-blocker but predominantly has alpha-blocking activities when given intravenously. It will lower blood pressure rapidly when given as an infusion and invariably causes severe postural hypotension with the patient being unable to get out of bed. Therefore we do not recommend it for parenteral therapy.

Nitroprusside

This is a potent vasodilator that invariably lowers blood pressure when given by intravenous infusion. The fall in blood pressure can be controlled by the rate of infusion. However, it must be given under very close supervision as severe hypotension can easily occur. It should be reserved for use in intensive care units or by anaesthetists. As well as causing the expected side-effects of any arteriolar vasodilator, i.e. flushing, postural hypotension etc., nitroprusside is metabolized to cyanide and thiacyanate. This is not important during short-term infusion, but toxicity can develop if the drug is given over several days, particularly when there is renal failure.

New solutions need to be made up every 4 hours and must be covered by light-proof paper to prevent photo-deactivation. The usual starting dose is 0.3 µg/kilogram/minute to a maximum of 6 µg/kilogram/minute. Blood pressure should be measured extremely carefully and the amount of nitroprusside should be carefully monitored. Precipitous falls in blood pressure can suddenly occur.

Hydralazine

Hydralazine can be given either intravenously or intramuscularly and was widely used but is now only used by obstetricians. The normal dose is 10 to 40 mg injected slowly. In most situations where it is used, oral hydralazine would be just as effective.

Oral therapy

For patients able to take drugs by mouth, most blood pressure-lowering drugs given orally act rapidly. For instance, nifedipine given in a 10 mg capsule, either bitten and held under the tongue or even swallowed, will cause blood pressure to fall within 10–15 minutes. The ACE inhibitor, captopril, when taken orally will lower blood pressure within 30 minutes. Oral beta-blockers, with or without hydralazine, reduce blood pressure over a period of 2–3 hours.

FURTHER READING

Carruthers SG, Lavochelle P, Haynes RB, et al. Report of the Canadian Hypertension Society Consensus Conference - 1 Introduction. *Canad Med Ass J* 1993; **149**:289–93.

The fifth report of the Joint National Committee on detection, evaluation and treatment of high blood pressure (JNCV) *Arch Inter Med* 1993; **153**:154–83.

Guidelines Sub-Committee. 1993 guidelines for the management of mild hypertension: memorandum for a World Heath Organisation/International Hypertension Society meeting. *J Hypertens* 1993; **ii:** 905–18.

Jackson R, Barham P, Bills T, et al. Management of raised blood pressure in New Zealand: a discussion document. *Br Med J* 1993; **307**:107–10.

Sever PS, Beevers DG, Bulpitt CJ, et al. Management guidelines in essential hypertension: report of the second working party of the British Hypertension Society. *Br Med J* 1993; **306**:983–7.

HYPERTENSION IN PRIMARY MEDICAL CARE

BACKGROUND

Other chapters in this book have dealt with the value of the investigation and reduction of high blood pressure. The next question is, who should actually deliver this potentially life-saving treatment? There is evidence that the quality and efficiency of blood pressure reduction on a long-term basis is a more potent predictor of a patient's life expectancy than the severity of the hypertension in the first place. Regrettably, practically every population survey in the UK, the USA and elsewhere has reported a depressing and woeful state of underdiagnosis, undertreatment and inadequate follow-up of hypertensive patients. The 'rule of halves' described in Chapter 1 means that less than 15% of all hypertensives are receiving adequate clinical care. The need for improvement in detection and management of hypertension ranks with the abolition of cigarette smoking as a major public health concern in developed countries. In the developing countries, this new epidemic is just around the corner, unless steps are actively taken to avoid it.

As most hypertensive people have only mildly elevated blood pressures, and complain of no symptoms, they are not likely to present to hospital specialists. The hospital-based services are, therefore, in no position to influence the problem of the rule of halves. The detection and management of millions of hypertensives (up to 20% of the adult population) must therefore be the responsibility of the primary health care system, with its increasing role in disease prevention and health promotion.

PRIMARY HEALTH CARE

The system for the delivery of primary health care varies from country to country. In some parts of the world, there is no systematic or established system for primary and preventive medical care, whereas a recognized speciality known as family medicine, or general practice, has been in place in some countries for many years. It is within the context of the primary health care team that the vast majority of hypertensives should be managed, so each nation has to adapt its health care resources to take on the challenge of managing millions of hypertensive patients. The pay-off is the prevention of deaths due to heart attack and stroke.

General practice

In the United Kingdom, every citizen has a named general practitioner (GP) who is responsible for the immediate care of a specified number of patients on his or her list. With the exception of accidents and emergencies, the individual patient has to go to the general practitioner as the first medical contact, and will only be referred on to a specialist if the GP considers it necessary. This system was established in 1947 and has undergone radical changes since that time, with a steady improvement in standards. General practice is now recognized as a speciality in its own right, with its own organized system of postgraduate training and qualifications. In addition, most GPs have now pooled their resources, and work in modern, purpose-built, community-based health centres or medical centres. With this trend towards group practices many individual GPs have tended to take up special interests, providing care for particular conditions for their whole group practice. There is increasing skill and expertise amongst the doctors in the primary health care system and this trend is to be encouraged.

Nurse practitioners

Perhaps the most significant development in the field of primary health care has been the establishment of the system of practice nurses. In many primary health care teams, the number of nurses has equalled the number of doctors. There is now increasing

Table 13.1
Estimated number of patients who are registered with an average British general practice who have a single casual blood pressure of 160/95 mm Hg or more. Figures in brackets denote the percentage of people in that age band with hypertension.

Age	Men	Women
0-19	7 (2%)	4 (1%)
20-39	25 (7%)	8 (3%)
40-59	70 (25%)	52 (18%)
60-79	66 (35%)	93 (37%)
80+	10 (50%)	26 (%)%)
total	178	183

evidence that appropriately trained nurses can take on the management of many chronic diseases such as diabetes mellitus, asthma and, of course, hypertension. In general, student nurse training has in the past tended to be geared mainly towards the care of acutely sick patients. Particular efforts are now necessary to organize suitable training schemes to enable nurses to fulfil an increasingly important role in the field of hypertension care. Nurses are ideally suited for counselling their patients on lifestyle changes which are now proven to aid in the prevention as well as in the treatment of all grades of hypertension. In addition, they have a major role to play in managing the other important risk factors for coronary heart disease.

Health maintenance organizations

There is an increasing trend in the USA for the development of a system of primary health care whereby the detection and management of chronic diseases and, where possible, their prevention is the main priority. These initiatives are carried out by Health Maintenance Organizations (HMOs) in a system not unlike that which exists in the UK. The speciality of family medicine is expanding in the USA; it differs from the system in the UK. in many respects but the objectives are similar. Private insurance schemes and occupational health programmes are intimately involved in primary prevention in the USA.

Primary health care in developing countries

Hypertension is emerging as a major cause of premature death in developing countries. With urbanization, blood pressures rise sharply and hypertension is now a common condition, particularly in the economically active segment of the population. This presents the health care systems of developing countries with a new problem, no less devastating than the epidemics of infectious disease and the problems of malnutrition. There is a need, therefore, to establish a system to deliver efficient primary health care in order to tackle the new epidemic of hypertension, diabetes mellitus, coronary heart disease and strokes. Each individual developing country must find its own solutions, but with the relatively small numbers of qualified doctors, it is likely that, as in the developed countries, there is an increasing role for various forms of paramedical staff, nurse practitioners and 'bare-foot doctors'. Again, training programmes are necessary in the skills of the detection and management of hypertension as well as its prevention, particularly with dietary and lifestyle advice.

SCREENING FOR HYPERTENSION

The symptomless nature of the earlier stages of hypertension means that some sort of screening initiative is necessary if hypertensive patients are to be detected and heart attacks and strokes prevented. The exact method to be employed depends on the primary health care system in individual countries. Most of the systems discussed below are relevant to the health care system in the developed countries but the basic principals are relevant for all nations.

Selective screening

A very strong case has been made for the selective screening of people who are at particular risk of developing the vascular complications of hypertension.

Family history

It should be the responsibility of patients as well as doctors to seek out symptomless relatives of those people who have been diagnosed as having hypertension or its complications, particularly heart attack and stroke. Many of these relatives will have raised blood pressure themselves and may benefit from antihypertensive treatment. Similarly, such patients should be screened to detect familial hyperlipidaemia. These high risk individuals need active counselling if they are to avoid the same fate as their unhealthy family members.

Previous complications

Patients who have already suffered a vascular complication of hypertension have a very high risk of recurrence. Second strokes can be prevented if blood pressure is controlled on a long-term basis. People who have already sustained a myocardial infarct need very active care. There is abundant evidence that heart attack recurrence can be reduced with active drug treatment using beta-adrenergic receptor blockers or verapamil, even if the patient is normotensive. Similarly, the management of hyperlipidaemia even at this late stage is definitely beneficial and smoking cessation is still worthwhile. Long-term low dose aspirin is of proven benefit in survivors of heart attack.

Diabetes mellitus

There is increasing awareness that in diabetic patients, the height of the blood pressure is often more important than the severity of the glucose intolerance. All diabetics should have regular blood pressure checks (Chapter 14).

Systemic diseases

The presence of hypertension substantially worsens the prognosis in a great many unrelated medical conditions and all patients with collagen vascular diseases, endocrine abnormalities and renal diseases need regular screening for hypertension (see Chapter 14).

Pregnancy

Another high risk group are pregnant women where hypertension remains an important cause of perinatal and maternal mortality. Here the efficient detection and management of high blood pressure is already an integral part of good routine obstetric care (see Chapter 16). The rest of the medical profession have a lot to learn from this.

Mass screening

The so-called 'well population screening' of fit populations is an emotive issue. Screening alone is not enough; there must also be efficient follow-up of abnormalities detected. Mass screening using mobile screening units is an efficient means of recruiting patients for clinical trials, but obviously if this is only a one-off exercise, it cannot solve an ongoing long-term problem.

Occupational screening

Screening of employees clearly has its place but this is available only to a minority of the population, mainly men who are employed in large firms or industries. There are also problems of confidentiality of clinical information, and usually industrial medical officers do not organize follow-up or drug treatment of chronic medical conditions.

Medical insurance companies

Private medical insurance has not in the UK addressed the problem of the early detection and management of cardiovascular risk factors even though this may prove cost-effective. In the USA and elsewhere the insurance industry has developed various forms of screening programmes and thus made an important contribution to the detection and management of hypertension and other coronary risk factors.

Casual screening

The provision of blood pressure measurement equipment and staff in supermarkets, department stores and public places can make only a small impact without follow-up and treatment. There is evidence that casual screening programmes such as these tend to attract hypertensive patients who are already diagnosed; people whose pressures have never been measured tend to ignore them. Increased public health education may alter this tendency but the system is certainly not ideal at present.

Screening the primary health care system

In developed countries, more than 75% of the adult population see a doctor for some reason at least once over a period of three years, and this almost invariably occurs in the context of primary health care. The methods to be used to screen for hypertension in primary care must vary from country to country but the system described below has the potential to detect almost all cases of hypertension and is adaptable for differing health care delivery systems.

In an ideal world, every person from childhood upwards would have his or her blood pressure measured as a routine procedure. Screening people below the age of about twenty would, however, yield relatively few hypertensive cases. Furthermore, the benefits of screening and intervention in very mild hypertension in childhood and adolescence are unknown.

Screening all people over the age of eighty would produce a very large number of abnormalities, but this would be in a group of patients in whom the benefits of

therapy of mild hypertension are less certain.

A reasonable compromise is for case detection programmes to be instituted for everyone between the ages of twenty and eighty. This represents about 1500 examinees in an average general practice in Britain, where there are about 2000 people on each general practitioner's list. Of those examinees about 20% (300 people) would have blood pressures above 160/95 mmH (Table 13.1). All such individuals need rechecking, and in many, blood pressures will fall. Only if blood pressures remain above this level after rechecking on four occasions should drug therapy be considered. Very severe hypertension is rare in general practice but clearly, when it is present, more urgent action is necessary.

Opportunistic screening

This system, which has been employed in many countries, relies on the observation that most people seek a medical consultation at least once in three years. This represents an ideal time to arrange for screening for hypertension as well as other symptomless medical conditions. In women, cervical cytology and breast examination can be organized at the same time.

The term 'opportunistic screening' implies that the doctor takes the opportunity provided by the patient's attendance to do routine checks. By this method, 75–80% of the population can be screened with no special efforts, appointments or clinics. Suitably trained nurses are probably the best people to conduct these routine tests and to discuss with the patients their lifestyles, cooking habits and perceived health problems. The system has proved workable: it can be ongoing and appropriate follow-up is easy to arrange (Fig. 13.1).

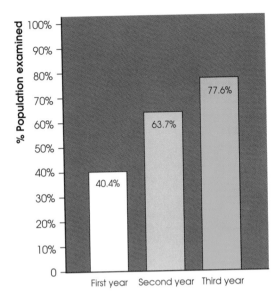

Figure 13.1
Proportion of eligible population examined by opportunistic screening in general practice in Scotland.

to continue the programme to include individuals who become eligible for screening over the ensuing years. For this purpose, the doctor should ideally have an age/sex register of the patients on the practice list. Patients reaching the age of twenty can thus be summoned for screening. One general practitioner in England sends his patients a birthday card together with an appointment for a blood pressure and general health check.

Moving house

In the UK, when an individual moves to live in a new area, he or she will usually visit the local health centre and join the list of that practice. In time his NHS medical records will be sent to his new doctor. If the patient has not undergone appropriate routine checks with his previous general practitioner, or if an abnormality was detected, the new primary health care team should arrange for routine checking as described above.

Appointments for eligible examinees

A faster way is to arrange appointments for all patients to have a routine blood pressure check. This will require extra paperwork and time spent on documentation, postage and screening clinics. However, it can achieve a complete screen over a period of a few months and is useful as a system to initiate a well population screening service and can take place at the same time as opportunistic screening.

Screening of newly eligible patients

Once the backlog of previously unscreened patients has been examined, it is important

Medical records

Efficient medical records are mandatory if patients are to receive good medical care. The advent of 'user-friendly' computerized record systems can greatly help in the detection, assessment and follow-up of hypertensive patients.

The creation of age/sex registers of all patients attached to an individual health centre and from this the creation of diagnostic lists or disease registers can greatly help in the management of patients and can be useful in creating an audit system.

However, even if a computerized system is not available, primary health care can be delivered with equal efficiency. In Britain,

HYPERTENSION RECORD CARD

SURNAME _____ DATE OF BIRTH _____

FORENAMES _____

ADDRESS _____

CONCURRENT COMPLAINTS _____

CONCOMITANT DRUGS _____

INITIAL SUPINE BP _____

RISK FACTORS		FACTORS IN TREATMENT ASSESSMENT (SIDE EFFECTS OR PRE-EXISTING)		INVESTIGATIONS CARRIED OUT		ADVICE GIVEN
SMOKER		WHEEZE		RBC		SMOKING
FAMILY HISTORY		BREATHLESSNESS		WBC		DIET
ALCOHOL		GOUTY ATTACKS		Hb		WEIGHT
EXERCISE		CHEST PAINS		Bl. SUGAR		EXERCISE
		IMPOTENCE		UREA		LIFESTYLE
		DEPRESSION		URIC ACID		ALCOHOL
OTHER VASCULAR DISEASE		COLD EXTREMITIES		LIPIDS		BOOKLET
		FATIGUE		ECG		
DIABETIC				IVP		
PERSONALITY TYPE				LFT		
				URINE		

	RETURN VISITS		
	DATE	BP	TREATMENT OR COMMENTS
PILL			
COMPLIANCE			
OVER 35			
PREVIOUS JAUNDICE			

Figure 13.2

Example of a hypertension record card.

DATE		4/6/94	16/6/94	20/7/94	22/8/94	7/9/94	2/10/94	7/12/94			
B.P.1		176/102	172/104	160/92	158/84	162/92	148/82	148/84			
PULSE		96	92	68	56	76	72	76			
B.P.2		172/100	172/102	154/88	162/86	152/88	142/80	142/76			
URINE		Nad									
WEIGHT	kg st lbs	84.0	83.5	83.0	84.2	85.6	84.2	82.9			
DRUG 1	Propranolol	/	start 40mgx2	40mg x2	STOP						
DRUG 2	Amlodipine	/			start 5mg	10mg	10mg	10mg			
DRUG 3		/									
DRUG 4		/									
DRUG 5		/									
DRUG 6		/									
INVESTIGATIONS		Cholest 6.7						urea 4.6			
NEXT VISIT		2/52	4/52	4/52	2/52	4/52	2/12	3/12			
DOCTOR'S SIGNATURE		DW	AB	DW	AB	DW	AB	DW			

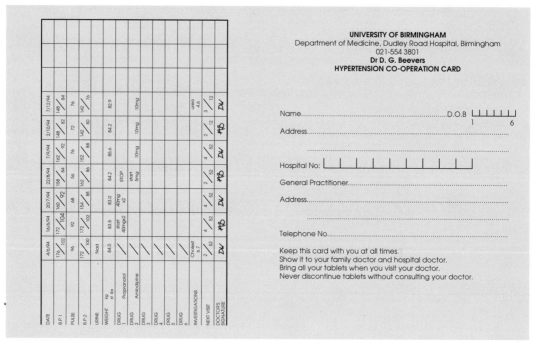

UNIVERSITY OF BIRMINGHAM
Department of Medicine, Dudley Road Hospital, Birmingham
021-554 3801
Dr D. G. Beevers
HYPERTENSION CO-OPERATION CARD

Name...D.O.B ⌐ ⌐ ⌐ ⌐ ⌐ ⌐ ⌐
                                                                                                        1   6
Address...

....

Hospital No: ⌐ ⌐ ⌐ ⌐ ⌐ ⌐ ⌐ ⌐ ⌐ ⌐ ⌐

General Practitioner..

Address...

....

Telephone No...

Keep this card with you at all times.
Show it to your family doctor and hospital doctor.
Bring all your tablets when you visit your doctor.
Never discontinue tablets without consulting your doctor.

Figure 13.3
Example of a blood pressure cooperation card.

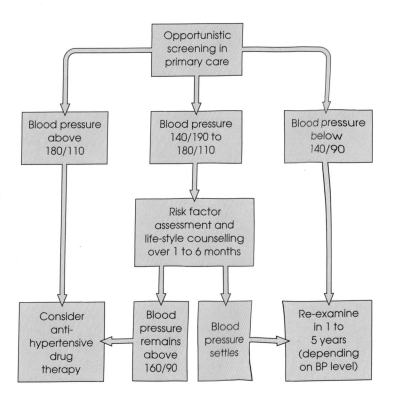

Figure 13.4
Suggested action in primary care during opportunistic screening programmes.

the general practitioner records system (the Lloyd George Envelope) is adaptable and can be used to draw attention visually to the records of patients requiring screening or, following screening, needing special care (Fig. 13.2).

Any type of sticker, or protruding section of an inserted card, renders individual patients' records readily identifiable. These can be used to draw attention to important diagnoses, not only of hypertension, and to identify patients due for blood pressure checking.

The system has been used in many practices and it is simple, cheap and effective.

The principle described here can be adapted for use in any health care system anywhere, so it is relevant to all countries. In view of the fact that computerized systems can on occasions break down, some sort of manual back-up system is probably desirable anyway.

Patient-held records

With increasingly mobile communities, it is sometimes useful for patients to have a copy of their medical records, in which blood pressure and the other cardiovascular risk factors can be recorded and follow-up data added (Fig. 13.3). This system can be used also to aid in the shared care of hypertensive patients who attend a hospital-based blood pressure clinic as well as their general practitioner. There is evidence that when patients are fully informed about their blood pressure and have an accurate list of the drugs they are meant to be taking, then compliance with medical advice is improved.

Blood pressure screening and subsequent action

When blood pressure is measured at first screening, there are three possible outcomes, i.e. triage (Fig. 13.4). The pressure may be entirely normal (diastolic pressure below 90 mmHg and systolic blood pressure below 140 Hg) so no action is necessary for some years. However, counselling on the avoidance of hypertension and cardiovascular disease may be worthwhile. The second possibility is that the pressure is found to be so high (diastolic BP of 110 mmHg or more, systolic BP 180 mmHg or more) that action is necessary more or less immediately. The large intermediate group represents patients who have mildly elevated blood pressures (140/90 to 180/110), many of which will settle on rechecking. This group needs very careful assessment in order to avoid over-treatment.

Mild hypertension

The guidelines of the United States Joint National Committee and the British Hypertension Society were both published in 1993. They strongly advocate the careful assessment of mild hypertensives before drug therapy is initiated.

There is evidence that whilst blood pressures fall on rechecking, this fall becomes less after the fourth visit, when pressures tend to bottom out. These follow-up visits, best organized by a primary health care nurse, can also be used as an opportunity to provide the patient with counselling about important dietary changes which may be necessary, together, where relevant, with advice on smoking cessation and alcohol moderation. Only if the diastolic blood pressure remains above 90 mmHg or the systolic pressure remains above 160 mmHg at the fourth visit, should blood pressure-lowering drugs be considered.

The schemes for reducing blood pressure are dealt with in detail in Chapter 12. The majority of hypertensive patients can be managed very adequately in primary care and in only a minority will blood pressure remain uncontrolled.

Investigations in general practice

The methods for investigating hypertensive patients are discussed in detail in Chapters 7 and 8. In general practice, all patients who require drug therapy should undergo routine first line investigations. Urine testing is mandatory, and a single non-fasting blood test should be taken for estimation of blood glucose and serum levels of cholesterol (including HDL), urea, creatinine, sodium, potassium, calcium, urate and gamma glutamyl transferase. In addition, all patients should have a simple 12 lead ECG. Chest X-rays are not particularly useful unless the radiologist reports the cardiothoracic ratio (CTR).

Audit

The marked improvements in medical records which have taken place over the last

10 years with the increased availability of computers now provides the clinician with an opportunity to conduct clinical audit. Audit should ideally be on going and the lessons learnt should lead to a feedback in order to modify clinical practice. All clinicians should, therefore, establish a system to investigate how effective they have been in screening their patients for hypertension and to ensure that all cases have undergone the appropriate investigations. Furthermore, it is important to check that all hypertensive patients have their blood pressures controlled with diastolic pressures below 90 mmHg and all systolic pressures below 160 mmHg. When audit demonstrates that this is not being achieved, clinical practice should be modified and, where relevant, made more efficient. Audit, or clinical enquiry, is now an integral part of good medical care and, of course, it also has a major pay-off in the generation of research data. In many countries, major randomized controlled drug trials of hypertensive treatment have been conducted in general practice. Sadly, however, apart from this, the impact of primary care on research into the epidemiology and treatment of hypertension has been disappointing. There is a great potential with the use of audit for an expansion of general practitioner input into research on the nature of hypertension and its response to treatment.

damage, e.g. proteinuria, renal failure or angina, which requires detailed hospital-based investigation. In addition, mild hypertensives under the age of 40 should probably be referred in order to undergo detailed investigations, even if the first line tests are unhelpful. Finally, if blood pressure remains uncontrolled despite adequate non-pharmacological and pharmacological therapy, then specialist referral is necessary.

CONCLUSIONS

Hypertension is a disease which should principally be detected and managed within the context of primary health care. Only a minority of cases require specialist referral. The efficient and effective control of blood pressure in general practice provides a great challenge but the practitioner should be aware that well controlled hypertension can bring about a 40% reduction in strokes and a 20–30% reduction in heart attack in hypertensive patients. This being so, when these events do occur, the clinician should question within the context of medical audit whether his management of the patient has been adequate.

REFERRAL FOR SPECIALIST ADVICE

About 10% of hypertensive patients need referral for specialist advice. These include those cases where first line investigations suggest the presence of some underlying cause for the raised blood pressure and also cases where there is evidence of end-organ

REFERENCES

Barber JH, Beevers DG, Fife R et al. Blood pressure screening and supervision in general practice. Br Med J 1979; i:843–6.

Coope JR. ABC of blood pressure management: management in general practice. Br Med J 1981; 282:1380–2.

Coope JR, Warrender TS. Randomised trial of treatment of hypertension in elderly patients in primary care. *Br Med J* 1986; **293**:1145–51.

The fifth report of the Joint National Committee on detection, elevation and treatment of high blood pressure (JNC V). *Arch Intern Med* 1993;**153**:154–3.

Fullard E, Fowler G, Gray M. Facilitating prevention in primary care. *Br Med J* 1984;**289**:1585–7.

Kurj KH, Haines AP. Detection and management of hypertension in general practice in north-west London. *Br Med J* 1984; **288**:903–5.

Sever P, Beevers DG, Bulpitt CJ et al. Management guidelines in essential hypertension: report of the second working party of the British Hypertension Society. *Br Med J* 1993; **306**:983–7.

4

Section Four

14 HYPERTENSION WITH OTHER DISEASES

BACKGROUND

No two hypertensive patients are alike, and very few of them resemble those cases which are included in the long-term randomized trials discussed in Chapter 9. In reality, patients differ in the severity of their hypertension, the frequency of pre-existing vascular complications of high blood pressure, and the presence of concomitant medical conditions which themselves substantially influence clinical management. By contrast, trial participants tend to be relatively low risk individuals, who are fit enough and have sufficient motivation to enter long-term studies. Clinical practice is often rather different. In this chapter, we discuss the impact of other diagnoses on the investigation and management of hypertension. First, we cover the presence of pre-existing vascular diseases which may in part be the consequences of the raised blood pressure; then we discuss the importance of related vascular risk factors, like diabetes mellitus and hyperlipidaemia, and their impact on antihypertensive therapy; finally we discuss the presence of important but unrelated medical conditions. There are practically no medical specialities where the presence of hypertension does not substantially influence the outlook, and all specialists need to be aware of the impact of hypertension on their clinical decision making. Furthermore, the frequency and importance of other medical conditions increases with advancing age as does the prevalence of hypertension itself.

HYPERTENSION AND ITS VASCULAR COMPLICATIONS

Hypertension and heart disease

As high blood pressure is an important risk factor for coronary heart disease, it is hardly surprising that many patients have cardiac damage particularly as they get older. Patients may have other causes for heart disease at the same time, including rheumatic heart disease, cor pulmonale or a cardiomyopathy. The beta-blockers and, more recently, the angiotensin converting enzyme (ACE) inhibitors are themselves used in the treatment of some forms of heart disease in patients with normal blood pressure as well as hypertensives.

Angina pectoris

Many hypertensive patients have anginal pain. This is only partly related to an increased tendency to develop coronary atheroma. Hypertensives with marked left ventricular enlargement may develop lateral ECG ischaemic ST-T changes in leads V4 to V6 due to relative ischaemia (sometimes called 'strain') where the cardiac enlargement is not accompanied by an appropriate increase in vascular supply. Many hypertensive patients with severe or unstable angina are found on coronary angiography to have very little coronary artery narrowing.

The effective lowering of blood pressure by any class of antihypertensive drug does reduce the severity and frequency of angina pectoris. However, the beta-blockers and the calcium channel blockers have specific anti-anginal effects, in addition to their antihypertensive effects. Beta-blockers remain the first choice but where these are ineffective, or contraindicated, the calcium blockers (nifedipine or amlodipine) are reasonable second line drugs. Both verapamil and diltiazem are also effective. If angina still persists, then long-acting oral nitrates (e.g. isosorbide mononitrate) should be added. All patients with angina should be assessed carefully, usually with an exercise ECG. If blood pressure is well controlled and angina persists, coronary surgery or angioplasty should be considered.

Myocardial infarction

All patients, and thus all hypertensive patients, who sustain a heart attack should be given a beta-blocker in addition to low dose aspirin unless there are contraindications. Both of these have been shown to reduce the reinfarction rate over the ensuing years. One recent report suggests that if beta-blockers are contraindicated, then a similar degree of secondary prevention can be achieved with verapamil. There is now increasing evidence that the ACE inhibitors are also beneficial in post-infarction patients, particularly if they have poor left ventricular function; not only is clinical cardiac failure prevented but there appears also to be a lower rate of reinfarction.

The above comments are relevant to all patients following a heart attack whether or not they are also hypertensive. If the patient is hypertensive, the clinician should be aware of some other factors which influence diagnosis and management.

First, the incidence of silent or symptomless myocardial infarction is greater in hypertensives compared with normotensives and the prognosis for hypertensives following a heart attack is bad.

Second, following myocardial infarction, blood pressure may fall so that the diagnosis of hypertension may be missed. Frequently, at follow-up blood pressures rise again. The clinician must be aware, therefore, that a patient whose pressures were normal or even low whilst in the coronary care unit may have hypertension which may reappear after recovery.

A third and important point is that the thiazide diuretics used in the treatment of hypertension may cause hypokalaemia and that heart attack patients with low serum potassium levels have a higher risk of arrhythmias and sudden death. A measurement of serum potassium at first presentation is mandatory in all heart attack patients, along with an assay of the cardiac enzymes.

On long-term follow-up of hypertensive patients, blood pressure must be controlled, and attention should be paid to concomitant risk factors such as hyperlipidaemia and cigarette smoking. Even at this late stage, correction of both of these risk factors has been proven to be of benefit.

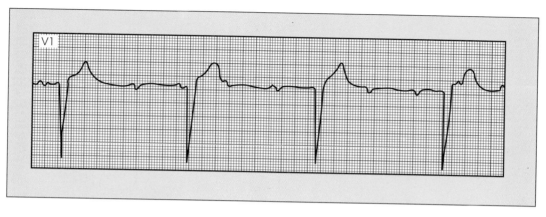

Figure 14.1
ECG showing complete heartblock.

Arrhythmias

The presence of any form of heart block is an absolute contraindication to beta-blockade or verapamil therapy (Fig. 14.1). The use of these two drugs together is particularly dangerous in post-infarction patients. The diagnosis of atrial fibrillation should raise the possibility of this being due to, or aggravated by, other medical conditions like hyperthyroidism or alcohol abuse, particularly if the fibrillation is resistant to digoxin. Atrial fibrillation can, on rare occasions, be due to raised blood pressure alone. It is now known that all patients with atrial fibrillation should be anticoagulated with warfarin, as even in the absence of mitral valve disease there is an increased risk of cerebral embolism. Most patients should be returned to sinus rhythm if necessary by cardioversion.

Heart failure

The ACE inhibitors are the only class of drug which have been shown convincingly to prolong life in patients with heart failure. The heart failure may be due to coronary heart disease or, rarely, to severe hypertension alone (Fig. 14.2). Other causes of heart failure and particularly alcoholic cardiomyopathy should be considered in hypertensive patients. Beta-blocking drugs and verapamil are absolutely contraindicated and there is an increasing view that all grades of heart failure should be treated by ACE inhibition. This must be introduced with caution, if necessary with a test dose of captopril 6.25 mg. Acute and very severe heart failure may rarely be due to very severe hypertension alone (e.g. diastolic pressures around 150 mmHg). If the blood pressure is lowered, the heart failure may improve. Sodium nitroprusside by infusion in a dose of 0.02 to 0.5 mg per minute can provide very accurate minute to minute control of blood pressure whilst avoiding precipitate and dangerous episodes of hypotension. In less severe cases, oral nifedipine may be used.

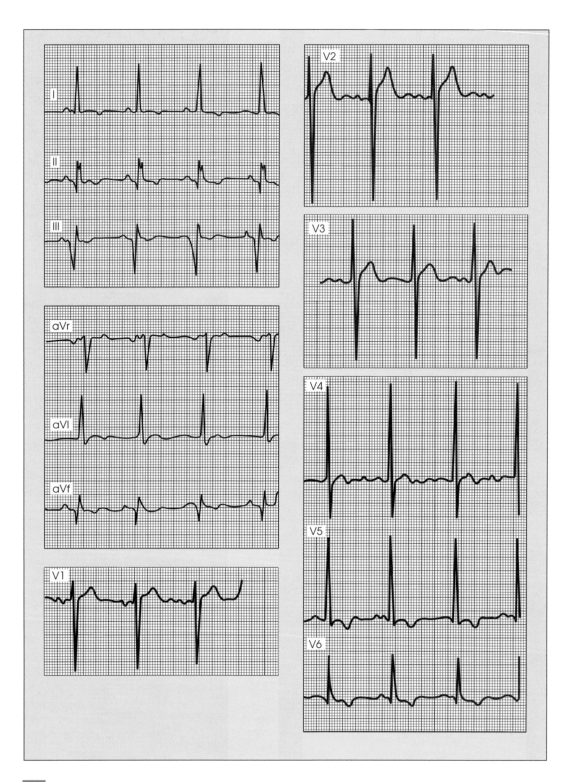

Hypertension and stroke

Whilst strokes are four times less common than heart attacks in middle-aged hypertensives, the incidence is roughly equal in the elderly. Antihypertensive treatment is particularly effective in preventing strokes in all age groups.

Stroke recurrence

In a hypertensive patient who has sustained a stroke, the mechanism is much more likely to be a cerebral infarction than a cerebral haemorrhage. A CT scan to confirm the diagnosis and differentiate between infarction and haemorrhage is desirable.

Immediate or rapid blood pressure reduction is dangerous. Following a stroke, cerebral autoregulation is broken down so that falls in blood pressure directly cause falls in cerebral perfusion. Antihypertensive medication is best withheld until the recovery phase when the patient is ambulant unless the blood pressure is very high (diastolic pressure 120 mmHg or more), when oral beta-blockade with atenolol in low dose may be considered. In stroke survivors, on a long-term basis the adequate control of moderate to severe hypertension is associated with a major reduction of the frequency of stroke recurrence (Fig. 14.3). If the cerebral lesion can be proved by CT

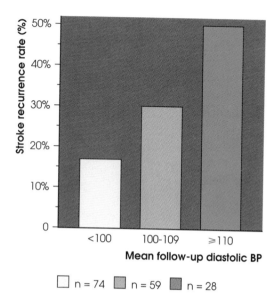

Figure 14.3
Stroke recurrence rates in relation to control of blood pressure in moderate to severe hypertension.

scanning to be an infarction, concomitant aspirin 75 mg daily should be prescribed. There is also a close relationship between strokes and cigarette smoking and heavy alcohol consumption, so, where appropriate, sympathetic constructive counselling is necessary.

Subarachnoid haemorrhage

There is a close association between hypertension and subarachnoid haemorrhage. Cigarette smoking is also a major risk factor. All patients need careful assessment to exclude the diagnosis of underlying autosomal dominant polycystic kidney disease (PKD). A detailed family history may reveal

Figure 14.2
ECG taken from a hypertensive patient with uncontrolled severe hypertension which shows gross left ventricular hypertrophy on an old inferior myocardial infarction.

relatives with renal failure or subarachnoid haemorrhage. The diagnosis of PKD is best made non-invasively with renal ultrasound scan.

Once the diagnosis of subarachnoid haemorrhage is confirmed, either by CT scan of the head or lumbar puncture, it is now known to be helpful to prescribe nimodipine in order to reduce or prevent spasm of the surrounding cerebral vessels. If the blood pressure remains high, a beta receptor blocker should be added in. If a berry aneurysm is found, neurosurgical treatment is mandatory. On a long-term basis, careful control of blood pressure is very important to prevent recurrence.

Peripheral vascular disease

Peripheral vascular disease is closely related to blood pressure, serum cholesterol levels and cigarette smoking. There is, as yet, little evidence from clinical trials that any drug therapy favourably influences the outcome, and some antihypertensive drugs have side-effects which make things worse (e.g., thiazides may further raise cholesterol and beta-blockers cause cold extremities).

Abdominal aortic aneurysm

There is a close association between hypertension and abdominal aneurysms, and some clinicians recommend the routine screening of all elderly symptomless hypertensive patients by abdominal ultrasound. If an aneurysm with a diameter greater than 6 cm is identified, elective surgical repair is worthwhile, as this procedure carries a lower mortality than an emergency repair of a ruptured aneurysm.

Claudication

All hypertensive patients and particularly those with calf pain should be examined for absent foot pulses and a femoral bruit. Many will also be found to have undiagnosed atheromatous renal artery stenosis (even if they are not hypertensive) so overenthusiastic drug therapy with large doses of ACE inhibitors can be hazardous. The calcium channel blockers may help to reduce the severity of claudication. Diuretics do not make symptoms worse but in high dose may cause glucose intolerance and raise serum lipid levels. Beta-blockers may worsen the symptoms in patients with claudication, as well as causing cold extremities. However, they may have little influence on claudication distance, even though they do reduce cardiac output. There are case reports of gangrene induced by beta-blockers in patients with severe arterial disease.

Raynaud's phenomenon

Although Raynaud's phenomenon is not associated with hypertension, where present it may be worsened by the use of beta-blockers. In such patients, beta-blockers are best avoided altogether, but, if they are considered necessary, a beta-blocker which has intrinsic sympathomimetic activity is the most sensible choice as it will cause less reduction in cardiac output.

If a hypertensive patient has Raynaud's phenomenon, then a diagnosis of underlying scleroderma should be considered. There may be skin thickening, telangiectasia, subcutaneous calcinosis, a tight fissured appearance around the mouth and possibly symptoms of oesophageal involvement. In scleroderma, once the blood pressure becomes raised and there is renal involvement, the prognosis is poor as renal function

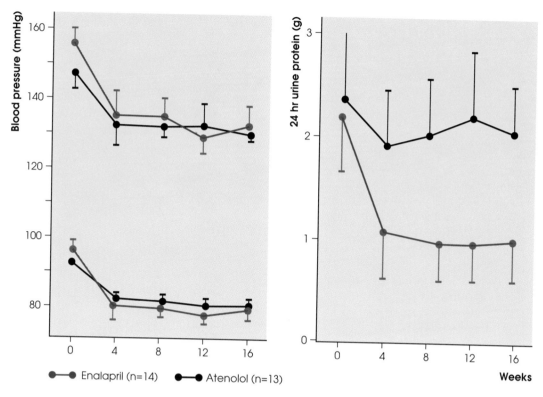

Figure 14.4

Comparison of atenolol and enalapril in patients with non–diabetic renal disease.

deteriorates rapidly. There is some evidence that the ACE inhibitor captopril is effective in delaying further renal damage so this must be regarded as the first choice, possibly in conjunction with a calcium channel blocker.

Renal disease

As stated in Chapter 7, patients with haematuria, proteinuria or renal impairment need detailed investigation. Many patients will be found to have intrinsic renal disease, including polycystic disease, IgA nephropathy, proliferative glomerulonephritis, polyarteritis and related conditions. However, a significant number of patients will be found to have no evidence of intrinsic renal disease and are considered to have hypertensive nephrosclerosis.

Intrinsic renal disease

Whilst raised blood pressure is not always found in patients with intrinsic renal disease,

201

where present it substantially influences the prognosis both for the vascular complications of hypertension and for progression of renal impairment. Until recently, however, the evidence that antihypertensive therapy prevented progression of renal impairment was not impressive. However, there is now increasing evidence that good control of blood pressure slows down the deterioration of renal function in some cases. Two recent studies have compared an ACE inhibitor with other classes of antihypertensive drugs. Whilst there were no important differences in the antihypertensive effects, ACE inhibition caused highly significant reductions in either microproteinuria or macroproteinuria (Fig. 14.4) and preliminary reports now provide evidence of preservation of renal function. The evidence in favour of ACE inhibition in diabetics with renal impairment is also impressive.

Chronic renal failure

Most patients with chronic renal failure are hypertensive and the raised blood pressure sets up a vicious cycle, causing further renal damage. The patient is rendered clinically unwell, with anaemia, metabolic bone disease, pulmonary oedema and the general systemic effects of uraemia. At this late stage, dietary protein restriction and control of blood pressure may delay but not prevent the otherwise inexorable trend towards end-stage renal failure. Detailed investigation is still worthwhile, however, in order to exclude any underlying vasculitis, and if renal artery stenosis is present, its correction, either by surgery or angioplasty, may help to control blood pressure and preserve some renal function.

In chronic renal failure, those drugs which are excreted by the kidney need to be prescribed in much reduced doses. The hydrophilic beta-blockers, like atenolol, are frequently given on alternate days and the doses of all ACE inhibitors need to be reduced. The ACE inhibitors can be hazardous if the patient becomes dehydrated, as they block any compensatory rise in plasma angiotensin II levels. The dihydropyridine calcium channel blockers are effective when used with care. When there is sodium and water retention, loop diuretics like frusemide or bumetanide are used and large doses may be necessary.

Chronic dialysis

Once the patient is on chronic dialysis, either haemodialysis or chronic ambulatory peritoneal dialysis, hypertension is almost universal. Furthermore, the incidence of heart attacks and strokes is much higher than would be expected on the basis of the height of the blood pressure or the presence of other risk factors. In most patients, blood pressure can be controlled relatively easily by removing salt and water during dialysis. Between dialyses, restriction of salt and water can help to control the pressure, but in many patients blood pressure-lowering drugs may be necessary.

In a small minority of patients in end-stage renal failure, the remnant chronically damaged kidneys substantially aggravate the hypertension. In these patients, the renin–angiotensin system becomes over-sensitive to sodium depletion. At the time of dialysis, plasma angiotensin II concentrations rise to very high levels and there is an intense vasoconstrictor-mediated rise in blood pressure. This rise in pressure can, in part, be controlled by drugs which either suppress renin disease (beta-blockers) or inhibit the generation of angiotensin II (the ACE inhibitors). If control of blood pressure remains difficult, bilateral nephrectomy is very occasionally necessary. Thereafter, the blood pressure becomes mainly volume dependent and can be controlled by dialysis alone, or with low doses of calcium channel blockers or beta-blockers.

Erythropoetin

The recent advent of erythropoetin for the correction of the normochromic normocytic anaemia of chronic renal failure has provided further problems in the control of blood pressure. The mechanisms of the erythropoetin-induced rise in blood pressure are complex. The rise in haematocrit as the anaemia improves may lead to a reduction of effective renal plasma flow, but also erythropoetin may have some properties in common with renin or angiotensin, acting as a direct vasoconstrictor. Whatever the mechanisms, when erythropoetin is given, the blood pressure should be carefully monitored and controlled with drugs if necessary.

Renal transplantation

Hypertension develops in around 75% of patients who have undergone renal transplantation and the reasons for this are complex. There is evidence that hypertension tends to follow the transplanted kidney. Hypertension is commoner in the recipient if the donor had hypertension or had a strong family history of hypertension. This finding has important implications for our understanding of the aetiology of essential hypertension and reflects the results of cross-transplantation experiments in rats.

In the early postoperative period, raised blood pressure may be due to the immediate host transplant rejection reaction, with the development of renal damage and an increase in renin and angiotensin release.

This hypertension may partly come under control with immunosuppressive therapy. There may, however, also be a volume expansion component to the raised blood pressure because there may have been pre-existing fluid overload prior to the transplant and if the transplant itself is rejected, it fails to excrete sodium and water. This problem is further compounded by sodium and water retention caused by the high doses of corticosteroids used to suppress rejection.

The advent of cyclosporin has been a major advance in the prevention of transplant rejection, but this also can raise blood pressure. Cyclosporin is also associated with hypertension following bone marrow and other non-renal transplants.

Following renal transplantation, raised blood pressure may be further aggravated by excess renin release from the host's own failed kidneys and sometimes bilateral remnant nephrectomy is helpful. On a longer term basis, transplant recipients have a greatly increased tendency to develop generalized arteriosclerosis. Atheromatous renal artery stenosis is common in transplanted kidneys and this can contribute to the development of hypertension. Occasionally the anastomosis of transplanted renal artery becomes stenosed, causing severe elevation of blood pressure.

The accurate control of blood pressure is important following renal transplantation. All the main classes of antihypertensive drugs may be used, but renal failure may develop and doses of drugs may need to be adjusted.

DIABETES MELLITUS

The relationship between hypertension and the two forms of diabetes (type 1, insulin-dependent diabetes mellitus or IDDM and

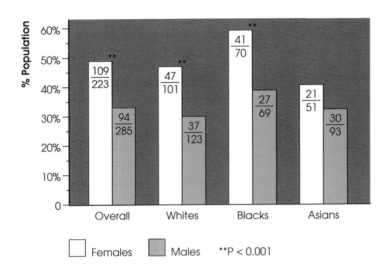

Figure 14.5
The prevalence of hypertension in white, black and Asian diabetics.

type II, non-insulin-dependent or NIDDM) is a close one, but this topic has, sadly, been neglected until recently.

Cardiovascular risk factors in diabetes

Hypertension is present in around 20% of patients with IDDM and in between 30% to 50% of patients with NIDDM. In patients of Afro-Caribbean origin and Indian subcontinental origin, the prevalence of raised blood pressure in NIDDM is around 60% (Fig. 14.5).

It is also important to note that hyperlipidaemia occurs in NIDDM at about twice the frequency of that seen in the general population. Furthermore, cigarette smoking is also common. This means that all three cardiovascular risk factors tend to be very common in diabetics and frequently they assume greater prognostic importance than the severity of the diabetes itself. The slavish

obsession with controlling the blood sugar, particularly in NIDDM, whilst ignoring or not even measuring the other cardiovascular risk factors, has been a feature of many cattle-market style diabetic clinics in the past, and patients have suffered accordingly.

The aetiology of hypertension in diabetes

The pathophysiology of the association between hypertension and diabetes has been the focus of much research. It is probable that the mechanisms differ in IDDM versus NIDDM although there may be some overlap. In IDDM, where plasma insulin levels are low on a long-term basis, diabetic microangiopathy develops and the raised blood pressure is mostly related to the development of diabetic nephrosclerosis with activation of the renin–angiotensin system and a largely vasoconstrictor- mediated hypertension. There may also be a small contribution from sodium and water retention although this is not apparent when estimating total exchangeable sodium or body water. By contrast, NIDDM is more closely related to volume expansion with increased total exchangeable sodium. Plasma renin and angiotensin levels are not usually high. This sodium retention is thought to be related to the degree of hyperinsulinaemia in NIDDM. In older patients with NIDDM, particularly if they are also cigarette smokers, there may be extensive large vessel atheroma and so atheromatous renal artery stenosis may contribute to the hypertension and renal impairment. Most patients with NIDDM are also obese, and even after correction for the tendency to overestimate blood pressure in obese arms, there remains a strong association between diabetes and hypertension.

Obesity itself is associated with hyperinsulinaemia which may itself be a factor in the development of raised blood pressure. The sulphonylurea drugs used in the treatment of NIDDM themselves cause weight gain and may aggravate the hypertension.

Reaven's syndrome or syndrome X

A unifying hypothesis to explain the concordance of hypertension, obesity, hypertriglyceridaemia and glucose intolerance has been put forward. It implies a prime role for insulin resistance and, therefore, hyperinsulinaemia in the elevation of blood pressure. The mechanisms are uncertain but insulin itself is a vascular proliferative factor and furthermore, under certain circumstances, insulin causes fluid retention.

It was demonstrated many years ago, that non-obese, non-diabetic essential hypertensives have modest impairment of glucose tolerance so that they are mildly insulin resistant. The same phenomenon is seen in

non-diabetic, non-hypertensive, obese individuals with a strong family history of hypertension. Could insulin resistance, therefore, be a final common pathway for the development of hypertension? However, if insulin resistance is an important mechanism in hypertension, then drugs which worsen insulin resistance would be expected to raise rather than lower blood pressure. This is clearly not so; the thiazides and, to a lesser extent, the beta-blockers have 'adverse' effects on insulin resistance but are very effective in lowering blood pressure and preventing heart attacks and strokes. Manufacturers of the calcium channel blockers and the ACE inhibitors are keen to point out that these drugs have no effects on glucose tolerance, but it remains uncertain whether this is an important consideration. The biguanide antidiabetic drugs, which improve insulin sensitivity, have no antihypertensive properties.

Treating hypertension in insulin-dependent diabetes

In view of the very poor outlook in patients with IDDM once they have developed hypertension, it is generally considered desirable to lower the threshold for starting antihypertensive drug therapy, although there are no reliable randomized trials to prove this is beneficial. If the diastolic blood pressure exceeds 90 mmHg on four occasions, a few weeks apart, despite all of the non-pharmacological manoeuvres outlined in Chapter 10, then blood pressure-lowering drugs should be instituted. Thiazide diuretics are best avoided in view of their metabolic side-effects. The beta-blockers are generally safe but may cause problems in very 'brittle' diabetics with frequent episodes of insulin-induced hypoglycaemia. The non-cardioselective beta-blockers interfere with both the autonomic and metabolic responses to hypoglycaemia. For this reason, the cardioselective beta-blockers, atenolol or metoprolol, are preferred.

Clinical experience with the calcium channel blockers and the ACE inhibitors in diabetics is less extensive. Both classes of drug have no adverse metabolic effects on glucose or lipid levels and when used carefully they are safe. The ACE inhibitors may, in the long term, confer special advantages in some diabetics as long as they are used prudently (see below).

Treating hypertension in non-insulin-dependent diabetics

Patients with NIDDM tend to be obese and hyperlipidaemic. Particular efforts should be made, with intensive dietetic back-up, to control these additional risk factors whilst also attempting to control the blood glucose by non-pharmacological means. We deprecate the early use of the sulphonylurea drugs, particularly for only modest elevations of blood glucose, without intensive dietetic management first. There is no evidence from randomized trials that these agents confer any benefit to the patient, and they frequently worsen obesity.

Whilst there may be some volume expansion in patients with NIDDM, the thiazide diuretics, even in low dose, should be avoided in view of their metabolic side-effects.

The calcium channel blockers and ACE inhibitors are effective in patients with NIDDM. These drugs are particularly useful when used in combination. Beta-blockers are still used extensively in NIDDM and are specifically indicated in the patient who has angina pectoris or has previously sustained a myocardial infarction.

Proteinuria and microproteinuria

The impact of antihypertensive drugs on renal function in diabetic patients is the focus of much research. Until recently, there was scant evidence that treating the hypertension or the diabetes had any impact on renal function. Once renal damage was present, it became progressively worse until the patient developed end-stage renal failure requiring dialysis or transplantation.

Once proteinuria on dipstick testing is present, the outlook is poor and there is now evidence that the presence of microproteinuria is also predictive but at an earlier stage. Microproteinuria is said to be present if the urine albumen concentration is between 30 and 300 mg/l, i.e. below the limit of urine dipstick sensitivity.

Well conducted, randomized trials in diabetic patients with proteinuria have shown that ACE inhibitors cause a significant reduction in urinary albumen excretion. One study has furthermore demonstrated a slowing of the rate of deterioration of renal function (Fig. 14.6). The beta-blockers and the calcium channel blockers, whilst equally effective at lowering blood pressure, showed less impressive or no effects on microproteinuria. Studies are now appearing of the use of ACE inhibitors in diabetic patients with proteinuria but with normal blood pressure and preliminary results look encouraging.

The reason why ACE inhibition appears to confer added benefits over other drugs for the same reduction in blood pressure may be related to the fall in angiotensin II levels causing glomerular efferent arteriolar vasodilatation and a reduction in intraglomerular pressure.

There is now sufficient evidence to recommend the routine use of ACE inhibitors in all hypertensive diabetics or all diabetics with proteinuria or even micropro-

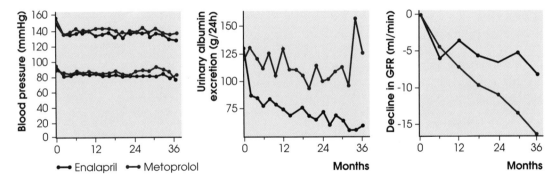

Figure 14.6
Comparison of enalapril and metoprolol in diabetic hypertensives with proteinuria.

teinuria. Further large-scale randomized controlled trials are necessary to prove that ACE inhibitors genuinely protect renal function on a long-term basis.

HYPERTENSION AND HYPERLIPIDAEMIA

This topic is covered in other chapters but is sufficiently important to merit special mention here. In a hypertensive patient, if hyperlipidaemia is also present, with high blood cholesterol levels and low HDL cholesterol levels, the risk of coronary heart disease is greatly increased.

Serum cholesterol levels of 8 mmol/l or more are seen in 8–10% of hypertensive patients (Fig. 14.7). Cholesterol levels above 6.5 mmol/l are seen in a further 20%. All hypertensive patients should be considered to be at high risk and have regular serum cholesterol testing. Dietetic treatment of hypertensive patients with raised or even

borderline serum cholesterol levels is mandatory. Cholesterol-lowering drugs (the fibrates or the HMG CoA reductase inhibitors) should be considered (preferably in conjunction with a lipidologist) if despite a low fat diet, the serum cholesterol remains above 8.0 mmol/l in high risk patients under 60 years of age.

Thiazide drugs and, to a lesser extent, the beta-blockers do worsen the plasma lipid profile and should, therefore, be used with caution and only in the lowest possible dose.

HYPERTENSION AND UNRELATED CONCOMITANT DISEASE

The majority of hypertensive patients have other medical problems which substantially influence the choice of antihypertensive drugs. This problem, like hypertension itself, becomes commoner with advancing age. Often the concomitant disease is more important than the height of the blood

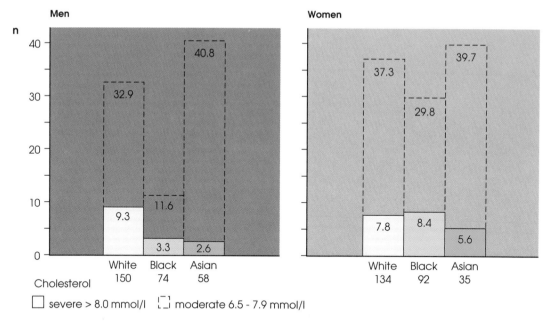

Figure 14.7
The percentage prevalence of moderate and severe hypecholesterolaemia in a hypertensive clinic.

pressure, so the clinician must balance the risks and benefits of treatment, taking into account the absolute risk of heart attack or stroke for his or her individual patient.

Asthma

In patients with any form of obstructive airways disease, beta-adrenergic receptor blockers are absolutely contraindicated. This is true for the third generation beta-blockers like celiprolol or bisoprolol although they do cause less bronchoconstriction than the earlier agents. Airways resistance is related to β_2-adrenergic function and beta-blockade makes things worse; these drugs may interfere with the action of the β_2-agonist inhalers like salbutamol.

All other antihypertensive drugs can be used safely and have no impact on airways resistance.

Patients on chronic low dose corticosteroid therapy for asthma probably do not sustain a significant rise in blood pressure although they do need careful monitoring. Short courses of high doses of prednisolone for acute asthma can cause elevation of blood pressure, but the hazards of this are greatly outweighed by the benefits of steroids in saving the lives of severe asthmatics.

Steroid therapy and beta agonists both tend to lower serum potassium levels which may be predictive of a poorer outcome in acute asthma. In patients who also have hypertension, the thiazide diuretics which also lower serum potassium levels should be used with caution.

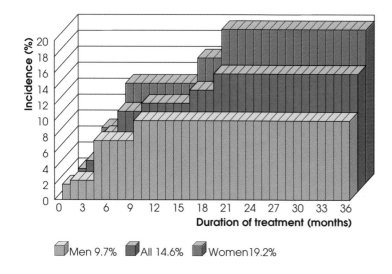

Figure 14.8
The incidence of cough in hypertensive patients receiving enalapril.

Men 9.7% All 14.6% Women 19.2%

Cough

There are no significant adverse effects of ACE inhibitors on airways resistance. However, the ACE inhibitors cause an irritating dry cough in about 10% of patients (Fig. 14.8). Middle-aged female non-smokers are particularly prone to develop this problem. The cough may be an early symptom of asthma, so such patients require careful assessment. If a cough develops with one ACE inhibitor, it will almost certainly occur with all others, so this class of drug has to be abandoned. If the cough does not go away, then ACE inhibitors were not the cause; more detailed respiratory tests are necessary and ACE inhibitors may be restarted with caution.

Gastrointestinal symptoms

All drugs may cause postprandial epigastric discomfort but this side-effect is sporadic and idiosyncratic. Only spironolactone persistently causes indigestion.

Constipation commonly develops in patients taking verapamil and frequently this drug has to be abandoned. If alteration of bowel habit persists, detailed gastrointestinal investigation is mandatory.

Dentists should be aware that the dihydropyridine calcium channel blockers can cause gum hypertrophy, particularly if there is poor dental hygiene.

Liver disease

Patients with liver disease generally do not have hypertension, but the association of alcoholism, raised blood pressure and stroke is important. Abnormal liver function tests with raised gamma glutamyl transferase levels strongly suggest this diagnosis. In cirrhosis of the liver, ACE inhibitors may be hazardous. Those ACE inhibitors which are hepatically metabolized (e.g. enalapril, metabolized to

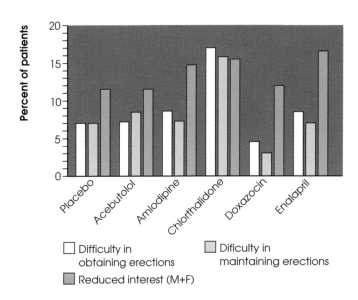

Figure 14.9
Blood pressure drugs and sexual function.

enalaprilat) may be less effective if there is impairment of hepatic function.

Urogenital disease

Sexual function

Impotence is common in anxious or sick hypertensive patients. The thiazide diuretics are an important cause of impotence and they should be avoided in sexually active men. The beta-blockers may also cause impotence but there appear to be no consistent effects on sexual function from the ACE inhibitors or the calcium blockers. The alpha receptor blockers are probably the best choice for men with problems with sexual function. Now that drugs are available which do not affect sexual function (Fig. 14.9), the clinician should specifically enquire about this topic and choose his antihypertensive therapy accordingly. There is no evidence

that any antihypertensive drug adversely affects fertility.

Prostatism

Patients with symptoms of prostatic obstruction need careful urological assessment. Alpha-receptor blockers may relieve symptoms a little, pending prostatectomy. Thus, these are logical drugs to use in men with hypertension and mild symptoms of prostatic enlargement. The dihydropyridine calcium antagonists such as nifedipine often cause nocturia and this side-effect needs to be distinguished from symptoms of prostatic enlargement.

Incontinence

Patients receiving the loop diuretic fruse-mide may develop urgency of micturition and female patients may develop urge or stress incontinence. Loop diuretics should be avoided particularly in women with a tendency to problems with control of bladder function. Many female patients have stress incontinence but are embarrassed to mention this to their cardiovascular specialist.

The alpha receptor blocking agents prazocin, doxazocin and terazocin may cause or aggravate stress incontinence in women. This symptom may not be volunteered by the patient so specific enquiry is recommended so that, if necessary, alternative antihypertensive drugs can be used.

The menopause

Blood pressures tend to rise in women after the menopause, so careful monitoring of blood pressure is advised. Hormone replacement therapy (HRT) is not contraindicated in hypertensive women but is best not given unless the blood pressure is well controlled; if it is given, regular three-monthly checks are necessary. No consistent tendency of HRT to cause raised blood pressure has been documented and it may even improve control of hypertension in some women.

CONNECTIVE TISSUE DISEASES

Systemic lupus erythematosus, polyarteritis nodosa, mixed connective disease and progressive systemic sclerosis (scleroderma) are all associated with renal damage and hypertension. Furthermore, corticosteroid therapy for these conditions can further elevate blood pressure. Antihypertensive drugs are often necessary and the calcium channel blockers

or the ACE inhibitors are the most suitable agents. There is some evidence that the ACE inhibitors have specific protective effects on the kidney in scleroderma.

Many drugs used by rheumatologists to relieve joint pains (e.g. ibuprofen or naproxen) or influence the progression of rheumatoid arthritis (e.g. indomethacin, gold or corticosteroids) can elevate blood pressure or interfere with antihypertensive drugs. A balance has to be struck between the harmful effects of these drugs on blood pressure and the benefits of pain relief and rheumatoid disease limitation. Indomethacin is only indicated in the acute phases of gout and, in the long term, for the inflammatory arthritides; it should not be used routinely for degenerative joint disease.

Gout

Hyperuricaemia and gout may be a mendelian dominant condition or may be associated with hypertension, alcohol abuse, renal failure or the thiazide diuretics. Mildly elevated uric acid levels are common in hypertension and should not be treated with allopurinol.

ANAESTHESIA

Patients who undergo surgery when they have diastolic blood pressures persistently in excess of 120 mmHg have a higher incidence of intraoperative or postoperative cardiac arrhythmias or myocardial infarction. This is often associated with concomitant coronary artery or generalized vascular disease. For this reason, elective surgery should not be carried out in these patients until they are fully assessed and the blood pressure controlled. The moments of greatest cardiovascular risk are during laryngoscopy and intubation, during hypotensive anaesthesia to aid haemostatis, and whilst the surgeon is manipulating the abdominal viscera. Spinal anaesthesia can cause profound hypotension.

In view of the pressor effects of the sudden discontinuation of clonidine therapy, this drug should be avoided in preoperative patients and other drugs substituted. Sudden withdrawal of beta-blocking drugs in patients with established coronary artery disease may cause exacerbation of angina, and these drugs should not be stopped in the perioperative period. The anaesthetist must be aware when a patient is taking blood pressure-lowering drugs: they may impair the physiological responses to blood loss. In particular, beta-blockers will block the increase in heart rate that occurs with fluid loss, the ACE inhibitors will block the compensatory response of the renin system, and in some cases with severe fluid loss profound hypotension may occur.

In the postoperative phase, while patients are resting in bed, receiving pain-relieving drugs, blood pressure usually remains low. Antihypertensive drugs should be restarted as soon as the blood pressure rises again and the patient is able to swallow them. Before this time, while the patient is receiving intravenous fluids only, intramuscular antihypertensive drugs are occasionally needed to control very high blood pressure.

Mild symptomless hypertension in an otherwise fit middle-aged person does not carry any excess cardiovascular risk during the pre-, intra- or postoperative period. All too often inexperienced anaesthetists needlessly cancel elective surgery on account of trivial hypertension or often a transient elevation of blood pressure on hospital admission in an anxious patient. If the patient is allowed to relax, careful measurement of the blood pressure may reveal much lower pressures and the surgical procedure can go ahead.

GLAUCOMA

Rapid falls in blood pressure may aggravate glaucoma. Thus, antihypertensive therapy should be given with care in patients with this condition. Beta-blockers are given topically to treat glaucoma, and a sufficient amount of the drug may be absorbed to induce systemic beta-blockade with some reduction of blood pressure.

PSYCHIATRIC DISEASE

Alcoholism

Alcoholics and heavy drinkers are more likely to be hypertensive than the general population and they should have their blood pressure monitored regularly, as they are particularly prone to develop strokes. See Chapters 3 and 10.

Anxiety states

Anxious patients may develop transiently raised blood pressure, particularly with high systolic pressures. There is, however, no evidence that chronic anxiety is a cause of hypertension. In anxious patients' treatment of the underlying psychiatric disease should be instituted, but because of the mild anxiolytic effects of beta-blockers these may be employed if the patient is truly hypertensive. Beta-blockers have been used in the treatment of schizophrenia.

The lipophilic beta-blockers like propranolol are probably the most effective in relieving symptoms of anxiety as they freely enter the brain. Atenolol is only very slightly lipophilic and it does have some useful effects in very tense and anxious patients.

Depressive disease

Once patients have been told they are hypertensive, they may develop anxiety or depression about their condition. These problems may be compounded by the use of the centrally acting drugs (methyldopa, clonidine and reserpine), all of which can cause depression. These drugs should never be used in depressed patients and are best avoided in all other patients. Beta-blockers do not cause depression but they may induce lethargy. This problem is particularly seen with propranolol, oxprenolol, metoprolol and timolol and possibly less with atenolol or nadolol. The ACE inhibitors may be associated with some improvement in wellbeing, and the complete absence of central side-effects makes them potentially useful in depressed patients.

In patients with bipolar depression or manic depressive psychosis, psychiatrists commonly use lithium therapy. If the patient is also hypertensive, thiazide diuretics are specifically contraindicated as they may cause a dangerous rise in plasma lithium levels. There are reports of a rise in serum lithium levels in some patients receiving ACE inhibitors.

CONCLUSIONS

It will be seen from this chapter that the management of hypertension is relevant to practically all branches of the medical and nursing professions. Specialists who do not have a prime interest in hypertension all too frequently neglect their patients' blood pressure or manage it inefficiently or incorrectly. Improved awareness of the importance of hypertension as a major cause of death or disability and of the sensible choice of antihypertensive drugs can greatly benefit hypertensive patients who have concomitant medical conditions.

FURTHER READING

Barnett AH. Diabetes and hypertension. Br Med Bull 1994; **50**:397–407.

Betteridge DJ. Questions about cholesterol. 'Lipid-friendly' antihypertensives. Postgrad Med J 1992; **68**:881–2.

Brown MA, Whitworth J. Hypertension in human renal disease. J Hypertens 1992; **10**:701–12.

Davey-Smith G, Eggar M. Who benefits from medical interventions? Br Med J 1994; **308**:72–4.

Kendall MJ, Lewis H, Griffith M, Barnett AH. Drug treatment of the hypertensive diabetic. J Hum Hypertens 1988; **1**:249–58.

Lip GYH, Beevers M, Churchill D, Beevers DG. Do clinicians prescribe hormone replacement therapy for hypertensive post-menopausal women? Br J Clin Prac 1994; **(In press)**.

O'Connell JE, Gray C. Treating hypertension after stroke. *Br Med J* 1994; **308**:152–4.

Prys-Roberts C. Anaesthesia and hypertension. *Br J Anaesth* 1984; **56**:711–24.
Reaven GM. Role of insulin resistance in human disease: Banting Lecture. *Diabetes* 1988; **37**:1595–1607.

Weston CFM, Penny WJ, Julian DG, on behalf of the British Heart Foundation Working Group. Guidelines for the early management of patients with myocardial infarction. *Br Med J* 1994; **308**:767–71.

Whelton PK, Klag MJ. Hypertension as a risk factor for renal disease. Review of clinical and epidemiological evidence. *Hypertension* 1989; **13 (Suppl I)**:I-19–I-27.

Winocour PH. Microalbuminuria: worth screening for in early morning urine samples in diabetic, hypertensive, and elderly patients. *Br Med J* 1992; **304**:1196–7.

15 HYPERTENSION IN THE ELDERLY

BACKGROUND

In all developed societies that consume large amounts of salt, blood pressure rises with age. One obvious consequence of this is that, in an aging community, the number of people with high blood pressure will increase unless they die prematurely from cardiovascular disease. If high blood pressure is defined as a single systolic measurement greater than 160 mmHg or a diastolic greater than 95 mmHg, over half the population over the age of 65 will have high blood pressure.

For many years it was felt that older patients 'needed' higher pressure to perfuse narrowed and stiffened arteries. This concept is totally incorrect. The risk of cardiovascular disease in the elderly from high blood pressure is identical to that in younger patients up to the age of 80 years. Indeed, the actual risk of dying from an event related to high blood pressure is much greater in the elderly because the chance of having a stroke or heart attack or dying is much greater as one gets older. In spite of this knowledge it had been argued in the past that treatment of high blood pressure in the elderly was not justified, because there was no evidence that treatment was beneficial. However, recent trials have now unequivocally demonstrated the immense benefit of lowering blood pressure in the elderly; indeed, there is a much greater benefit in the short term in preventing strokes, heart attacks and heart failure than in younger patients. Older patients, therefore, at least up to the age of 80 years, with high blood pressure must be treated. However, care needs to be taken in the choice of the right drugs, using lower doses and avoiding postural drops in blood pressure.

THE RISE IN BLOOD PRESSURE WITH AGE

Blood pressure, as pointed out in Chapter 3, rises with age in developed societies. The rise in systolic pressure tends to be greater than that in diastolic pressure and, indeed, in many patients diastolic pressure may fall after the age of 65 years, giving rise to a widened pulse pressure. However, epidemiological evidence clearly shows that the systolic pressure is a very potent predictor of risk for coronary heart disease, heart failure and stroke in the elderly irrespective of diastolic pressure and, indeed, is a much better predictor than diastolic pressure. Not only is blood pressure an important predictor but the actual risk of having a stroke or heart attack or dying from a complication of these is much greater in the elderly than in younger patients.

ASSESSMENT OF THE PATIENT

In the majority of elderly patients blood pressure measurement is straightforward. However, in a few, there may be a systolic gap and systolic pressure may be underestimated. Elderly patients are much more likely to have concomitant disease, either related to the hypertension, e.g. heart failure, previous ischaemic or cerebrovascular disease, or conditions unrelated to blood pressure itself, including chronic chest disease, cancer etc. Clearly, in assessing these patients one needs to be careful not to miss these other important concomitant diseases that need treatment which may alter the type of drugs or the sort of treatment that is given.

Important changes occur in the elderly which influence drug treatment. There is a gradual reduction in glomerular filtration rate as age increases, so that renal function declines. Indeed, on average, at the age of 70 years, renal function is about half that of a younger person. Therefore, drugs that are excreted or metabolized by the kidney tend to accumulate and dosage adjustments must be made. Elderly patients also tend to have a less reactive renin system and this results in their blood pressure being more responsive to changes in volume, particularly when diuretics or salt restriction are used.

Elderly patients often have some impairment of postural reflexes that maintain blood pressure when they stand up. This may lead, in some patients, to postural drops in blood pressure without drug therapy which may be worsened when drug therapy is added.

SECONDARY CAUSES OF HYPERTENSION IN THE ELDERLY

Secondary causes of hypertension in the elderly are just as common as in younger patients, contrary to what many experts have said in the past. Nevertheless, as in younger patients, the majority of patients do not have an underlying cause but routine investigations need to be done to exclude adrenal adenomas (plasma potassium), and in those where there is severe hypertension or any unusual story that suggests a phaeochromocytomas (24-hour urinary catecholamine). By far the most common cause of secondary hypertension in the elderly is renal artery stenosis due to generalized peripheral vascular disease. These patients have usually been heavy cigarette smokers in the past or currently. They usually have some degree of renal impairment and evidence of peripheral vascular disease either with intermittent claudication or absent pulses in the legs, as well as previous evidence of ischaemic heart disease or cerebrovascular disease.

INVESTIGATIONS IN THE ELDERLY HYPERTENSIVE

The same routine investigations that are done in younger patients should be done in older patients. Clearly it is important to check kidney function with serum urea and creatinine and electrolyte levels. Heart failure tends to be common in these patients due to a combination of ischaemic heart disease and high blood pressure. Patients where renal artery stenosis is suspected should be referred to a specialized centre, as investigation of these patients, usually with renal angiograms, carries some risks and is only justified, where there is a worsening renal failure, uncontrollable hypertension or heart failure which may be secondary to the renal artery stenosis.

EVIDENCE FOR THE BENEFIT OF TREATMENT IN THE ELDERLY

Until recently there had been a lot of discussion about how beneficial it was to treat the elderly, as previous studies such as Hamilton's classic studies in 1964 in very severe hypertensives and the Veteran's study with more moderate hypertension did include some people over the age of 60 years, but it was unclear whether this group did specifically benefit. Other suggestive evidence from the HDFP study and the Australian National High Blood Pressure study also suggested that the elderly might benefit. However, recently several randomized controlled studies in the elderly have clearly demonstrated the immense benefits of treatment.

European Working Party on Hypertension in the Elderly (EWPHE) 1985

This was a large hospital-based study in Europe in patients over the age of 60 who were randomized either to receive thiazide combined with triamterene or placebo. The study showed that blood pressure could be lowered without significant adverse effects although there were some metabolic problems with the thiazide diuretics. Patients were included who had systolic pressures of 160–239 mmHg and diastolic pressures of 90–119 mmHg. The study clearly demonstrated a reduction in cardio-vascular mortality. A study done at around the same time in general practice in the UK, where patients were randomized either to a beta-blocker or to observation only, showed very similar results, with a reduction in strokes but no reduction in total mortality rates when the two groups were compared.

Medical Research Council study in the elderly

This was a randomized study in patients of age 65–74 years. Entry criteria included diastolic pressures of less than 115 mmHg, and systolic pressures of 160–204 mmHg. The study was a comparison of the beta-blocker atenolol or a diuretic against placebo and included over 4,000 patients. The study clearly demonstrated the benefit of treatment in the elderly. Diuretics, in particular, reduced cerebrovascular disease as well as coronary heart disease. The beta-blocker group had a similar reduction in cerebrovascular disease, i.e. strokes, but no reduction in coronary heart disease (Fig. 15.1). The exact reasons for this are not clear and have been disputed. However, what is clear is that beta-blockers were not as effective in lowering blood pressure as a diuretic, which may partially explain the difference in the two drug treatments.

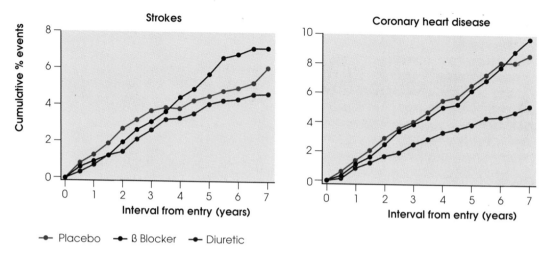

Figure 15.1
Results of treatment in the MRC trial of hypertension in the elderly.

Swedish Trial of Old Patients with Hypertension (STOP-H Trial)

This trial from Sweden again clearly demonstrated the benefits of treatment in elderly hypertensives with either a beta-blocker or a diuretic combined (Table 15.1). A subgroup analysis of the two different treatments has not been published so it is impossible to say whether one form of therapy is better than another in this particular study.

Systolic Hypertension in the Elderly Program (SHEP)

This study was specifically set up to look at elderly patients who had raised systolic pressure with normal diastolic pressure. In order to recruit these patients a very large number of people had to be screened and the patients who were eventually studied were a very highly selected group of people who had isolated systolic hypertension but who were otherwise well. The study was a randomized controlled study using diuretics with a beta-blocker added if blood pressure was not controlled, against placebo. The study clearly demonstrated a reduction in strokes and coronary heart disease. In the placebo group the average systolic blood pressure after the run-in of the study showed an average systolic pressure of 155 mmHg, and in the actively treated group 144 mmHg, with a diastolic pressure of 71 mmHg in the placebo group and 68 mmHg in the treated group.

The group that received active treatment had a highly significant reduction in strokes and coronary heart disease compared to those given placebo. However, before accepting these entry levels of blood pressure and assuming that the whole of this elderly population should be treated, it should be remembered that these were selected patients. Nevertheless, it does suggest that even quite mild degrees of

Table 15.1

Results in the STOP-H trial.

		Placebo	Active (ßB or Th)
Entry characteristics	numbers	812	815
	age (>70)	76	76
	BP (DBP>90)	195/102	195/102
Outcome (No/1000pt. yr)	ALL MI	16.5	14.4
	Fatal MI	4.5	3.4
	All stroke	31.3	16.8
	Fatal stroke	8.3	2.3
	Other CV deaths	3.4	1.7
	Total deaths	35.4	20.2

systolic elevation of blood pressure in the elderly, which certainly carry a risk for cerebrovascular and cardiovascular disease, may benefit from treatment.

INDICATIONS FOR TREATMENT IN THE ELDERLY PATIENT

Taking into account these trials, where there is no doubt that it is now beneficial to treat the elderly, there are still some open questions, particularly over the age of 80 years and in mild degrees of isolated systolic hypertension. Balanced against the benefits of treatment there must be consideration of the problems of blood pressure treatment in the elderly, the side-effects of drugs and particularly the postural hypotension that can occur and can result in death from fractured hip.

Accelerated hypertension or very severe hypertension

This should always be treated irrespective of age. As in the younger population, very good results can be obtained.

Patients with hypertension and congestive heart failure

These patients should always be treated, as the lowering of blood pressure may bring about a dramatic relief of their heart failure.

Patients up to the age of 80 years

Any patient who has high blood pressure, whether systolic or diastolic, should be given non-pharmacological advice. If diastolic pressure, in spite of non-pharmacological advice, remains consistently over 95 mmHg, then they should be treated, provided there are no obvious contraindications (Fig. 15.2). Systolic pressure should also be treated if it is consistently, after non-pharmacological advice, greater than 170 mmHg.

Patients over the age of 80 years

In those studies which included patients over the age of 80 years there were benefits in both stroke and heart attack prevention, although the number was quite small. There is no reason why these older patients should not benefit from reduction in blood pressure but in view of the limited evidence it is probably better to only treat those whose systolic pressure is greater than 200 mmHg or diastolic pressure is greater than 110

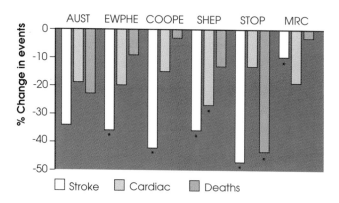

Figure 15.2

Comparison of six clinical trials showing the decrease in stroke and cardiac events and death.

mmHg. The benefits of treating hypertension in the very old are currently being investigated in a randomised control trial (HYVET, see Chapter 9).

DOES TREATMENT OF THE ELDERLY DIFFER FROM THAT OF YOUNGER PATIENTS?

Non-pharmacological treatment

All patients should be advised about non-pharmacological treatment in the same way as younger patients (see Chapter 10). Reduction of salt intake is likely to be particularly effective in older patients in view of their less reactive renin system. Many older patients tend to take large amounts of salt in their food and may find initial difficulties due to a decrease in sensitivity of salt receptors in the mouth with increasing age. Our experience, however, is that if a careful explanation is given and they are told that it will take time to adjust, the elderly, like younger patients, will find that they can get used to less salty foods and, indeed, after a while much prefer them. Many elderly patients are eating inadequate amounts of potassium-rich food and it is important to try and encourage a greater consumption of fresh fruit and vegetables. This particularly applies if thiazide diuretics are being given. Excess weight and excess alcohol should clearly be dealt with in the same way as in younger patients.

Which drug should be used in the elderly?

In general terms the same drugs are used as in younger patients. However, lower doses should be used initially owing to a decreased clearance or metabolism of the drugs by the liver and kidneys with increasing age.

Thiazide diuretics

All of the controlled randomized trials in the elderly use thiazide diuretics and there is no doubt that they do reduce both strokes and, perhaps more surprisingly, coronary heart disease. Low dose thiazide diuretics are particularly effective in the elderly and have the advantage that they will have less of the metabolic side-effects. However, these metabolic side-effects should be looked for, particularly a fall in plasma potassium, as elderly patients tend to have low potassium intakes. Whether it is justified to add in a potassium-sparing diuretic such as amiloride or triamterene is a matter of debate. In our view it is better not to do this unless the plasma potassium falls. Salt restriction will also prevent large falls in plasma potassium. Thiazide diuretics may occasionally cause postural drops in blood pressure and are more likely to cause a reduction in renal function, so this needs to be monitored.

Beta-blockers

Beta-blockers on their own are less effective in lowering blood pressure in the elderly. However, the trials in the elderly do seem to clearly indicate that, when combined with a thiazide diuretic where they are additive, they are useful. Low doses of these drugs should be given, as with the thiazide diuretics. They are, of course, more likely to cause problems with peripheral blood flow in that many of these patients already have peripheral vascular disease. They should be avoided in patients with peripheral vascular disease. Many elderly patients will complain of cold hands and feet on beta-blockers, and the insidious side-effects of beta-blockers, on mentation, exercise etc., are just as likely to occur in the elderly as in younger patients.

ACE inhibitors

ACE inhibitors on their own are not as effective in older patients as in younger patients. Nevertheless, when combined with a thiazide diuretic or a calcium antagonist, they become very effective, especially if elderly patients are prepared to restrict their salt intake. These drugs are particularly useful in congestive heart failure in the elderly. Elderly patients who smoke and have evidence of peripheral vascular disease are likely to have renal artery stenosis, and ACE inhibitors may cause a deterioration in renal function. It is essential in these patients that renal function is checked before and after 2 or 3 weeks if an ACE inhibitor is used.

Calcium entry antagonists

These drugs, like the diuretics, appear on their own to be more effective in the elderly and are used in exactly the same way as in younger patients, but again lower doses of these drugs should be used, particularly as initial treatment.

FURTHER READING

Beard K, Bulpitt CJ, Mascie-Taylor H, et al. Management of elderly patients with sustained hypertension. *Br Med J* 1992; **304**:412–6.

Bulpitt CJ, Fletcher AE, Amery A, et al. The hypertension in the very elderly trial (HYVET). *J Hum Hypertens* 1994; **6**:631–2.

MRC Working Party. Medical Research Council trial of treatment of hypertension in older adults. *Br Med J* 1992; **304**:405–12.

Potter JF. Hypertension in the elderly. *Br Med Bull* 1994; **50**:408–19.

SHEP Cooperative Research Group. Prevention of stroke by antihypertensive drug treatment in older person with isolated systolic hypertension. Final results of the Systolic Hypertension in the Elderly Program (SHEP). *JAMA* 1991; **265**:3255–64.

Staessen J, Bert P, Bulpitt CJ, et al. Nitrendipine in older patients with isolated systolic hypertension: second progress report on the SYST-EUR trial. *J Hum Hypertens* 1994; **7**:265–71.

16 HYPERTENSION IN PREGNANCY

BACKGROUND

Hypertension in pregnancy remains one of the most mysterious medical conditions facing the clinician. Whilst it is relatively common, medical science has, to date, failed to provide a coherent mechanism and clinical research has provided only a limited amount of information to guide the clinician when managing individual patients. There are clearly several quite distinct forms of hypertension in pregnancy and they differ not only in terms of pathogenesis but also in terms of treatment. In England and Wales, hypertension ranks equally with pulmonary embolus as the commonest cause of maternal death, with a rate of 10 per million pregnancies (Fig. 16.1). It is also the commonest cause of fetal and neonatal death.

The relative paucity of therapeutic trial data on which to make clinical decisions means that on some occasions obstetricians and physicians have tended to base their opinions on extrapolations from published data concerning older non-pregnant women or even from men. There is every reason to believe that this is dangerous and can lead to the mother and baby being exposed to antihypertensive drugs which are at times useless and may even be harmful.

There are now some alarming data on the use of some beta-blockers and the ACE inhibitors in pregnancy. The decision to use these drugs is all too often made on the basis of an inadequate understanding of the mechanism of the hypertensive syndromes of pregnancy and a failure to respond to advances in our knowledge of the hazards of treatment as well as the benefits.

CLASSIFICATION OF THE HYPERTENSIVE SYNDROMES IN PREGNANCY

There have been several attempts to classify the hypertensive syndromes in pregnancy. None are entirely satisfactory but it is important to attempt to ascertain which syndrome is present in individual patients so that appropriate treatment can be given.

Pre-existing essential hypertension

About 5% of women of childbearing age have chronic pre-existing, usually mild,

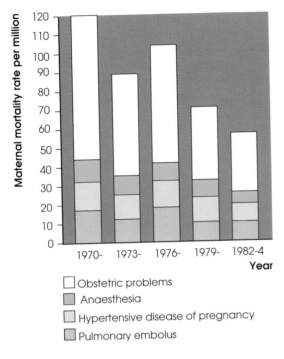

Obstetric problems

Anaesthesia

Hypertensive disease of pregnancy

Pulmonary embolus

Figure 16.1

Causes of maternal mortality in England and Wales.

essential hypertension, as defined by the World Health Organization criteria, of a blood pressure of 140/90 mmHg or more. In women in their late thirties and early forties, this figure approaches 10%. When these women become pregnant, blood pressure frequently settles during the first trimester but may rise to pre-pregnant levels during the third trimester. Unfortunately, pre-pregnant blood pressure measurements are frequently not available to the clinician so it is difficult to be certain whether a blood pressure rise in mid to late pregnancy is due to early pre-eclampsia, to pregnancy-induced hypertension or to pre-existing mild hypertension.

It is important to note that mild essential hypertension in pregnancy does not carry a bad prognosis for mother or fetus and its early treatment does not convincingly prevent the onset of pre-eclampsia or protect the mother or baby (Fig. 16.2).

Secondary hypertension in pregnancy

The topic of secondary hypertension is covered in other chapters of this book. Primary hyperaldosteronism is very rare and there is little information available on its management in pregnancy. If present, there will be hypokalaemia and a high or high normal plasma sodium level. Phaeo-chromocytomas are well described in pregnancy and are associated with both maternal and fetal death. Hypertension associated with renal disease may cause renal impairment, in which case the patient may be sub-fertile. When pregnancy does occur, the outcome is bad as uraemia has direct effects on the fetus and, furthermore, there may be a deterioration of renal function across the pregnancy. Fortunately, this problem is rare in routine clinical practice.

Pregnancy-induced hypertension

This term refers to those women whose blood pressures are documented to be normal both before and after pregnancy, who sustain a rise in blood pressures in late pregnancy, but who do not develop pre-eclampsia. There are varying criteria for diagnosing pregnancy-induced hypertension (PIH) and none are entirely satisfactory. The International Society for the Study of Hypertension in Pregnancy (ISSHP) defines

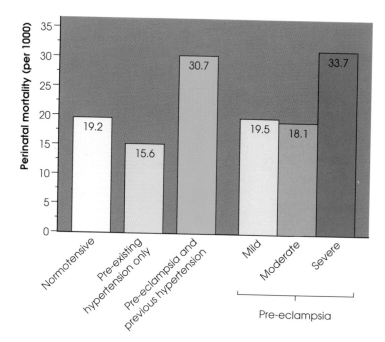

Figure 16.2
Perinatal mortality in relation to blood pressure in the British Births Survey.

PIH as a single diastolic blood pressure (Phase 5) of 110 mmHg or more or two readings of 90 mmHg or more at least 4 hours apart occurring after the 20th week of pregnancy in a previously normotensive woman. An American Working Group defines it as a rise of more than 15 mmHg diastolic or 30 mmHg systolic compared with readings taken in early pregnancy. If PIH is mild and does not proceed to pre-eclampsia, then the prognosis is good. It develops in up to 25% of women in their first pregnancy and in 10% of subsequent pregnancies.

Pre-eclampsia

This syndrome above all others carries a bad prognosis and requires careful assessment and treatment. Pre-eclampsia is diagnosed if the mother develops proteinuria (more than 300 mg/l) associated with a blood pressure that rises to above 140/90 mmHg after the 20th week of pregnancy. The third feature of pre-eclampsia, namely oedema, is much less reliable as mild pre-tibial and facial oedema is common in entirely normal pregnancies. The prevalence of pre-eclampsia is 4–5% in mothers during their first pregnancy and about half this figure in later pregnancies if the father is the same.

Eclampsia

Eclampsia is a major obstetrical emergency associated with a high incidence of both maternal and infant mortality. Blood pressures are almost invariably high and protein-uria of more than 300 mg/l (i.e. dipstick proteinuria one plus or more) is almost always present. There may be gross facial and peripheral oedema, headaches, irritability and, in extreme cases, convulsions. In addition, there may be cerebral and pulmonary oedema, renal failure, hepatic failure, retinal detachment and strokes. This terrifying syndrome occurs in around one pregnancy in 500 in the developed world but is commoner in countries which lack efficient antenatal care.

DIAGNOSIS

Some of the diagnostic categories above are open to variations in criteria or guidelines laid down by various expert committees and there is often an overlap. Some of the diagnoses can only be made with confidence in retrospect once the pregnancy is over and the mother is assessed 3 months later.

The presence of proteinuria is critical to the diagnosis of pre-eclampsia or eclampsia. The accurate measurement of blood pressure is also of paramount importance but this topic is sadly neglected.

BLOOD PRESSURE MEASUREMENT IN PREGNANCY

The first recorded measurement of blood pressure in pregnancy was by Frederick Akbar Mahommed in 1874 at the London Fever Hospital. The invention of the mercury sphygmomanometer by Riva Rocci in 1898 and the discovery of the Korotkov sounds

in 1905 meant that the measurement of blood pressure in clinical practice was relatively easy. Sadly, however, standardization of methods, equipment and the posture of the patient for optimum assessment has not been achieved.

The topic of blood pressure measurement is covered in detail in Chapter 6. In pregnancy, the main sources of variation are the methods for measuring the diastolic pressure and the posture of the patients.

Measurement of diastolic blood pressure

In the past, obstetricians, along with all other clinicians, have tended to take the diastolic blood pressure at the phase of muffling of diastolic sounds (phase 4) rather than the phase of disappearance of sounds (phase 5). This has lead to considerable confusion and still remains the source of some debate. It was argued that in the hyperdynamic state that occurs in pregnancy, faint diastolic sounds are often heard at very low pressure levels, or even at 0 mmHg. It was recommended, therefore, that it would be better to measure the diastolic pressure at the phase of muffling. However, intra-arterial blood pressure measurement has clearly demonstrated that the true intra-arterial diastolic pressure is closer to the phase of final disappearance of sounds (phase 5). More recently, it has been shown that the tendency for phase 5 diastolic pressures to be improbably low was somewhat overestimated (Fig. 16.3). The median difference between the muffling and disappearance phases (i.e. phase 4 minus phase 5) in pregnancy was 2.7 mmHg, whilst in non-pregnant women it was 0.7 mmHg. Furthermore, a recent survey amongst obstetricians and midwives demonstrated that almost half favoured phase 5 and

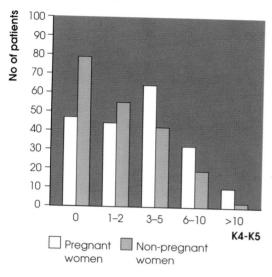

Figure 16.3

The difference between muffling and disappearance of sounds when measuring diastolic blood pressures (K4 minus K5 in mmHg).

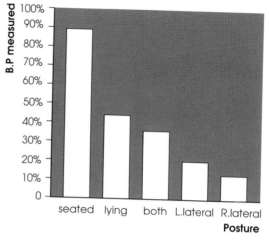

Figure 16.4

Posture favoured by midwives and obstetricians when measuring blood pressure, demonstrating lack of agreement as to the best method.

half favoured phase 4 so there clearly is diagnostic anarchy. Analysis of the techniques reported in the international obstetric literature shows, however, an increasing trend to adopt phase 5. We strongly advocate the universal use of phase 5 for recording diastolic pressure, with the caveat that phase 4 should be used if the K4–K5 difference exceeds 20 mmHg.

Posture

As in the non-pregnant state, we strongly advocate the routine measurement of blood pressure in the seated position (Fig. 16.4). In late pregnancy, when women lie flat on their backs, the gravid uterus may cause some vena caval compression, leading to a reduction of venous return, a fall in cardiac output and a fall in blood pressure; when the patient lies on her side, blood pressure rises. This assessment of blood pressure by the 'roll over test' is now obsolete and provides no useful information.

Blood pressure should be measured at least monthly for the first two trimesters and thereafter weekly. If the pressure is 140/90 mmHg or more it should be re-measured after 5 minutes' rest in the seated position in a quiet room. If this second blood pressure measurement exceeds 140/90 at any stage of pregnancy, accurate clinical assessment of the patient is crucial and if the pressure exceeds 160/110 mmHg, this should be done on an inpatient basis in most cases.

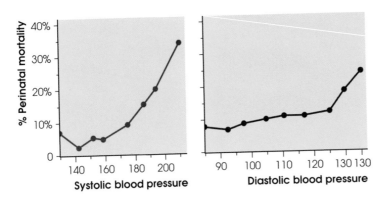

Figure 16.5
Perinatal mortality in relation to systolic and diastolic blood pressure in 4404 women with pre–eclampsia.

PROGNOSIS

The prognosis for the various hypertensive syndromes in pregnancy varies according to category. There are only a limited number of reports of perinatal or maternal mortality in relation to accurate assessments of blood pressure in the three trimesters of pregnancy. This is partly because, in developed countries, maternal and perinatal mortality is so low that risk factors have to be investigated using national surveillance statistics and these data tend to rely on casual and often inaccurate blood pressure measurement by thousands of observers.

Very high blood pressure in pregnancy can affect the mother and the baby. In the mother, there is an increased risk of pre-eclampsia but also an increased risk of stroke and renal damage. The consequences to the fetus are reduced uteroplacental blood flow, placental ischaemia, intrauterine growth retardation, premature delivery, abruptio placentae (acute partum haemorrhage) and fetal death (Fig. 16.5).

National surveillance data demonstrate that the perinatal mortality in pregnancies associated with mild essential hypertension and mild pregnancy-induced hypertension is, in fact, somewhat lower than in the majority of pregnancies where the blood pressure remains persistently normal. By sharp contrast, there is a high perinatal mortality in those pregnancies complicated by proteinuric pre-eclampsia. The reasons for the good outlook in the mild hypertensive woman with no pre-eclampsia are uncertain. It may be because those mothers who were diagnosed as having mildly raised blood pressure received a higher quality of obstetrical care. Alternatively, the mothers with lower blood pressure included a subgroup who had other diseases, like asthma or chronic infections, which may have reduced their blood pressures.

Whatever the mechanisms of the lack of adverse effects of mild hypertension alone, there are important clinical implications. First, mild hypertension with blood pressure below 150/100 in pregnancy should not be treated with antihypertensive drugs. Clearly, careful observation is crucial as in some cases blood pressures may rise to levels where drug therapy is necessary and the clinician is not able to predict whose pressures will rise and whose will not.

There is no convincing evidence that the treatment of very mild hypertension in pregnancy has any effect in preventing pre-eclampsia, or reducing the incidence of intrauterine growth retardation or preterm delivery.

AETIOLOGY

Hypertension in pregnancy has been called the 'disease of theories', mainly because a great many hypotheses have been advanced but none convincingly fit the bill. Clues may be obtained from investigating the epidemiology of pre-eclampsia and also from studies of its pathology.

Epidemiology of hypertension in pregnancy

Large-scale studies have demonstrated that certain mothers are particularly prone to developing pre-eclampsia. Their identification can aid in their management.

Genetic factors

Pre-eclampsia undoubtedly runs in families and this is likely to be due to genetic factors as well as a tendency for relatives to be subjected to similar environmental influences. However, an autosomal dominant inheritance has been postulated.

Age

There is an increased incidence of pre-eclampsia in young teenage girls and also in women aged over 35 years.

Parity

Pre-eclampsia is commonest in first pregnancies and also in women with five or more pregnancies, with a rate of about 6%. The syndrome remains common in second or third pregnancies if they are by a different father.

Multiple pregnancies

Pregnancies associated with both monozygotic and dizygotic twins have a raised rate of pre-eclampsia.

Previous pre-eclampsia

Mothers who have had pre-eclampsia in their first pregnancy have an increased chance of this developing in subsequent pregnancies although the risk is low.

Previous oral contraceptive-induced hypertension

It is generally held that women who have had raised blood pressure from the oral contraceptives have an increased risk of hypertension in pregnancy. It is uncertain whether this is true for the newer low oestrogen or progestagen-only contraceptive. Similarly there is some doubt whether women developing hypertension in pregnancy have a greater chance of developing raised blood pressure if they subsequently use oral contraceptives.

Ethnic origin

Pre-eclampsia is commoner in black and Asian people in Britain but it is uncertain whether this is due to environmental and social factors or to any genuine genetic difference.

Obesity

Maternal obesity is associated with pre-eclampsia as well as a greater tendency to develop essential hypertension. If appropriate sized arm cuffs are used in blood pressure measurement, the effects of obesity are less pronounced. It is uncertain whether women who gain more weight during pregnancy are at greater risk of pre-eclampsia.

Socio-economic factors

People of low socio-economic status are more prone to most diseases and this is true for hypertension in general as well as for hypertension in pregnancy. Assuming only a modest genetic determinant of pre-eclampsia, then the socio-economic gradient is likely to be related to obesity, poor quality diet and overcrowding. Paradoxically, cigarette smoking does not cause pre-eclampsia, nor does it cause hypertension in non-pregnant people.

Other factors

Pre-eclampsia is commoner in diabetic women, those with hydatidiform mole and Rhesus isoimmunization. Pregnancies leading to male babies have a slightly higher risk of eclampsia.

Pathogenesis

Pre-eclampsia appears to be a syndrome associated with a defect of implantation of the placenta and thus has its origins in early pregnancy, before any clinical features are detectable. At this early stage, there is histological evidence of a reduced number of uteroplacental arteries and a failure of the spiral arteries, in particular, to dilate, lose their muscularis, and thus provide for an increase in blood flow which will become necessary later on in pregnancy as the fetus grows. The placenta and fetus are thus ischaemic at an early stage. Subsequently, the development of atherosis, fibroblastic proliferation and fibrinoid necrosis causes more acute ischaemia with vascular occlusions and placental infarctions. Non infarcted areas of the placenta look pale and gritty. The fetus is ischaemic, and hypoxic, growth is retarded and, in severe cases, the fetus dies. Renal involvement with the development of proteinuria and elevation of blood pressure are late phenomena and should be regarded as secondary to the basic underlying disease of the placenta.

MECHANISMS

The search for the mechanisms of pre-eclampsia has centred on investigations of vasoactive substances and intravascular clotting factors. As with similar studies in non-pregnant hypertensives, it is often difficult to be certain whether the findings are a cause or a consequence of the raised blood pressure.

The renin–angiotensin system

Renin is generated by the kidney but there is also good evidence that there are local renin–angiotensin systems in the placenta and uterus. Thus circulating renin and angiotensin levels may not reflect the true role of the renin system in pregnancy. In normal pregnancy, plasma renin substrate (angiotensinogen) levels are high, and renin is consumed to generate angiotensin II so that plasma renin activity is raised. In hypertensive pregnancies, these trends are less pronounced and plasma renin activity is lower, but still not as low as in the non-pregnant state. Thus in normal pregnancies the circulating renin–angiotensin system is activated, and in hypertensive pregnancies it is less active. The lower levels of angiotensin II may be related to increased vascular sensitivity to endogenous and exogenous (infused) angiotensin II.

The local renin–angiotensin systems have received less attention, but may promote vasoconstriction, vessel wall growth and failure of dilatation of the spiral arteries.

Other vasoactive substances

There is evidence of disturbance of function of many vasoactive systems in pre-eclampsia. These include increased vascular responsiveness to adrenaline and noradrenaline, reductions in vasodilator prostaglandin production, and low levels of kallikrein-kinin activity; also, a possible role for the newly discovered vasoconstrictor, endothelin, has been suggested. These abnormalities are clearly all interrelated and their individual significance is uncertain.

Coagulation

A certain degree of activation of the coagulation system, with thrombin-mediated fibrin generation, is a feature of normal pregnancy. In pre-eclampsia, fibrinolytic activity may be impaired and platelet aggregation is increased. In extreme cases, a consumptive coagulopathy develops with thrombocytopenia, microangiopathic haemolytic anaemia, a rise in circulating fibrin degradation products and a prolonged prothrombin time. Measurement of these features is used in monitoring the clinical management of pre-eclamptic mothers.

Haemodynamics

In a normal pregnancy, there is a rise in plasma volume and cardiac output and a fall in total peripheral resistance. There is a slight tendency of blood pressure to fall in the first half of normal pregnancy. In mothers with pre-eclampsia, cardiac output is reduced, plasma volume falls and peripheral resistance rises. Resistance to blood flow in the uteroplacental circulation increases and this further compounds the tendency to fetoplacental ischaemia.

CLINICAL MANAGEMENT

As outlined above, accurate blood pressure measurement is essential because even small elevations of pressure do radically affect the patient's care. Similarly, the patients need very careful general assessment to check for underlying causes for the hypertension and to detect other clinical conditions which may influence the choice of antihypertensive drugs.

Hypertension before pregnancy

It is now generally agreed that it is the responsibility of the primary health care team to ensure that all adults have their blood pressures measured regularly. This has lead to an increasing number of women of childbearing age being diagnosed as having hypertension. Clearly, decisions on what to do depend on the degree of elevation of the blood pressure and whether it is associated with underlying renal or adrenal disease. It should be remembered, however, that relatively young pre-menopausal women do not necessarily have a high hypertension-related, absolute cardiovascular risk; i.e. their actual chance of developing a heart attack or a stroke is minimal, particularly if they are non-smokers with a benign family history. The clinician is faced with the question as to whether drug therapy should be started. The British Hypertension Society guidelines for the management of hypertension also give the clinician a mandate to withhold drug therapy in very low risk, very mild hypertensives. Many women of childbearing potential fall into this category although they must be monitored regularly. If the clinician does opt to prescribe antihypertensive drugs then he or she must bear in mind that the patient may opt at some time to become pregnant. There should be a natural reluctance to prescribe any drugs in 'potentially pregnant' women. In particular, the clinician should remember that the ACE inhibitors are absolutely contraindicated in pregnancy as they are associated with a high perinatal mortality. The calcium channel blockers are relatively contraindicated, diuretics should not be used in pregnancy and some (but not all) beta-blockers are associated with adverse fetal outcome.

The assessment of hypertensive patients who are not pregnant is covered in Chapters 7 and 8, and in young women special efforts must be made to detect underlying causes. It should, however, be remembered that radiological procedures like intravenous urography should only be conducted either during or immediately after a menstrual period in order to avoid radiation damage to a recently conceived fetus.

There are very few women who should be advised to avoid becoming pregnant on account of their hypertension. With modern antihypertensive drugs, the risk of stroke in pregnancy can be greatly reduced. If women with severe hypertension do become pregnant, then early expert obstetrical medical care is necessary.

Hypertension before 20 weeks of gestation

If women are found to have blood pressures of 140/90 mmHg or more at the first antenatal booking visit, they should preferably be referred to a joint antenatal–hypertension clinic. It is probable that hypertension at this stage is really due to underlying chronic, essential or secondary hypertension, especially if obesity is present. A strong family history of hypertension would certainly suggest that the patient has essential hypertension. All such patients should undergo routine dipstick urine testing and a blood sample should be taken for a haematological profile and serum levels of urea, creatinine, uric acid, sodium and potassium as well as a random blood glucose. A 24-hour urine test for catecholamine excretion should also be started. If the blood pressure exceeds 160/110 mmHg, then it may be preferable to admit the patient to the antenatal wards for more detailed assessment. If the blood pressure remains at this level, antihypertensive medication should be started, usually with labetalol or methyldopa. The choice of antihypertensive drugs is described later in this chapter.

The use of antihypertensive drugs in the treatment of mild hypertensives in early

Table 16.1

The results of a trial with labetolol or methyldopa or no therapy in mild hypertension in early pregnancy

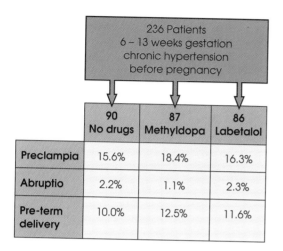

	90 No drugs	87 Methyldopa	86 Labetalol
Preclampia	15.6%	18.4%	16.3%
Abruptio	2.2%	1.1%	2.3%
Pre-term delivery	10.0%	12.5%	11.6%

pregnancy has not been shown to be useful (Table 16.1). One study employing atenolol provided worrying results, as the fetuses subjected to atenolol rather than to placebo were 1 kg lighter (Table 16.2). If, therefore,

blood pressure remains at 150/100 mmHg or less, antihypertensive drugs should not be prescribed.

If both hypertension and proteinuria are present before 20 weeks of gestation, then it is likely that there is some underlying renal pathology like glomerulonephritis or pyelonephritis. Bacteriological examination of the urine is essential and, where relevant, antibiotic drugs should be given.

Hypertension after 20 weeks of gestation

Elevation of the blood pressure for the first time after 20 weeks of gestation is likely to be due to pregnancy-induced hypertension (PIH) or, if proteinuria also develops, the mother may have pre-eclampsia. The clinical problem is that the clinician may not be sure which of these two symptoms is developing.

Pregnancy-induced hypertension

If there is a modest blood pressure rise in the second half of pregnancy and this is not

Table 16.2

The results of a randomized trial of atenolol versus placebo in mild hypertension in early pregnancy.

	Gestation at entry (weeks)	BP at entry (mmHg K5)	In trial BP (mmHg K5)	Birth weight (kg)	Placental weight (g)	Weight at one year (kg)
Atenolol (n = 15)	15.8	144/86	132/74	2.62	454	9.26
Placebo (n = 14)	15.9	148/86	136/81	3.53	633	9.82

associated with proteinuria or severe oedema, then the outlook is good. If the pressure exceeds 160/110 mmHg, then admission to hospital and antihypertensive medication would be recommended. If the pressures are between 140/90 and 160/110, then many women can be managed at home, with rest – but not bedrest. Those who are still at work should stop. The midwives or obstetricians should check the blood pressure twice weekly. If the blood pressure remains above 150/100, and there is no proteinuria, then most clinicians would start antihypertensive medication on an outpatient basis. The limited number of clinical trials of the use of beta-blockers, labetalol and methyldopa suggest no adverse outcome when treating this level of blood pressure in late pregnancy but there was no evidence of prevention of pre-eclampsia. This level of pressure is associated with an appreciable risk of stroke particularly in high risk, older mothers. The risk is, however, too small for any single clinical trial to have the power to detect a difference between placebo or active drug therapy.

Pre-eclampsia

This syndrome is serious and is associated with intrauterine growth retardation or death as well as maternal morbidity and mortality. If blood pressure rises after 20 weeks of gestation and proteinuria develops, the mother should be admitted to hospital immediately for full assessment and antihypertensive medication. Whilst strict bedrest is of no value (and may be harmful), the simple process of admitting the patient may cause a fall in blood pressure.

The clinical progress should be monitored with 4 hourly blood pressure readings, twice-weekly measurements of serum creatinine and uric acid levels and platelet counts as well as twice-weekly 24-hour urine collections for protein estimations.

If pre-eclampsia develops very near to the end of the pregnancy then the optimum treatment is to deliver the baby whilst maintaining good blood pressure control until 7 days post partum. Mothers should also be prescribed diazepam or phenytoin to prevent eclamptic convulsions. Severely pre-eclamptic patients who have blood pressures over 160/110 and show signs of cerebral irritability or headaches should be admitted to an intensive care unit. Furthermore, if the pregnancy is not far advanced (i.e. less than 35 weeks), the mother should be admitted to a hospital with excellent paediatric back-up with a special care baby unit.

Eclampsia

With improvements in antenatal care, this syndrome should become increasingly uncommon. The mother's life is in great danger. In addition to anticonvulsant drugs, blood pressure should be reduced with parenteral medication with magnesium sulphate or labetalol miniboluses (50 mg) or infusions of intravenous hydralazine (20 mg). In milder cases, rapid control of blood pressure can be achieved with oral nifedipine (not slow release). However, precipitate drops in pressure should be avoided as this can worsen cerebral, cardiac, renal and placental ischaemia.

The management of full-blown eclampsia is the responsibility of the obstetrician together with an anaesthetist and a paediatrician and is covered in more detail in obstetrical textbooks.

INVESTIGATIONS
Renal function

Serum urea and creatinine levels should be measured at first antenatal booking in all mothers and again if the blood pressure rises. A serum urea of more than 5 mmol/l and a serum creatinine of 100 mmol/l or more is highly abnormal in a pregnant woman and suggests a diagnosis of renal impairment.

and increased fibrin degradation products. These parameters should be monitored regularly. If coagulopathy is present, the outlook is bad and emergency lower segment caesarian section should be considered.

Electrolytes

Plasma potassium may be reduced due to diuretic therapy, which anyway should not be prescribed in pregnancy. In primary aldosteronism serum potassium is low and serum sodium is moderately elevated.

In severe pre-eclampsia, serum sodium and potassium may fall to low levels due to intense hyperaldosteronism induced by renal ischaemia and hepatic dysfunction.

Ultrasound scans

Fetal progress should be monitored throughout pregnancy by serial measurements of crown-rump length (CRL) by ultrasound. In later pregnancy, fetal growth is monitored by serial measurements of biparietal diameter (BPD). This is the best method of diagnosing intrauterine growth retardation.

Uric acid

Serum uric acid levels are sometimes modestly raised in essential hypertension so this test should be done, at first booking, in all hypertensive mothers. In pre-eclampsia, hyperuricaemia frequently develops and this may be used to confirm the diagnosis and monitor progress. The value of serial measurements of serum uric acid levels is debatable as they tend only to become abnormal in clinically obvious pre-eclampsia.

Cardiotocograph

Once the pregnancy has advanced beyond 20 weeks, patients should be monitored by cardiotocography. This should demonstrate physiological beat-to-beat variation of fetal heart rate and the response when the baby kicks or there is a spontaneous uterine contraction. If there is fetal distress there is a loss of variability of heart rate and also sudden decelerations. As with all antenatal monitoring, this test has a high level of specificity (i.e. few false positives) but low sensitivity (i.e. many false negatives).

Haematological indices

In severe pre-eclampsia and eclampsia, there is a consumptive coagulopathy which is associated with thrombocytopenia, a prolonged prothrombin time (or raised INR)

Proteinuria

The detection of proteinuria is crucial to obstetrical care and, when it is present, the 24-hour urine excretion should be measured. At the present state of knowledge, the measurement of microproteinuria as a method of diagnosing early pre-eclampsia cannot be recommended.

ANTIHYPERTENSIVE REGIMES

The information available on the safety of antihypertensive drugs in pregnancy is very limited and with the newer agents like the ACE inhibitors and the calcium channel blockers there is so little published data that these drugs should be avoided. It should be noted that the manufacturers of these drugs specifically state that they are contraindicated in pregnancy. The clinician should, therefore, be very conservative in the choice of drugs and should think hard before prescribing anything.

Rest and sedation

Bedrest is of no value. With rest blood pressure settles but, as soon as the patient mobilizes again, the pressure rises and nothing has been achieved. There is no published evidence that bedrest leads to a favourable outcome in pregnancy and it may lead to an increased risk of venous thrombosis or pulmonary embolus. A less strict form of rest, by stopping work and 'taking things easy' at home or in the ward can, however, be advised although its blood pressure-lowering effects are not impressive.

Sedatives and tranquillizers are similarly of no value unless the patient is agitated or distressed. These drugs may sometimes produce an uncontrolled and prolonged fall in blood pressure and may cause hypotonia

and hypothermia in the fetus. The technique of treating hypertension in pregnancy with bedrest and sedatives represents archaic obstetrical practice which is known to be useless.

Diazepam may, however, be used as an alternative to phenytoin in patients with eclampsia or severe pre-eclampsia as they have a high risk of developing convulsions.

Salt restrictions

There is little information on the value of salt restriction in pregnancy. Extreme salt restriction may reduce intravascular volume and stimulate renin release so it is best avoided. It seems sensible to suggest a maximum sodium intake of around 100 mmol per day, this being about two-thirds of the average intake in the northern European and American population. This salt intake is easily achievable by avoiding adding salt at the table and restricting notoriously salty foods.

Weight restriction

Rigorous dieting should be avoided in pregnancy but obese patients should be advised to try to avoid excessive weight gain in pregnancy and to moderate their calorie intake.

Antihypertensive drugs

A comprehensive review of antihypertensive drugs is to be found in Chapter 11. The review here concentrates on the use of drugs in pregnancy but the other aspects of each pharmacological group should be borne in mind.

Diuretics

The thiazides are said to be contraindicated in pregnancy. Women with pre-eclampsia have relatively contracted plasma volumes and diuretics will cause further contraction and worsen the impairment of uteroplacental blood flow. However, a recent review has suggested that diuretics are not as harmful as they were originally thought to be. Diuretics, particularly frusemide, may, of course, prove necessary if there is severe heart failure or gross fluid retention due to renal failure.

Centrally acting drugs

Methyldopa has, for many years, been the mainstay of obstetrical antihypertensive treatment. There is good evidence that it is entirely safe in pregnancy for both mother and baby but the drug is now falling from favour because it causes severe dose-related sedation and lethargy. Methyldopa probably does remain the first line drug in women with asthma, where beta-blockers are contraindicated. Doses of up to 2 g daily can be used but sedation can be minimized with no more than 750 mg daily.

In theory the use of methyldopa in pregnancy might be associated with the development of postnatal depression.

Labetalol

This drug has been used extensively in pregnancy and there is no evidence of any adverse effects. The starting dose is usually 100 mg twice daily, doubling if necessary. If, with a total of 400 mg daily, blood pressure remains uncontrolled, then it is usual to add in either hydralazine or nifedipine.

The beta-blockers

The published data on the use of beta-blockers which lack intrinsic sympathomimetic activity (ISA) are alarming, with reduced fetal blood flow and smaller babies. Drugs like atenolol and propranolol should now be regarded as contraindicated in pregnancy. Oxprenolol and pindolol, both of which have ISA, may be safe but are not used much nowadays.

Hydralazine

When given by injection, hydralazine is useful in the treatment of severe pre-eclampsia and eclampsia. Its use in the milder grades of hypertension has declined as newer drugs have become available. Oral hydralazine is a safe alternative to beta-blockers or methyldopa in the earlier stages of pregnancy.

Calcium channel blockers

There is too little information on the use of the calcium channel blockers in pregnancy to justify their use, except in special circumstances. Nifedipine has been used safely in some severely hypertensive women, either as add-on therapy or where other drugs were contraindicated or not tolerated.

The ACE inhibitors

These agents are absolutely contraindicated in pregnancy or, for that matter, in women who are planning to become pregnant. Where they have been used, there are reports of congenital abnormalities, growth retardation and intrauterine death.

The alpha-blockers

The world experience suggests that prazocin is not harmful but there are no reliable data on the use of the newer, long-acting alpha-blockers (doxazocin and terazocin) in pregnancy.

Aspirin

There is increasing evidence particularly from the CLASP study that the use of low dose aspirin is associated with a reduced risk of placental ischaemia and fetal problems. However, this treatment should be used only in mothers who are at particularly high risk and must be started early in the second trimester. Women with hypertension alone need not take aspirin unless there are other factors indicating a high obstetrical risk.

POSTNATAL HYPERTENSION

Antihypertensive drugs

If hypertension is due to pre-eclampsia alone, blood pressures usually return to normal within a few days after the baby is born. Thus antihypertensive drugs can gradually be withdrawn gradually over 2 or 3 days. However, blood pressure sometimes remain mildly raised for weeks or months following delivery. Usually it is not high enough to merit drug therapy but patients must be monitored carefully. If the raised blood pressure was due to pre-existing hypertension, with or without pre-eclampsia, therapy should be continued although frequently the dosage of antihypertensive drugs can be reduced. As thiazides are useful antihypertensive drugs when used in combination with beta-blockers, these may be reintroduced.

Further investigation

All women who have had hypertension of any cause in pregnancy should be referred soon after delivery to a blood pressure clinic. In those women who had pure pre-eclampsia, blood pressures usually return to normal and, apart from a careful history and examination, no further action is needed. If blood pressures remain even slightly elevated, then a full work-up with intravenous urography is mandatory. The methods of managing such patients are covered in Chapter 7.

Further pregnancy

Women who had pure pre-eclampsia can be reassured that a further pregnancy may not be complicated by the same troubles. However, it is important that, as soon as they become pregnant again, they should attend a joint antenatal and blood pressure clinic. Women with pre-existing hypertension can usually be advised that it is safe to undergo a further pregnancy, but only with careful supervision as they do have an increased risk of stillbirth. Perhaps only women with hypertension complicated by chronic renal failure should be advised to desist from further pregnancies.

SPECIAL SITUATIONS

Chronic renal disease

If the mother has pre-existing chronic renal disease, with or without hypertension, special care is necessary. Superadded pre-eclampsia is common and it is important to measure the 24-hour urinary protein content at an early stage, usually during a brief in-patient stay. Aggressive control of blood pressure is mandatory but, even then, as many as 45% of pregnancies may end with a dead baby. The help of a nephrologist or hypertension specialist should be sought as soon as pregnancy is diagnosed.

Phaeochromocytoma

This is an important but rare cause of maternal as well as fetal death. A 24-hour urine collection for urinary metanephrines or VMA should be routine in all hypertensive pregnancies. If phaeochromocytoma is suggested by this test, then abdominal ultrasound should be undertaken to locate the tumour. It is mandatory that the mother is treated with both alpha- and beta-blockers throughout the whole of the pregnancy. Delivery of the baby is best by caesarian section; a surgeon should be present with a highly qualified anaesthetist as well as a physician and a paediatrician. If all goes smoothly, it is probably best to remove the phaeochromocytoma electively a week or two after delivery, through a more appropriate abdominal incision, and after CT scanning has confirmed the site of the phaeochromocytoma.

Coronary heart disease

Occasionally, hypertensive women with angina become pregnant. Beta receptor blockers with or without calcium channel blockers and nitrates are mandatory. Vaginal delivery should be avoided, as should excessive blood pressure falls during epidural anaesthesia.

Asthma

This is a common problem. The asthma is treated along conventional lines, with monitoring of blood theophylline levels if this drug is used. Reliance should be placed more on inhaled beta-agonists, steroids and atropine-like drugs than on oral therapy. Beta-blockers should never be used as even the most cardioselective blockers increase airways resistance. High blood pressure should be treated with methyldopa, hydralazine or possibly nifedipine.

Diabetes mellitus

Both insulin-dependent and non-insulin-dependent diabetes are associated with an increased perinatal mortality rate and there is some evidence that rigorous control of blood glucose levels is associated with a more favourable outcome. Hypertension may frequently be present and it is generally considered that this also should be treated aggressively. The ACE inhibitors are frequently used in diabetic hypertensives because of their presumed renoprotective effects. However, in pregnancy, these agents are specifically contraindicated. Atenolol, also commonly used in diabetic patients, should probably be replaced by labetalol.

ORAL CONTRACEPTIVES

Women who have had raised blood pressure in pregnancy are not doomed to develop raised blood pressure when taking the oral contraceptive. However, they should be monitored carefully before starting the pill and thereafter every 6 months.

HYPERTENSION IN LATER LIFE

It is probable that women who have had pre-eclampsia are more likely to develop essential hypertension in later life. They should be regarded as a group to be selectively screened for hypertension in primary care at least once per year.

FURTHER READING

Lowe S, Rubin PC. The pharmacological management of hypertension in pregnancy. *J Hypertens* 1992; **10**:201–7.

National High Blood Pressure Education Program Working Group Report on High Blood Pressure in Pregnancy. *Amer J Obstet Gynaecol* 1986; **163**:1689–712.

Perry IJ, Beevers DG. The definition of pre-eclampsia. *Br J Obs Gynaecol* 1994; **101**:587–91.

Perry IJ, Stewart BA, Brockwell J, et al. Recording diastolic blood pressure in pregnancy. *Br Med J* 1990; **301**:1198.

Shotan A, Widerhorn J, Hurst A, Elkayam U. Risks of angiotensin converting enzyme inhibition during pregnancy. *Am J Med* 1994; **96**:451–6.

17 BLOOD PRESSURE IN CHILDREN

BACKGROUND

From a clinical point of view, the topic of blood pressure in children has been rather neglected, being mainly of interest to paediatric nephrologists. Only a tiny minority of children need antihypertensive drug therapy and most of these have identifiable renal or vascular abnormalities requiring detailed and expert management.

Long-term, follow-up studies of cohorts of normal infants and children strongly suggest, however, that the origins of adult essential hypertension are to be found in early childhood or even in the antenatal period. These studies, which are difficult to conduct, are in a position to provide an insight into aetiology and may also provide guidance for early non-pharmacological management as well as the primary prevention of hypertension.

BLOOD PRESSURE MEASUREMENT

The principles of blood pressure measurement in children are largely the same as in adults and the reader is referred to Chapter 6. The main differences are related to arm size, which precludes conventional sphygmomanometry below the age of about 5 years and influences the choice of cuff in all children until they have stopped growing.

Doppler ultrasound blood pressure measurement

In neonates and children up to the age of 5 years, the measurement of blood pressure is best performed by Doppler ultrasound equipment. This only provides a measure of the systolic blood pressure but results are reproducible and accurately reflect the intra-arterial systolic pressure. False elevations of blood pressure can be avoided if the child is quiet, relaxed and not crying. Limited availability of equipment means that this technique is only performed in specialized paediatric units. As conventional sphygmomanometers are not suitable in children under the age of 5 years, the routine measurement of blood pressure cannot be recommended in the context of primary health care.

Oscillometric blood pressure measurement

The use of oscillometric systems for measuring blood pressure is feasible in children of all ages (Chapter 6). There are, however,

Table 7.1

Cuff sizes for use in children

Age	Bladder width (cm)	Bladder length (cm)
Newborn	2.5–4.0	5.0–9.0
Infants (6 months to 3 years)	4.0–6.0	11.5–18.0
Children (3 years to 10 years)	7.5–9.0	17.0–19.0
Small adult size	12.5–13.5	22.0–23.5
Alternative adult size	13.5	33.5

few published reports of its application on a large scale. Oscillometric manometers generally measure the diastolic blood pressure more closely to the fifth phase of Korotkov sounds.

Cuff sizes

The topic of cuff sizes in all age groups is not yet fully resolved. It is generally recommended that the rubber bladder inside the cuff should encircle at least 80% of the upper arm. If too small a cuff is used, blood pressure will be overestimated. It remains uncertain whether it matters if the cuff is too big, encircling more than 80% or even overlapping around the arm. Ideally, the paediatrician needs a variety of cuffs to allow for different lengths, as well as circumferences, of childrens' arms. The clinician must use which cuffs are available and this will differ from country to country. In the United Kingdom, there are four cuffs suitable for use in children and, of course, in older children the conventional 'normal adult' cuff will be suitable (Table 17.1). If there is any doubt, the arm circumference should be measured and the most appropriate cuff employed.

Stethoscope

In very small children, a stethoscope with a paediatric size chest piece is necessary. The stethoscope diaphragm may be more suitable than the bell.

Systolic end-point

The height of the systolic blood pressure can be measured either by palpation of the radial artery or by listening over the brachial artery in the conventional manner. Systolic pressure is taken at the first appearance of the Korotkov sounds.

Diastolic end-point

There remains confusion as to whether muffling or disappearance of the Korotkov sounds provides the most accurate or reproducible estimate of the diastolic blood pressure in children. In adult practice, the disappearance of sounds (Korotkov phase 5) is now universally accepted as the correct method for measuring diastolic pressures.

Many paediatricians still take diastolic-pressures at the phase of muffling of sounds (phase 4) but we know of no evidence as to whether phase 4 is nearer to the true intra-arterial diastolic pressure than phase 5 in children. If diastolic muffling cannot be identified, then the disappearance of sounds must be employed anyway.

Arm position

It is critical that the arm cuff is at the same level as the heart. The posture of the child will depend on its age. Blood pressures are best measured seated, with the child either in a chair or on the mother's lap.

The flush method for measuring blood pressure

This technique is now obsolete. It depends on the use of a tourniquet and occlusion bandages to render the arm bloodless so that the clinician can then identify at what level of systolic pressure blood returns to the arm as the cuff is deflated.

Leg blood pressure

All children with raised blood pressure should be checked to exclude the diagnosis of aortic coarctation. Blood pressure must be measured in the legs. The child is placed lying on its tummy and a suitable cuff is applied around the thigh, to encircle at least 80% of the circumference. The stethoscope is applied in the popliteal fossa and blood pressure is measured in the conventional auscultatory manner.

Number of readings

As in adult medicine, two blood pressure readings should be taken at each consultation, and the second reading used for clinical decision making. In all but a tiny minority of children with very high blood pressures, rechecking is necessary on at least four occasions before long-term therapeutic decisions are made.

BLOOD PRESSURE IN NORMAL CHILDREN

The results of long-term follow-up studies from the UK and USA are summarized in Figure 17.1. In neonates, blood pressure rises sharply soon after birth from around 90/70 mmHg to 110/80 at about 6 weeks of age. Then blood pressures seem to level off until the age of about 5 years, when a slow steady rise in blood pressure with advancing age is seen, and this trend continues on into adult life. It is not known whether breast-fed babies differ with respect to blood pressure, when compared with bottle-fed babies, but there is evidence that babies weaned onto a low salt diet have a smaller rise in blood pressure over 6 months (2 mmHg) compared with normal salt intake babies. The role of salt in the rise in blood pressure with age is discussed in detail in Chapter 3. The development of essential hypertension is intimately linked to the rise in blood pressure in normal people with advancing age. This phenomenon is not seen in low salt eating societies. Clearly, therefore, the origins of hypertension are to be found in childhood even in children whose pressures, whilst technically normal, are above average for their age.

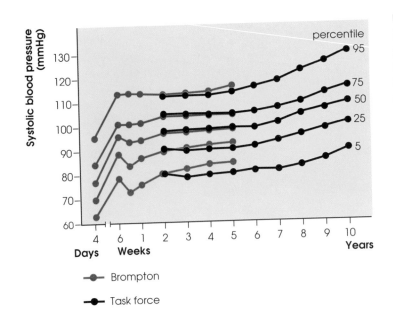

Figure 17.1
Percentiles of systolic blood pressure from the Brompton study and the Task Force for blood pressure control in children.

Tracking

The term 'tracking' implies that those individuals with blood pressures in the upper, middle or lower parts of the normal range will retain their rank and, as their pressures continue to rise with age, some will cross the arbitrary line and will be considered to have hypertension. Tracking is seen in studies of schoolchildren and young adults but there is no convincing evidence of tracking of individual pressures in neonates and infants. Thus, it is not possible to predict the onset of clinical hypertension in the blood pressures of neonates and, anyway, a great many other genetic and environmental factors will influence blood pressure over the ensuing decades.

There is also some evidence of a 'vicious cycle effect'. Not only do blood pressures tend to rise with advancing age, but there is evidence in adults, at least, that those individuals with the higher pressures sustain a steeper rise than those whose pressures are in the lower part of the distribution. Again, this effect cannot be detected in neonates and infants but it is seen in studies of adolescents and young adults. The salt restriction study of Hofman et al (Fig. 17.2) strongly suggests that the rise in pressures is due to environmental factors which should be preventable and possibly reversible.[4]

Genetic factors

Comparison of parents with their adopted and natural children suggests that all children have pressures which are positively correlated with those of their parents but that adopted children correlate less closely. Thus, both genetic and shared environmental (mainly dietary) factors are related to the blood pressure of normal children (see Chapter 3).

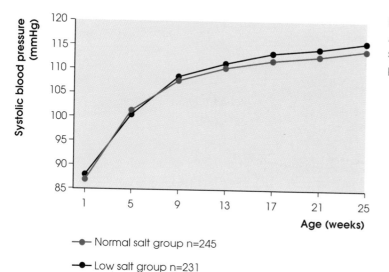

Figure 17.2
A randomized trial of low sodium intake and blood pressure in newborn infants.

Birth weight

Recent research has drawn attention to the fact that the birth weight of children is negatively related to blood pressure in later adult life. Paradoxically, therefore, the low birth weight babies are the ones who will develop hypertension in adulthood. As high blood pressure in adults is positively correlated with obesity, this implies that high blood pressure will be particularly seen in those individuals who start out being underweight (and with lower than average pressures) and who later become overweight. The origins of essential hypertension might, therefore, be traced back to the intrauterine environment. Early undernutrition, related to poverty and a poor diet, together with later overnutrition, with obesity and an equally poor but different diet, may both influence the development of hypertension.

CRITERIA FOR ABNORMAL BLOOD PRESSURE

As stated in the earlier chapters, it is difficult to define a normal blood pressure. All blood pressures in Western societies are too high; the rise of blood pressure with age is not a natural phenomenon and it should be preventable. No obvious threshold between the normal and the abnormal can be identified. Similarly, the pragmatic definition of hypertension in children cannot be applied as no randomized therapeutic trials of blood pressure reduction have been conducted. There is no level of pressure where clinical trial data dictate the use of blood pressure-lowering drugs. Children with raised blood pressure and renal impairment are given antihypertensive drugs in the hope of preventing the development of renal failure. It would be unethical to withhold such treatment, even though no randomized trials are available.

Table 17.2

Definitions for normal and raised blood pressure recommended by the second task force on blood pressure control in children 1987.

Term	Definition
Normal BP	Systolic and diastolic BPs below 90th percentile for age and sex
High normal BP	Average systolic and/or diastolic BP between 90th and 95th percentile for age and sex
Hypertension	Averasge systolic and/or diastolic BP equal to or greater than 95th percentile for age and sex (measurements on at least three occasions)

In paediatric practice, a great many parameters like height and weight are considered on the basis of percentiles obtained from surveys of large numbers of individuals (see Figure 17.1). These criteria depend on the source of the individual 'normal' children but do provide sensible guidance on what levels of blood pressure require action. The USA Second Task Force on Blood Pressure Control in Children in 1987 produced a classification of hypertension and criteria for defining children as 'normal, high normal or hypertensive' (Table 17.2). These criteria are applicable to all Western countries and paediatricians should respond to them.

THE VALUE OF SCREENING

The role of well population screening in children is uncertain. By the percentile definition of hypertension mentioned above, at all ages 5% of children will be considered to be hypertensive. No clear guidelines are available on whether all children should undergo routine blood checks. Routine blood pressure measurement in all adults is now clearly indicated but as yet no information is available on the cost/benefit ratio of examining children, or on the problem of the feasibility of screening. There is no doubt, however, that some children should undergo routine checks in the context of either paediatric clinical practice, children's welfare clinics or the primary health care team (i.e. general practice).

Screening sick children

All children who are ill enough to be referred to see a paediatrician should have their blood pressures measured at any age. In particular, children presenting with failure to thrive, those with any evidence of renal or adrenal disease and those requiring oral corticosteroid therapy need accurate blood pressure assessment. All children with diabetes mellitus should have regular blood pressure checks at least once per year.

Opportunistic screening in hospital practice

Children who are admitted to hospital for non-serious disease and, in particular, all those who are admitted for minor surgical conditions should have blood pressures measured at any age.

Screening children with high personal risk

Children who are obese have a high probability of having raised blood pressure and they should have their blood pressures measured.

Table 17.3
Classification of hypertension by age group.

Age group	Significant hypertension (mm Hg)	Severe hypertension (mm Hg)
Newborn	Systolic BP ≥ 96	Systolic BP ≥ 106
8–30 d	Systolic BP ≥ 104	Systolic BP ≥ 110
Infant (<2 yr)	Systolic BP ≥ 112	Systolic BP ≥ 118
	Diastolic BP ≥ 74	Diastolic BP ≥ 82
Children (3–5 yr)	Systolic BP ≥ 116	Systolic BP ≥ 124
	Diastolic BP ≥ 76	Diastolic BP ≥ 84
Children (6–9 yr)	Systolic BP ≥ 122	Systolic BP ≥ 130
	Diastolic BP ≥ 78	Diastolic BP ≥ 86
Children (10–12 yr)	Systolic BP ≥ 126	Systolic BP ≥ 134
	Diastolic BP ≥ 82	Diastolic BP ≥ 90
Adolescents (13–15 yr)	Systolic BP ≥ 136	Systolic BP ≥ 144
	Diastolic BP ≥ 86	Diastolic BP ≥ 92
Adolescents (16–18 yr)	Systolic BP ≥ 142	Systolic BP ≥ 150
	Diastolic BP ≥ 92	Diastolic BP ≥ 98

High familial risk children

Healthy children who by virtue of family history are considered to be at high risk of having hypertension should all be screened. All children of parents who have polycystic kidney disease (PKD) should actively be tracked down and screened for hypertension.

These children should also undergo an ultrasound scan of their kidneys. The affected relatives of patients with PKD are frequently found to have abnormalities requiring clinical action. Similarly, children of parents with phaeochromocytoma and primary hyperaldosteronism (both of which can be familial) should have their blood pressures checked.

Routine screening of all children

At the present stage of knowledge, it is not possible to justify the routine measurement of blood pressure in normal healthy children. In children under the age of 5 years, the Doppler ultrasound equipment is not generally available so screening is hardly feasible anyway. In children aged 5–18 years, the establishment of a system for measuring blood pressure on a population-wide basis is only justifiable as a research exercise or as a study of feasibility. At the age of around 18 years, the routine examination is probably worthwhile and possible, at the time of entry into higher education or prior to taking up employment.

Referral

All children with blood pressures at or above the 95th percentile need careful assessment and are best referred to a paediatrician. They may be classified as having 'significant' or 'severe' hypertension by the United States Second Task Force criteria (Table 17.3).

RECOMMENDATIONS FOR INVESTIGATING CHILDREN

Children whose blood pressures are between the 90th and 95th percentiles need investigation only if there is a suspicion of some underlying disease. Children whose blood pressures are at or above the 95th percentile always need detailed investigation and they should preferably be referred to specialized units. The method of investigation is along similar lines to those recommended in Chapters 7 and 8. Full haematological and biochemical profile, chest X-ray, intravenous urography, ECG, urinary metanephrines or VMA and a midstream or clean-catch specimen of urine for microscopy and culture are all that is routinely needed. Further investigation depends on the results of these tests.

A good case can be made for measuring plasma renin levels routinely in all children with raised blood pressure, as this may help to detect renal hypertension.

THE AETIOLOGY OF HYPERTENSION IN CHILDREN

If the diastolic pressure exceeds 110 mmHg, it is most likely that there is an underlying renal, renovascular or adrenal cause for the hypertension. In cases where the diastolic pressure is below 100 mmHg it is most likely that no underlying cause will be found and, as in adults, such cases are classified as essential hypertensives.

There follows a brief classification of underlying causes which should be considered when investigating hypertension in children, with comment on each of the important clinical features.

Coarctation of the aorta

Narrowing of the arch of the aorta occurs either immediately before, at the level of, or just after, the ductus arteriosus. There may also be other cardiac defects, including patent ductus arteriosus, bicuspid aortic valves, ventricular septal defects or transposition of the great vessels. The femoral pulses may be absent or delayed and leg blood pressures are low or normal in spite of raised arm pressures. Coarctation in adults carries a poor prognosis with a high risk of myocardial infarction and subarachnoid haemorrhage. For this reason, surgical correction should be carried out as soon as feasible and optimally at the age of about 4 years. Even with early surgery, blood pressure may not completely be normalized, so long-term follow-up is important.

Arterial disease

Hypertension may occur with congenital aortic hypoplasia. Many acquired arteritic diseases may also be complicated by hypertension. These include scleroderma, systemic lupus erythematosus, juvenile rheumatoid disease, polyarteritis nodosa and pulseless disease.

Renovascular disease

In children, renal artery stenosis is rarely congenital. Acquired stenosis is usually due to fibromuscular hyperplasia of renal or intrarenal arteries rather than atheroma. Fibromuscular hyperplasia may be seen in other vessels, including mesenteric, iliac or femoral arteries. Detailed investigation and surgical correction is mandatory. The further investigation of renal artery stenosis is discussed in Chapter 8.

Renal disease

Renal and renovascular hypertension in children may be associated with biochemical evidence of secondary aldosteronism, with hypokalaemia and high plasma renin and aldosterone levels. These children may present with nonspecific symptoms, including general malaise and failure to grow normally or, in babies, failure to thrive. Hypertension may complicate acute nephritic syndrome, nephrotic syndrome, chronic glomerulonephritis, particularly IgA nephropathy, chronic pyelonephritis and obstructive or reflux uropathy with or without urinary tract infection. Various forms of unilateral or bilateral renal hypoplasia, including the Ask-Upmark kidney (segmental renal hypoplasia), may cause hypertension, which may be very severe. Adult-type, polycystic kidney disease (Mendelian dominant) causes familial hypertension, renal failure and subarachnoid haemorrhage. The rarer, recessively inherited, form of polycystic disease is also associated with renal failure and high blood pressure.

Very rarely, a benign renin-secreting tumour (haemangiopericytoma) may be identified. These are often small renal tumours which can usually be excised by heminephrectomy. Hypertension may also complicate renal tumours (Wilm's tumour or Grawitz tumour).

Endocrine disorders

Both primary aldosteronism and phaeochromocytoma may present in childhood. The diagnostic guidelines are similar to those described in Chapter 8. In children hypertension may also complicate Cushing's syndrome, due to pituitary causes, adrenal hyperplasia, or corticosteroid or ACTH therapy. The very rare congenital adrenal diseases, including 11-β-hydroxylase deficiency and 17-α-hydroxylase deficiency, are associated with abnormal sexual development and hypertension which is related to mineralocorticoid excess. Hypokalaemia and renin suppression, but with normal plasma aldosterone levels, are strongly suggestive of this form of mineralocorticoid hypertension. As discussed in Chapter 14, hypertension may complicate diabetes, hyperparathyroidism and possibly myxoedema.

TREATMENT

The object of antihypertensive treatment should be to reduce diastolic blood pressure to below 90 mmHg. Careful monitoring of serum creatinine levels is necessary, since the aim of treating hypertension in children is primarily to prevent the onset of renal failure. We recommend following the algorithm in the report of the Second Task Force on blood pressure control in children (Fig. 17.3).

Salt restriction with the substitution of potassium-rich foods may be sufficient to control blood pressure in some mildly hypertensive children without renal impairment. Even in children who are receiving antihypertensive drug therapy, this dietary approach should be followed, as there is an additive effect of low salt diet with most antihypertensive drugs. Hypertensive children often tend to be obese, and calorie restriction should be advised where this is relevant.

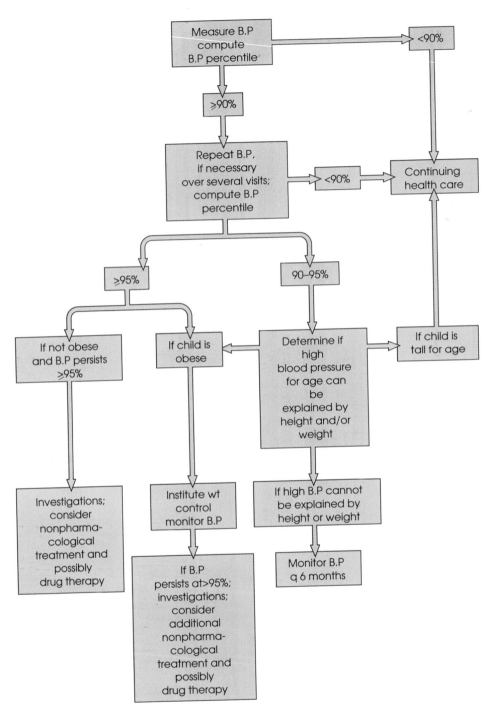

Figure 17.3
Algorithm for identifying children with high blood pressure.

Table 17.4

Paediatric doses of antihypertensive drugs (Check manufacturer's recommendations before prescribing).

Class	Dose range in relation to body weight	Comments
1. Beta blockers		
Atenolol	1–2 mg/kg	All beta-blockers are safe in children but they must not be used in asthmatics. If there is renal failure, smaller doses should be used
Metoprolol	1–4 mg/kg	
Propranolol	1–2 mg/kg	
2. Thiazides and other diuretics		
Bendrofluazide	0.1 mg/kg	These agents have long-term metabolic consequences and are not usually used as monotherapy
Hydrochlorothiazide	2.5 mg/kg	
Frusemide	0.5–2 mg/kg	For use with an ACE inhibitor
Spironolactone	1–2 mg/kg	Used only in aldosterone excess
3. Calcium channel blockers		
Nifedipine	1–2 mg/kg	Safe in all hypertensive syndromes
4. ACE inhibitors		
Captopril	0.5–2 mg/kg	Must be used with great caution in children with renal or renovascular disease
Enalapril	0.25–0.5 mg/kg	
5. Alpha blockers		
Prazosin	0.05–0.2 mg/kg	Safe in all hypertensive syndromes
6. Centrally acting agents		
Methyldopa	1–10 mg/kg	Safe but causes sedation
7. Vasodilators		
Hydralazine	1–5 mg/kg	Best avoided due to risk of lupus syndrome

Drugs for juvenile hypertension

The same rules as for the treatment of adult hypertension apply. The thiazide diuretics, beta-blockers, ACE inhibitors and calcium entry antagonists are all suitable first line drugs (Table 17.4). The long-term metabolic consequences of thiazides make these drugs less desirable and they are also less effective in younger patients. Minoxidil causes hirsutism and is contraindicated unless all other drugs have failed. The centrally acting drugs methyldopa, clonidine and reserpine may cause undue sedation. Dosages of drugs must be corrected for the weight and age of the child as recommended in the manufacturers' literature. The pharmacy departments of most specialized paediatric units are able to make up special elixirs containing very small amounts of the ACE inhibitors. These drugs may cause over-rapid falls in pressure in children with renal or renovascular disease so they must be used with great care; on a long-term basis they may preserve renal function more than other drug groups.

PREVENTION

There is some evidence to suggest that essential hypertension is related to a genetically determined increased sensitivity to dietary salt. For this reason, there is a good case to be made for restricting salt intake in children with a strong family history of hypertension.

One carefully controlled study in newborn babies has shown that those given a lower salt intake had significantly lower systolic pressure at 6 months of age (see Fig. 17.2). Since, as mentioned above, hypertensive children, or those who have above average blood pressures, tend to be obese, weight reduction is also an important preventive approach. The measures that follow should contribute to the prevention of adult hypertension in the community.

Definite

(a) The regular monitoring of blood pressure in all children with diabetes and those with a history of renal disease.
(b) The measurement of blood pressure and the regular follow-up of all children who have hypertensive parents.
(c) Salt restriction and, where relevant, calorie restriction in children whose parents are hypertensive.

Possible

(a) The routine measurement of blood pressure of all children of school age.
(b Advice on salt and calorie restriction for all children whose diastolic pressures exceed 80 mmHg.

Unproven

A good case could be made for restricting the salt intake of the whole population, but no studies have been carried out in children that prove this to be worthwhile. There are two studies of salt restriction applied on a population basis in adults; one showed no benefit but one showed a reduction of the average blood pressure of the whole community.

We feel there is cause for concern that many children in the developed countries now consume large quantities of salt in convenience foods, including sausages, hamburgers and canned foods as well as snacks, potato crisps and salted nuts. The salt content of sauces and potato crisps is very high. In relation to their body weight, many children in Western countries now consume as much salt as the north Japanese; a population with the highest recorded incidence of stroke. This public health issue needs further investigation and action.

Conclusions

There is a urgent need for more information on the topic of blood pressure in children. Most of our knowledge is based on paediatric nephrological practice and a limited number of epidemiological surveys. As the origins of essential hypertension are closely related to lifestyle factors in childhood as well as genetic factors, more long-term research is needed on the value of preventative strategies. Children whose blood pressures exceed the 95th percentile for their age need referral to hospital specialists and detailed investigation.

FURTHER READING

Berenson GS, Wattigney WA, Bas W, et al. Epidemiology of early primary hypertension and implications for prevention: The Bogalusa Heart Study. *J Human Hypertens* 1994; **8**:303–11.

Dillon MJ. Investigation and management of hypertension in children. *Pediatr Nephrol* 1987; **1**:59–68.

Gruskin AB, Dabbagh S, Fleischman LE, Atiyeh BA. Application since 1980 of antihypertensive agents to treat pediatric disease. *J Human Hypertens* 1994; **8**:381–8.

Report of the Second Task Force on Blood Pressure Control in Children. *Pediatrics* 1987; **79**:1–25.

INDEX

abdomen
  examination, 85
  x-ray, 96
accelerated hypertension *see* malignant
    hypertension
ACE inhibitors, 48, 49, 159–62, 174
  and anaesthesia, 212
  clinical trials, 126
  contraindications, 174, 209–10, 232, 237–8
  dosage, 160, 174
  mode of action, 160
  side-effects, 160–1, 209
  use, 161–2, 174
    children, 251
    connective tissue disease, 211
    diabetics, 174, 206–7
    elderly, 221
    heart failure, 161, 197
    malignant hypertension, 178
    myocardial infarction, 196
    psychiatric patients, 213
    renal disease, 201, 202–3
acebutolol, 153, 154, 173
  dosage, 153
acromegaly, 83, 107
Addison's disease, 50
adenomas, tests, 96, 97
adrenal gland disorders, 99–107
  adenomas, 100–1
  bilateral hyperplasia, 102
  children, 249
  Cushing's syndrome, 50, 82, 83, 99, 103
  enzyme deficiencies, 103
  phaeochromocytoma *see* phaeochromocytoma
adrenaline (epinephrine)
  blood pressure regulation, 47–8
  excess, 54
  excretion, 97
age
  blood pressure and, 18–19, 29–32, 215–16, 243–4
    extreme old age, 30
    primitive societies, 31–2
    Western countries, 29–30
    women, 35–6
  and cardiovascular risk, 24

and pre-eclampsia, 229
alcohol consumption
  and blood pressure, 38–40, 81, 140
  as cardiovascular risk factor, 8, 9, 25, 138, 212
  excess, 139–40
  and hypertension, 39–40, 81, 138–9
  maximum recommended, 139, 140
  reduction, 139–40
alcohol withdrawal, effects, 138–9
aldosterone, 49, 50
  plasma, 99
aldosteronism
  primary, 53–4, 99–102
    biochemical features, 100
    children, 249
    clinical features, 100
    investigations, 100–1
    treatment, 101–2
  secondary, 99, 100, 103
allopurinol, 211
alpha-blockers, 163–4, 175, 210, 211
  central, 164–5
  clinical trials, 126
  combined with beta-blockers, 164
    dosage, 163
  dosage, 163
  phaeochromocytoma, 106
  use
    children, 251
    pregnancy, 238
amaurosis fugax, 80
amiloride, 102, 149, 151–2, 172, 221
  dosage, 147
amlodipine, 156–7, 174, 196
  dosage, 155
anaemia, 88
  microangiopathic, 88
anaesthesia, 211–12
aneurysms
  abdominal aortic, 200
  berry, 5, 200
  Charcot-Bouchard, 5
  hypertensives, 5, 11–12
angina pectoris, 6–7, 196
  pregnancy, 239